Champagne Baby

# Champagne Baby

How One Parisian
Learned to Love Wine—and Life—
the American Way

LAURE DUGAS

BALLANTINE BOOKS
NEW YORK

Published in the United States by Ballantine Books,
an imprint of Random House, a division of
Penguin Random House LLC, New York.

BALLANTINE and the HOUSE colophon are
registered trademarks of Penguin Random House LLC.

ISBN 978-1-101-88463-8
ebook ISBN 978-1-101-88464-5

Illustrations by Dowotaki

Printed in the United States of America on acid-free paper

randomhousebooks.com

2 4 6 8 9 7 5 3 1

First Edition

*Book design by Elizabeth A. D. Eno*

For my parents and my Uncle Alain

# CONTENTS

# Introduction

When I was a baby in Paris, my mother would dip her finger in champagne and rub it on my lips, to acclimate me to the taste and smell, she told people, because our family was from Champagne. I have no memory of this. The modern parent would be horrified. *You are getting your baby drunk! You are giving her brain damage!* But I'm sure she did it in good fun, and I don't feel too much the worse for it.

My mother's grandparents cultivated our family's first vines in Champagne in the 1930s before the war, and good wine still comes from our vineyard (a small one not found in many guides). My paternal grandfather managed all the wine distribution that came through Bercy during the war. My father went in a slightly different direction, selling fine spirits throughout France. His brother, my Uncle Alain, is a respected vintner in the esteemed Châteauneuf-du-Pape geographic appellation of the Rhône Valley. Wine is most definitely in my blood.

So you might think I am some kind of wine princess, that I was schooled in everything there was to know about wine from the moment I could speak, that in my youth I could have recited the great vintages of France the way the child of the Church knows her catechism. *Oh pfft*, you say, *no wonder she is writing about wine: She's French! Her family is in the business!* And you would be right about my family, but not about me. I don't deny that I grew up surrounded by wine. As a girl I watched my mother open a bottle of her family's champagne at nearly any excuse. A friend stopping by the house? *Champagne!* The sun coming out after a little rain? *Alors! Champagne!* But the truth is that I knew almost nothing about it, except that there was plenty in the pantry. My pedigree, as it were, came with no "special" understanding at all, simply proximity.

And so what it comes to is this, and I have no compunction about sharing it with you right away: entitlement is the very opposite of what makes for the most rewarding, most open experience of wine. Growing up, I drank only one kind of champagne—my family's—and could not have described any other, or even what made ours any good (though it benefits from some of the best *terroir* of Champagne, in Ambonnay).

Being French is not the answer, either. While France, in my opinion, possesses the tradition and know-how to make the best wines in the world, that doesn't mean every French citizen can tell the difference between a Chablis and a Pouilly-Fumé (just as, despite what I learned as a child, from the TV show *Dallas*, not every

American knows how to herd cattle). Being French can, in fact, actually breed complacency. I've seen plenty of my fellow country-men and -women act a certain way to suggest they're naturally gifted when it comes to wine, when that couldn't be further from the truth. Nationality alone is not enough.

I'm a prime example. If you'd told me as a little girl that I would one day operate my own wine bar and store, premised on the pleasures of French wine, I'd have laughed out loud. It was the last thing I wanted to do, having grown up in a family like mine. And anyway, credentials guarantee nothing—in life as in wine. By the time I was nearly finished with university, I was still naïve about both. And I did not learn, really learn, what it means to *love* both until I left my family and my country at twenty-three, and moved to New York City.

This is the story I want to tell you.

# FRENCH WINE REGIONS

PART I

Planting / Racine

# 1.

## Nobody Knows Everything

*On ne peut pas tout connaître*

I've always had the unfortunate tendency to leap before I look. It's not very French of me, but I can't help it. So when my uncle pulled me aside after a family dinner in the summer of 2006 to offer me the chance to work in the U.S., I didn't say I would think about it or consult with others. I said yes. He'd heard I wanted to learn English, and he needed someone to work with his new American wine importer, which was based in New York. Never mind that to do the job well I would need a minimum of two things, neither of which I had: a minimal competency in the English language, and a much deeper understanding of French wine. Never mind that I had a boyfriend in Paris, Jules, who had already patiently waited for me as I studied in Spain for a year. Never mind also that my uncle needed someone for only the first six months of 2007, after which I would be on my own.

I said yes immediately, before I could think twice. Even my uncle was surprised; after a moment he asked if I'd heard correctly that this would mean traveling around *les États-Unis*—the whole country. I assured him I had, and he laughed and said that in that case we'd have to make our preparations.

My answer might have been different if he had told me that in January I'd find myself in front of a hundred and fifty sales representatives in Seattle, conducting a tasting of his wine with a shaky hand. I'd never spoken in front of even fifteen people, but there I was, not only expected to speak but to speak intelligently, while secretly knowing that I had only a fraction of the experience of every other person there. When it came to wine, all my uncle and I had in common was a last name.

I stood outside the tasting room unable to feel my toes out of nervousness, mouthing a script I'd gone over a hundred times. The opening monologue describing Château la Nerthe and what made it special was easy enough. It was the prospect of then having to walk the sales reps through the wine itself that worried me. If you'd handed me a glass of wine that morning, I could have instinctively told you whether it was good or bad—but not why. If you'd asked me to describe what I was tasting, I wouldn't have known where to start.

*Now we will taste the Châteauneuf-du-Pape red of Château la Nerthe. [Wait for others to pour. Hold up glass.] The color you see is a bright ruby with a raspberry tint. The nose is fresh with red fruit, a touch of black pepper. [Wait for others to smell.] The palate is frank. [Wait for others to sip.] What you are holding is a complex wine, with hints of cherry, blackberry, black currant, and spice. The tannins, as you can tell, are elegant. [Wait for others to spit.]*

There were a hundred ways for me to screw it up. The scripted pauses, which I needed to remember *not* to say out loud. I didn't even know what fruit the English words "black currant" referred to. And what *was* a ruby color, exactly? I'd never seen a ruby in real life.

I'd have turned around and *walked* back to France if my audience hadn't been expecting me. I opened the door, with only one thought echoing in my head: *What have you gotten yourself into?*

As I've said, it's how I've always been, pressing on first and asking questions later. I said yes to my uncle, and yes to myself, that summer, and decided I'd move to America early, in November. That way, I thought, I'd be able to find a place to live, learn English, study wine, and conquer New York City, all in the two months before my job was to start. I was certain it would be plenty of time.

❧

Over the years I've noticed that people commonly think about wine in one of two ways: Some believe that its secrets are possessed by a select few. For the French, who have been making wine since before the Roman Empire, this often takes the form of snobbery: *Only we (and maybe some Italians) know anything about wine.* All experts are tempted to believe that their knowledge is special and not easy to attain. Let's call this the "a few people know everything" camp.

The other extreme is a response to this elitism: a conviction that experts are a fraud, that the industry is a charade. You may have heard about taste tests that show no real difference between a one-hundred-dollar bottle of wine and a ten-dollar bottle of wine. Reports like this are meant to assure people that they shouldn't feel ashamed if they don't know much about wine— after all, a ten-dollar bottle is all you ever need! We can call this the "nobody really knows anything" school.

This is what I want to say before I get to what happened in New York: Neither is right. The truth is in the middle. There is indeed a lot to learn, but anyone can do it. I once watched as a celebrated winemaker failed to detect his own wines in a blind taste test. His own wines! But did that mean he was a fraud? Hardly. He had been making quality wines for two decades. All it meant was that *tasting wine is complicated, even for experts*. It didn't mean that there is no such thing as an expert.

There are no flash cards here. There are no bite-sized facts to memorize and recite at dinner parties. If you are looking for either a complete encyclopedia or an easy cheat sheet, you can stop reading now. This is about my experience—what I learned about wine and about myself when I moved to America. So a better approach might be to say that "nobody knows everything." Wine is too mysterious, too influenced by nature and by the smallest decisions of the people who produce it, to be easily pinned down. There is always more to learn. But with a few specific principles and a commitment to take it seriously, anyone—whether you have no experience at all, or are an elite pedigree but with no formal understanding—can start a lifelong journey in the art of enjoying wine.

I'm living proof.

What would have happened if I'd turned my uncle down and stayed in France? Who knows? I certainly could never have predicted that I'd one day have the U.S. to thank for much of my success and happiness. Americans seeking the French secret to the good life have launched a thousand bestsellers—but a Frenchwoman improving herself by way of America? Blasphemous! I might still have ended up working with wine, but without the influence of a culture that prizes ingenuity and experimentation, I'd be a very different person.

I'd originally imagined living in England, not the U.S. London was both closer to home and culturally more familiar. I had yet to complete my undergraduate degree, but my time in Spain had only increased my wanderlust. New York was so far, and in the days after telling my uncle yes, I had second thoughts. Jules—patient, encouraging Jules, my boyfriend of four years, who had already waited for me over one of them without complaint—wouldn't hear of it. "You have to go," he said. "It's the chance of a lifetime. You'll be back soon." He would turn out to be right about one of those things.

I'd never been so excited and scared at the same time—it was confusing. I'd only just returned from Spain, and there was so much to do before I left again. I went to the south of France to visit my uncle, who walked me around the vineyards pointing out where the grenache was planted and where the syrah was, and in the cellar he let me taste some wine directly from the barrels that wasn't ready for bottling—the kind of in-depth tour I'd never cared to do in all my childhood visits to my mother's family in Champagne. He even signed me up for a six-week wine course to at least reduce the likelihood that I would make a total fool of myself. Though you cannot become an expert in anything in six weeks, learning the basics gave me the slightest boost in confidence.

By the time I returned to Paris there was only a month left to spend with Jules. My closest childhood friend, Vera (who had been the one to introduce me to Jules), knew someone I could stay with in New York. I could not imagine being so far from both of them, but when it was time to leave I was too anxious to allow either to accompany me to the airport—only my mother, whose relative silence I knew was for my sake.

As for the flight itself, my memory is a blank. I do remember my first sight of Manhattan through the clouded Plexiglas of the taxicab divider, the gray outline of buildings that rose up closer to the sky the closer we got. And then we were in the city. I'd always pictured Manhattan as an array of immaculate, shining skyscrapers from end to end but had never really imagined the streets themselves; it was like picturing a person only from the neck up and completely ignoring everything below. So I was surprised to be dropped off on a desolate, narrow stretch of East Eleventh Street, at the far reaches of the East Village. The sidewalk could hardly fit my two giant suitcases, myself, the tree planter dotted with dog excrement, and the trash cans so full the lids would not close. The plain brick and stone row houses lining the street were no taller than six stories. For a second, I could have believed I'd stepped into an alternate, dirtier version of Paris, not the glass and metal towers I thought would be awaiting me.

This was the neighborhood that introduced me to New York—and, despite my first impressions, where I would eventually make my home, the place I chose over every other neighborhood in the city. I waited, biting my nails, for a few minutes before I spotted Vera's friend approach from down the street. Because she was the friend of a friend we kissed cheeks, but the greeting felt mechanical. Rose was French as well, and officially the first person I met in the U.S. She was also, it quickly became clear, my polar opposite, starting with appearance: she was tiny, blond, and sharply featured where I am tall and brown-haired and round-nosed. She was taking a break from work to let me in, and I could see the tension in her shoulders and lips, even though her eyes were cool and unreadable—unnervingly so for an open book like me. (Pinocchio had his nose; I have my cheeks, which turn helplessly red at the smallest provocation.) "Come, come," she said in her clipped Parisian French, beckoning me to follow her into the building. She was doing Vera a favor, it was obvious, and little more.

I let out an involuntary moan of relief when I saw the building had an elevator, and Rose glanced back at me questioningly. "My suitcases," I said. "I brought too much!" and laughed with embarrassment. There was barely room for the four of us; I had to stand very close to Rose and her stern face as we ascended the six flights.

The apartment was a two-bedroom she shared with her boyfriend. The décor was minimalist and modern—black couch, black coffee table, uninterrupted white wall except for a few framed black-and-white photos. Everything was tidy; everything matched. "This is very classy," I said. Her lip twitched in satisfaction. She led me to the spare bedroom, which looked into the concrete courtyard at the rear of the building, weeds sprouting from the cracks. This, at least for a short time, would be my view of the city.

"Here is your key," she said, waiting for me to turn from the window, "and sometimes, just so you know to be careful, you have to flush the toilet twice. I must return to work. I will see you tonight."

And with that, she was gone.

Though a part of me wanted to draw all the shades and hide, I drummed up enough courage to return to the street to find something to eat. I had no way to orient myself, however—I had been lulled into overconfidence by Manhattan's grid. But "Eleventh Street" meant nothing to me. Neither did "Avenue C," where I next found myself. Had I known better I would have turned west toward the rest of the city, but instead I wandered eastward until I was suddenly facing a highway. Had I already reached the end of Manhattan? I backtracked and turned to walk along Avenue D, where a power station loomed to the north, and to the east housing projects blocked my view of the water. Figures in the twilight burst out of a corner store, startling me with their laughter. I walked a few more blocks, reminding myself not to be frightened by every noise. Everything was strange and growing stranger in the dark. I hurried back to Rose's apartment, in shock, and still hungry.

This was the first moment I realized how unprepared I was. I'd believed it would be better to come early, with many ideas but few concrete plans. It hadn't occurred to me that this was like bringing a bottle of wine home with no way to store it until you are ready to drink it. I spent three nights with Rose and her boyfriend, Nicolas, who was as warm and friendly as she was cool, and he helped me go through Craigslist looking for places to live. His English was very good, and he would launch into spontaneous and unprompted vocabulary lessons—"this is a *sofa*"; "this is a *pen*"; "*today, tonight, tomorrow*"—most of which I immediately forgot, having no way to practice. He did teach me some basic phrases beyond the few that I knew, and told me if I ever wanted more time to think about what to say in English, I shouldn't make the usual raspberry sound, or shrug, like we do in France. His preferred method instead was to start sentences with, *"The thing is . . ."*

"This phrase tells your listener that what you are about to say is important, and they'll wait for you to complete the thought while you're coming up with what to say," he said to me in French. (From then on, whenever I heard him speak in linguistically mixed company I noticed every time he used his favorite trick. *The thing is . . . the chicken looks delicious,* he'd say. Or *the thing is . . . the situation in Iraq is no good.*)

Rose tolerated our lessons, and sometimes even contributed a word or two at Nicolas's urging, but she seemed preoccupied. On the third day she told me, almost casually, that her parents were coming to visit the following week.

"How nice!" I said, not sure what else to say.

After a pause, she continued, "I'd like for them to stay with me."

I nodded. "I understand."

"The only thing is we want to paint the room first."

I kept nodding, even as my heart sank into my stomach. She didn't say when exactly she wanted me to leave—and in fact she never actually said that I had to go at all—but I packed up that morning regardless. (It was my first lesson in Rose's uncanny ability to make everything clear without having to spell it out.) I had nowhere to go. Nicolas told me I didn't have to leave right at that moment, but I was too proud not to—a running theme in my story, I should let you know now.

"Call us if you need anything," he said. "Where are you staying?"

"Oh, I'll just go to a hotel," I lied. I had a very limited budget and didn't want to ask my parents for help. Over those three days, no permanent lodgings had materialized—the few people I'd met through Craigslist wanted a lot of money up front, or proof of current employment, or both. I had neither. And I'm sure I made a poor impression, stuttering my way through the pocketful of English I knew, unable even to understand what "security deposit" meant.

The realization I'd had about my poor preparation was even truer than I'd imagined. I don't know how I got through the next two weeks; a mix of determination and luck, I suppose. From Rose and Nicolas's I moved to a youth hostel on 14th Street. I signed up for an English class near Madison Square Garden, an area that was more like the New York of my imagination—bustling side-walks, enormous buildings—but the class itself was terrible. Most of the students were from China, South Korea, or India and had even less of a head start than I did. Yet the teacher would pair us off for hours at a time to practice our conversation, as if two bad English speakers would add up to one good one. Instead, as you might expect, one partner would thoroughly mangle the language, and the other, not knowing any better, would just cheer them on. The room was full of people sitting across from each other, one side spouting nonsense and the other saying, "Good! Very good!"

After each day's class I met potential landlords and roommates, but the answer was always the same. Then every evening the hostel clerk would ask, "Are you sure you don't want to reserve a few days in advance?" and, ignoring his concern, I would always reply, "No, this might be my last day here." I was stubborn. I talked to Jules on Skype using the common area Wi-Fi and admitted that things were a bit slow, while trying not to alarm him. I worried that he'd say to forget the whole thing and come home, and I'd be tempted to listen. It was not the advice I wanted to hear. At night

I climbed into my bunk bed, envious of the excited whispers of the tourist girls around me, and cried quietly.

Of course, the inevitable happened: one evening I returned from class to reserve my bed for the night and the clerk said, in a tone that was both sympathetic and I-told-you-so, "We're booked up."

"Oh," I said, considering what he would do if I sat right there on the floor and refused to move.

"Let me call the one on Bowery and see if they have space."

I pushed my two baby-elephant-sized suitcases down the sidewalk in the chilly November dusk. The beds at the new place were in individual cubicles with walls tall enough to block the view but not the sound. I lay down and listened to the ambient noise of the guests I couldn't see, the throat-clearing, the occasional laughter. The bathroom wasn't far from my cubicle, and I heard every flush of the toilet. I'm sure there were people staying there that night in far more dire straits than me, but I was too busy feeling sorry for myself to wonder about them.

I dreamed I was back in Spain, in the small coastal town not far from Valencia where I had studied. I was on a hill overlooking the sea, with a picnic of bread, ham, and a floral Spanish white wine that replenished itself with every glass I drank. A cat came up to my blanket, but instead of mewing, it let out a blaring noise. The cat wouldn't stop making that noise. I'm not sure how much time passed before I woke up to the fire alarm screaming on the wall above my head. I hurried outside with the other guests, a coat hastily thrown on over my pajamas, as we waited for the fire department. My feet were freezing. Then it started to rain.

As I stood in the downpour, miserably waiting to return to a bed that was only mine for the night, my mind went, as it does in hard times, to the most popular comic strip in France. *Asterix and Obelix* is to France what *Peanuts* is to the U.S. But instead of a lonely boy and his dog, the heroes are mismatched friends in ancient Gaul who spend their days rebelling against the Roman Empire. All they have on their side is pluck and a magic potion. It's a very French comic, but it would take me too long to tell you exactly why.

The important thing to know is that Asterix is small and clever, while Obelix is big and strong, if a bit naïve and impulsive. As a baby, clumsy from the start, Obelix fell into a vat of the village's magic potion, rendering him nearly indestructible. Obelix had his potion, and I had my champagne—the point is that I am much more like Obelix than like Asterix. And when I find myself in difficult situations, I usually end up blaming our shared traits for my troubles. I, too, have always stumbled along belly first without thinking and can have a bit of a temper. Look where it had gotten me. The next time my family compared me to Obelix, how would I ever refute them?

But if Obelix benefits from the clever presence of his friend, I had no one to help me but myself. Something had to change if I was going to make it to January. I quit the English class. I had to forfeit the rest of the week's tuition, but I'd rarely been so sure about a decision. Sitting at a café, surrounded by New Yorkers productively typing away on their laptops—how I wanted to be one of them!—I Googled "French restaurant East Village" and wrote down every address. (I would keep that pen for years, as a good luck charm.) My plan: walk into every single one until I got a job. There's a reason restaurant work is the obvious path for new arrivals with poor English skills, and I wished I had thought of it earlier.

It was also my last, best hope, and I didn't dare imagine what I'd do if it didn't work out.

At the first restaurant on my list, a bistro and jazz bar on Second Avenue, the manager didn't even look up as he turned me down, just waved me away and kept going over his receipts. The whole thing took less than a minute, and then I was on the sidewalk again, trying to suppress my sense of panic, to keep from hailing a cab to JFK right there. It was probably half an hour before I started walking in the direction of the second restaurant.

L'Éléphant, on First Street, was a Thai place with a charming blue-and-yellow awning, and I soon found out why it had come up in my search—it was French-owned, and half the menu was French-influenced. I took a breath and approached the man standing in the back, and, taking a gamble, spoke to him in French. I told him I had a passion for Thai food (not true) and a strong work ethic (true).

When I finished, he thought for a moment, and said only: *"Mais, avez-vous de l'expérience?"*

Yes, I lied, I had experience.

He nodded.

"You're in luck," he said. "Someone just quit and I need help with lunch. You can start now? Here's an apron."

Luck had found me! And I'd done my best to give it a chance to. L'Éléphant was my first exposure to working in hospitality, and though I stayed there only until the end of December, the experience has paid off to this day. I loved the restaurant. It was my introduction to the multiplicity of New York: a French manager

who oversaw a staff of French and American servers and a head
chef who had emigrated from Mexico as a teenager and now
cooked Thai food. I spoke French to the manager, teased the chef
in Spanish, and repeated to customers the same three English
phrases:

"How are you today?"

"Do you know what you'd like to order?"

"How is everything?"

Even now these are the three sentences I can say with the least
trace of an accent. My English rapidly improved as I interacted
with diners—faster than I could have ever hoped had I remained
in that overheated classroom by Madison Square Garden. I
worked nearly every day, mostly the lunch shift and sometimes
dinner. When it was quiet in the afternoon, I sat at a back table
and studied the Château la Nerthe materials.

My biggest disappointment with L'Éléphant was that whenever I went down to the basement I saw the restaurant's wine
stacked with the other dry goods in boxes next to the boiler. It was
stifling hot and damp down there—a terrible environment for
wine, which is best kept sideways in a cool, dark spot. One afternoon I poured myself a glass, and it was awful, warm and vinegary.
It had overoxidized, and every other bottle that was sitting by the
boiler had likely suffered the same fate. But in all the time I was
there, I never heard anyone complain.

I said nothing to Jean, the manager, not wanting to risk my
position. It wasn't worth it. The job had allowed me, finally, to
find a room in a three-bedroom apartment off Second Avenue.
The leaseholder, Carl, was about my age or a little older, from
California and living in New York to finish a novel he was working on. He was the first Californian I'd ever met, and he looked

the part: blond, tan, and always in knee-length shorts, even as winter approached. He interviewed me in his living room, arms thrown over the back of the couch and one leg propped up on the coffee table while I sat, hands in my lap, in a chair across from him.

After we'd spoken for a while I asked, "Your novel, what is it about?" He yanked his leg off the table and sat up straight, and I realized that no other candidate had asked him this.

"It starts out a roman à clef," he said, gesticulating urgently. "You know what that means, of course, you're French. It's the life of a normal guy, normal childhood in the San Fernando Valley. Then"—he came even more alive, his hands moving wildly—"it turns into, like, a thriller. He discovers a secret organization that runs all of Hollywood, Silicon Valley, *and* the agriculture industry, and a conspiracy involving movie revenues and the water utility. But the thing is, no one will believe him," he said, his voice dropped to a hush. He sat back again in satisfaction. "It's a satire," he finished.

"Of what?" I said. I recognized the word "satire," which though pronounced differently, is the same in French.

"The *system*, of course," he said, as if there were no other answer. He had only one more question for me. "So what do you do?"

I could feel myself beaming uncontrollably. "I'm a waitress."

In the larger scheme, getting an apartment was the most minor of accomplishments, something thousands of people do every day in New York. But I was ecstatic to finally have something good to tell

Rose, who had texted me a few times to see how I was doing. I'd replied only *"Bien!,"* not wishing to say any more, since nothing really was any good. The last thing I wanted was to confront her guilty and pitying gaze. But once I signed on the apartment, I agreed to meet for coffee and ended up telling her everything, not only about my improved situation, but the days I'd been stuck in that dead-end English class, sleeping at the hostel. She put her small hands over her mouth in horror. I told her things I hadn't even told Jules, and it all poured out in one breath. When I was done, she told me about her parents' visit and complained briefly about her job and how she hadn't been able to take any time off, then sighed as if she had just exerted herself. I didn't know if she'd really wanted to share, or just reciprocate a bit, but I appreciated it all the same.

She hesitated for a moment. "This Friday my friend Maya is having a party," she said. "You should come. She is French, too. There will be a lot of French people. And also some people who are not French."

I tried not to show my excitement. "That sounds very nice," I said.

In my new room in Carl's apartment, I made Jules, on Skype, help me choose a dress to wear. He didn't understand why I was trying so hard for a house party with people I didn't know. I told him that was exactly why I had to try so hard.

I left my new apartment far too early to be fashionable and killed time by walking around the East Village. It was a mild evening and it felt like everyone was out, enjoying the last of autumn. On one street, I passed groups of young people in leather jackets and belt chains and piercings. Then I turned a corner and everyone was in skinny jeans and flannel shirts, buttoned all the way up. I reached the building, walked around the block twice more, and rang the bell. No one answered. I texted Rose, then called her. I checked and rechecked the little piece of paper on which I had written the address until the creases started to tear. Ten minutes passed, then twenty. I sat on the steps in a panic.

How quickly everything can turn! I'd been so hopeful, and now was overwhelmed by dark thoughts—that the party had been canceled and she forgot to tell me or, in a nightmare right out of high school, that I'd been invited as a joke. Or did I have the wrong night?

A couple approached the building and I frightened them by asking in garbled English, tears in my eyes, about the party whose hosts I did not know the names of. They had no idea what I was talking about, and went up without letting me in. I sat back down on the stoop and cried. After the job, the apartment, I'd been sure that a social life would be next, and now I was paying for that optimism.

Forty minutes after I first rang the bell, forty despairing minutes during which for some reason I didn't go home, Rose called me back. The background was loud; there was music. "People have been coming up, I don't understand how we missed you," she said. Seconds later, she appeared—across the street. I'd had the address wrong. She waved and smiled and laughed.

We often place too much emphasis on first impressions, when the second is truly more important. I met other people at that party who would become a part of my life, but I remember it mostly as the night that set Rose and me on the path to great friendship. For all I've lamented my poor planning, it's the surprises that have stayed in my mind. I'd come seeking a metropolis and, although I didn't know it yet, ended up in a village.

My roommate Carl, to whom I wrote the rent checks, was odd, but easygoing and clean. Our third roommate, Shaina, was a

woman of Indian descent who worked in finance and had lived
there only a month longer than me. One weekend early on, we all
went out to bond as roommates, but the bar was a little too loud
and crowded for me, and I left early. When Carl and Shaina returned late that night, they were drunk and laughing, and in the
morning did a poor job of pretending they hadn't slept together.
Then they stopped speaking completely. I had no way of telling
whether this was just a normal part of living in New York or not.

At the end of December, I quit the restaurant. It had been a
nearly perfect experience—busy at nights and easy at lunch. I told
Jean I'd be leaving by Christmas, and he was nonplussed. "Sure,
sure," he said. "Thanks for letting me know." One thing he didn't
know, however, was that in my last couple of weeks I started trying
to steer customers away from the overheated wine. If a diner ordered a glass, I'd say very casually, "We have nice beer, too; it will
go with the food even better." Sometimes it worked, sometimes it
didn't. If they still wanted wine I watched from a distance as they
took a first sip, always hoping they would say, "This is terrible!
Let me talk to the manager!" But no one did.

"You suddenly care so much about the wine," my mother said.
We were talking regularly again, after a stretch of brief and inconsistent calls when I was having a hard time and didn't want to
admit it.

"Well, I don't want anyone to have a bad experience."

"Is that all?" she said cryptically.

"Plus, if I'm going to be helping Uncle Alain, I should at least
play the part."

"If you say so."

I knew what she was getting at, although we never said it out
loud. Neither she nor my father (they divorced when I was a little

girl but remain close) ever pressured me into seeking a career in wine. This was the first time she hinted that she may have hoped I would.

## Thinking About Wine

A bottle of wine is always a surprise. This is one of the reasons why nobody can know everything. Not even the winemaker knows what she'll find inside. You can make an educated guess; you can have expectations, based on the producer, the vintage, the grapes, the region of origin, and, most important, your past experiences. But you can't know for sure.

So when you greet a newly opened bottle of wine, do so with care and attention. Evaluate it the way you would anyone you've just been introduced to: with generosity, but a critical wariness. After all, any recent acquaintance can end up being a dud. Do the wine the honor of sizing it up. Don't just drink it blindly—a lot has gone into giving it a specific personality, and who doesn't want to be recognized for who they are?

**Pouring.** Before you pour, make sure you have the right setup. Are you using wine glasses? Good. Have they been stored for a long time in a closet? Bad. Rinse them out. Take a look at the cork, if there is one. It won't tell you everything, but if it smells moldy or vinegary, that's not a good sign. Wine is not inert—it is alive, always changing. These details are important.

**Smelling.** This is an underrated step. Don't just sniff for the sake of sniffing; put your nose into the mouth of the glass and inhale deeply. You can tell so much about a wine by its aroma, before it ever touches your tongue. You often see people swirl their wine before smelling it. Next time, try taking a whiff *before* swirling—this is your first impression. See if the wine reveals anything to you so soon after pouring, if you can detect the aromas typical of the appellation, or of the grapes. (The "appellation" is a government-controlled designation based on geography and character—there are appellations for cheese, as well, though in France wine is the largest and most famous system.) At this point, the wine might not have much to say, or it might have a lot. Now swirl it around the glass, helping it get a little air, so it can really begin to speak for itself. Bring it to your nose again—if you still don't smell much, the wine probably isn't *open* yet, and is a little shy! Give it time to reveal its character. You can either sit and wait patiently, or decant it in a carafe. A carafe can be a wine's best friend, whether the wine is red or white, especially if it is good quality and/or a recent vintage—if it's young, no wonder it's a little hesitant. If you don't have a carafe, pour some into your guests' glasses so there is more air in the bottle, letting more wine open up at once. (I hope you didn't open the bottle just five minutes before dinner.)

**Looking.** All this time, you've also been taking in the wine with your eyes. You'll have noticed that a young red wine will be redder, brighter, more purply, and that older reds will have a slightly orange hue. Young whites will have a yellow-green glow, older wines softening into a brownish tint. Anything very dull and faded-looking may be past its prime—or gone bad. But you won't know for sure until the next step.

**Tasting.** Now you will really see what a wine is made of. As you take your first sip, let it coat your entire tongue. You don't shake someone's hand with one finger, but with your entire palm. Let every one of your thousands of taste buds encounter the saltiness, the sweetness, the bitterness, the acidity. Let the wine move all around your mouth and notice how the flavor progresses with every passing second. Then swallow. Congratulations! Take another sip. Have another glass. The last glass in a bottle will taste different than the first—with wine, time affects everything. Pay attention.

**Remembering.** This is the step the experts don't talk about enough. *Remember* what it is you tasted, and how you responded. What sort of fruit pleases you the most, and how much of it? Maybe you like earth tones, licorice, and spice. If you liked this wine, where is it from, who makes it, and how old is it? The most important thing is identifying what you like, so that you can purchase the right wine and drink it on the right occasions. This doesn't happen at once. Like all wisdom and self-knowledge, it takes time, and concentration, and care. Keep a wine journal. Take pictures of the labels with your phone. Anything. Just don't forget. The wonder of wine, like everything else in life, is in the details.

# 2.

## Youth Has Its Virtues

### *La jeunesse a ses vertus*

The French see their wine, much as they see themselves, as defined by elegance, refinement, tradition. That we have a long and proud tradition is indisputable, but the truth is that not all French wine is elegant, and not all French people are refined. I recently tried to help a Frenchman who drank only Burgundies look for something new. I recommended a juicy Sancerre made from pinot noir grapes, and he shook his head to cut me off. "No, no," he said, "I don't like pinot noir"—and I was obliged to inform him, as politely as I could, that all of Burgundy uses pinot noir.

It's easy to criticize youth for being brash, opinionated, and immature. But it's just as easy to find fault in the old for being condescending, unadventurous know-it-alls. I wanted to live in England more than the U.S. because it was more familiar, more refined. More *Old World*. America—well! You know the stereo-types as well as I do. I'm not proud to admit it, but even though I was excited about what awaited me across the Atlantic, my expec-tations of a worthy cultural experience were not very high. If you are thinking, with a bit of irony, that this plays right into the stereo-type of the snobby French girl, you're right. I wouldn't have un-derstood this then, as I had very little conception of what it was *to be French*, or how we looked to the outside world. After all, I'd been French all my life and had no reason to wonder what it meant.

I would soon learn that there were many ways I wasn't so tra-ditionally French after all, and had I known this earlier I may have been more open-minded. My family had always teased me about my outbursts, my impulsiveness, the way I sought out new things—for being youthful, for being very "Obelix," who is hardly *une personne typique française*. (My émigré life soon showed me there were others out there who also broke the French mold: a few months after I arrived in New York, Nicolas confessed his deepest shame one night over dinner. A perfect Parisian in every other way, the man hated cheese. Have you ever met a Frenchman who hates cheese? No, because they are either hidden in caves by the government or they run away to America.)

Wine also inspires stereotypes. One of the simplest is a prefer-ence for older vintages—the idea that if you have to choose be-tween a 2009 and a 2010 you should always go for the 2009. But this isn't true! There are many factors you must take into account, including the quality of the vintage, which we'll get into later, and, most important, what kind of wine it is and what kind of wine you *want*. All wines change as they age, but some change for the better over a long period, and some—you may be surprised to discover—hit their peak rather quickly.

There's more to youth than just being pre-old. Well-aged

wines, like older people, are complex and often marvelous. But wines meant to be enjoyed young, like many of the varietals from Beaujolais, for example, are perfect with the right food and on the right occasion: fresh, fruity, and fun. And, like Beaujolais, youth can easily be misunderstood, dismissed offhandedly for the very qualities that make it great.

Not so unlike the U.S.

L'Éléphant was my first substantial glimpse into American culture. I saw all of New York pass through the doors in those weeks: people of every age, of every color and creed, people who I imagined lived rich American lives as bankers and lawyers and students and artists. In the interests of educating myself, I tried to eavesdrop as much as I could, but could understand only snippets that made no sense in isolation. It was overwhelmingly new, and so much to process that I would walk home at night in a daze, going over everything I had seen and heard.

I was amazed at how fast everything moved. At lunch, people ate and left in a rush, and lingered only a little longer at dinner. It was nothing like France or Spain, where meals are long and leisurely. In Paris, if you sit down for dinner at eight you're free to stay until midnight. (The first time I was asked to leave a restaurant because the next party had reserved the table, I was shocked.) Here, we saw dozens of diners every night, and we turned over tables as quickly as possible.

I was also confused by all the rituals of politeness. I had to ask, "How are you today?" and "How is everything going?" Every stage of the interaction between waiter and customer was acknowledged with a smile. The service in French restaurants is nothing like this, though I wouldn't go so far as to call it rude. They just have different priorities—and most French diners, in fact, would see this level of attention as bordering on harassment.

After I quit, I went home for several days for Christmas. It was a short break before the new year and my start with my uncle's new importer, the importer and champagne house Moët Hennessy. I almost didn't return to Paris at all, not wanting to spend the money or disrupt my acclimation in the States, and I felt sheepish flying back having accomplished nothing more than finding a place to live and waitressing for just over a month. But my father insisted on paying for one leg of the flight, so I gave in, admitting to myself how much I missed my family after so short a time.

We spent our usual Christmas Eve and morning together— with great food, yes, but even better drink. Imagine, my mother bringing the champagne, my father the cognac, my uncle the Châteauneuf-du-Pape—some of the best libations France has to offer on one dining room table. I answered their questions without lingering over my first miserable weeks. I didn't want them to know how close I'd been to giving up before the real job had even begun.

Jules came to pick me up to spend Christmas afternoon with his family. I can't talk about my homeland without talking about Jules, who was the most quintessentially *French* person I had ever met: sardonic, intelligent, intense, proud. If I was a young spirit, he was an old one, cool, with strongly held beliefs that had grown and taken hold like tree roots over many years. And there he was waiting for me, standing beside his run-down Mobylette motorbike with his hands in his pockets and his brown leather jacket on,

looking much like the first time I'd ever seen him: James Dean
with a strong Gallic nose and deep-set eyes, his hair cut close to
his scalp.

"*Salut, mon coeur*," he said, playing it as cool as if he'd just seen
me yesterday, until I got close enough for him to throw his arms
around me and lift me up.

He had just started design school when we'd met four years
earlier. My friend Vera had invited him along to see a movie, and
we watched him come chugging up on his motorbike in that same
leather jacket. All the other students had fancy scooters they parked
outside their pricey rented flats, but Jules had his old Mobylette
that was a pain to start, and he lived with his parents. I was especially charmed by his slightly bashful demeanor, which would flash
at moments when he was unsure of himself, his wide mouth breaking into a shy smile and his long lashes blinking rapidly.

A few days after the movie we met again at a party, and a few
days after that we had dinner together, just the two of us. We still
didn't know much about each other, but I wondered what Vera
had told him about my background because he made sure to hold
the wine list himself, as if to impress me. He didn't know how far
from a connoisseur I was and that he had no reason to try to prove
himself. But it seemed presumptuous to say something, so I stayed
silent as he scanned the list with his finger, making thoughtful
sounds. He glanced up once to gauge my reaction, and I tried to
convey with a smile that I knew no more than he did.

Then his index finger stopped, and he said to the waiter, "This,
this one."

The waiter paused, and said, "This one?"

Jules looked briefly annoyed. "Yes, yes," he said, and the waiter
gave a tiny shrug and left. "You'll like it," Jules continued. "It's

from Dordogne, where *my* family is from," he said. The way he placed the emphasis on *my* all but confirmed that he'd heard about my family's business.

The waiter returned and poured a taste of the white wine. I will never forget the look on Jules's face as he sipped it.

"No, no," he said to the waiter. "This is very sweet."

The waiter presented the label to Jules again. "It's a Monbazillac. You have chosen a dessert wine," he added, with a hint of glee.

"Well, we can't drink this. It's too sweet for our dinner. We must switch it for something else."

"Is the wine spoiled, *monsieur?*"

"No, it's just too sweet."

"I'm sorry, *monsieur*, if there is nothing wrong with the wine we cannot take it back."

We were nineteen-year-old students with no money—ordering another bottle was out of the question. "It's fine," I said in a hurry. "We'll drink it." Jules's face steadily turned red as the waiter filled my glass and then his with the Monbazillac. I sipped and, wanting to reassure him, said, "It's good." It was good—sweet, of course, reminiscent of peaches and apricots with a hint of spice—though I wouldn't have known at the time how to articulate all that. I hadn't even heard of Monbazillac, though I now frequently recommend it as an affordable alternative to France's most famous sweet wines: the Sauternes of Bordeaux, which are rich, floral, luscious.

"It doesn't go with the duck." Jules frowned.

This was an important moment in those early days of our romance. I was young, but there are some things a woman learns to spot very quickly, and one is the particular disappointment of men. Especially if paired with embarrassment, it can soon turn pouty, or angry, and then you know you are in the presence of a man who doesn't handle obstacles very well. I sipped my wine nervously as he took a slow draught and let it sit in his closed mouth for a few seconds before swallowing.

Then his eyes relaxed and brightened, his forehead smoothed out, and his brow lifted in amusement. "Oh well, *tant pis!*" he said. *Too bad!* And we both laughed for a long time.

It was at that moment I felt he was someone I could love.

After an early Christmas dinner in his family's apartment above the suburban school where his parents taught, we rode the Moby-lette back into Paris. It was cold; Paris winters are not as cold as New York's, but the air is moist, which I've always found unpleas-ant. We parked near the Hôtel de Ville so we could spend some more time together before I had to go home. Walking around the city had always been the easiest way for us to be alone when we were both living with our parents. He knew the Paris streets bet-ter than anyone else, and liked to point out to me the places where bits and pieces of history had happened.

As we began to walk, I tried to explain Manhattan to him, the way nearly all of its streets were arranged in a grid, making it im-possible to get lost (for the most part).

"Sounds boring," he said.

I found myself feeling a little defensive.

"It's elegant, in its way," I said.

We were holding hands, and he turned a little to look at me with disbelief. For most French people, complaining about every-thing, especially their own country, is a part of the national character. But Jules was a true patriot and believer in the French state as the most advanced society in the world, and he never failed to compare it favorably to the U.S. (which he had never visited). And whatever skepticism the French may have about the American way of life, they generally admire New York as a symbol of human potential, and as a place where people arrive from all over the world to make new lives. Jules was exempt. To him, New York was just a denser concentration of all the things that already made him suspicious about America; in particular, he railed against Wall Street as a glorified money-launderer for the military-industrial complex. Our generation had been sensitive teenagers on 9/11—Jules and I met just months afterward—and we'd been in college during the disastrous American war in Iraq. It had left my peers trying to understand the world through a prism of disillusionment.

Though we had discussed planning a visit during the six months I would be working for my uncle, we had yet to decide when. I needed to know my job's travel itinerary first. I also worried that he would back out, since he had already vowed (years before my uncle's offer ever came up) never to step foot or spend money in a country where George W. Bush was president.

We walked from Notre Dame to the Bastille. We saw each other again the next day, and the next—the day on which it started to feel as though I maybe had never really left, like Alice waking up on her side of the looking glass. But the end of the week approached and I realized that I would soon have to step back through the mirror again, back to the view of bustling Second Avenue just outside my East Village window, to Rose and Nicolas, to the smell of laundry on my way to the subway, to the café where I liked to get a chai latte on cool mornings.

Once again I didn't let Jules take me to the airport. "But you are coming to visit, right?" I asked pointedly the last night when he dropped me off at home.

"Six months isn't really so long, is it?"

He was joking, but I wasn't, and I made him soothe me for a minute in his arms before letting him off the hook. I watched him round the corner on his Mobylette, feeling my chest tighten when I could no longer see him.

The first time I'd landed in New York, just two months before, I had been perfectly helpless, but now I knew where to go, and— a fact that thrilled me when I remembered it—in my purse was a key to the door of the New York City apartment where I lived.

One thing I needed to do before the new year was buy some professional clothes. My waitress uniform of black shirt and jeans wasn't going to cut it; neither were the shorter skirts I'd brought with me in anticipation of spring. I took the train uptown to the Fifth Avenue department stores but ended up just looking at the opulent Christmas window displays alongside the tourists, feeling happy not to be counted among their ranks. I'd never been on such crowded sidewalks, even on the Champs-Élysées. It was all very lively, but I knew without even going inside that I wouldn't be able to afford anything at Bergdorf's or Saks. I walked all the way down Fifth to the Flatiron District. There, at a more modest store, I bought three simple outfits to rotate through until my first paycheck.

Back at the apartment, I put one outfit on and walked from one side of the room to the other, sat on a corner of the bed, crossed my legs. Carl came in without knocking, as he often did, and sat down on the other corner eating an apple and complaining about the holidays. Not the upcoming holidays—all holidays. He'd gone home to California for a short time; I didn't know what his relationship with his family was like, but it must have been pretty good if they were sending him enough money to write his novel and pay rent without starving. Shaina was in Virginia for another week; the two of them had yet to start speaking again. I was probably the only person he talked to regularly except for the coffee shop baristas.

I ignored him for a few minutes and then, while examining my new professional look in the mirror, said, "Carl?," interrupting his stream of thought.

"Yeah?"

"You have to knock before you come in."

He looked around as if just realizing where he was. I'd never asked anything of him before, because he liked to remind me just how many people had applied for my room and that I'd been lucky to get it.

"Oh, sorry," he said. He was holding the apple core in his hand and moved to throw it away in my trash, but thought better of it and ambled out.

Fifth Avenue aside, nothing could have prepared me for the glamour and luxury I would encounter in my first two weeks of preparation for my role as Château la Nerthe's brand ambassador. The Tuesday after New Year's I went to the Moët offices in the West Village to meet my liaison and travel manager, Luc, the son of

French immigrants whose nearly perfect French and totally perfect American English was a combination I'd never encountered.
He would be my main contact and help me arrange everything
with the regional wholesaler offices I'd be visiting—the ones
who'd be doing the actual on-the-ground selling of Château la
Nerthe around the country.

But before I began my six-month tour, I had to do two weeks
of training with Moët's top Manhattan salesperson, a woman
named Elise who, like me, was born in Paris but had lived in the
U.S. for five years. "Have fun out there. You have a lot in common," Luc said as he introduced us. I couldn't tell if he was joking.
Elise was blond and statuesque and intimidatingly beautiful. I
thought at first glance she was about thirty, but after our first day
together I realized she must have been only a year or two older
than me—perhaps twenty-four or twenty-five. Her assurance and
polish had deceived me. She was one of those women who could
get away with wearing black and white every day and look different every time. She favored sleeves with wide cuffs that floated
around her wrists as she moved. I might as well have shown up to
work in sweatpants and braces.

Elise's task was to introduce me to clients and show me how
her job worked. How her job worked, I learned, mostly involved
eating at the nicest restaurants in New York and chatting up the
chefs and sommeliers so that they would buy more wine. And she
was very good at it, seeming to be friends with everyone we met,
never a word or strand of hair out of place. I didn't see how I could
ever do what she did.

That first day, as we lunched at a three-star restaurant, she
leaned over and whispered in our mother tongue, "Rule number
one, don't forget." I sat at attention, ready to absorb her hard-

earned wisdom. "Always. Be. French." I looked around to see if any of the waitstaff were in earshot, but they'd positioned themselves at a respectable distance.

"Pardon?" I said, not understanding. I'd spent the meal being careful not to be poked by one of her high heels whenever she crossed her legs, and now I had to refocus in order to process this advice.

"You must use your Frenchness!" she said emphatically.

"Use it?"

She leaned over even closer.

"It's your secret power," she continued, raising her eyebrows.

"My power?"

She sat back and looked at me with impatience. "Do you know," she said, sipping her Chablis, "my American accent has actually become quite good. But I would never use it at work. I have more *authenticity* speaking with a heavy French accent. Your uncle's wine is expensive. Restaurants and stores want to trust who they buy it from. They will trust you. Why? Because you are French. And being French gives you authority."

I was so surprised by what she'd said about her accent that I didn't speak for a few seconds. "But I don't know much about wine," I blurted out, and immediately regretted it.

She waved off my concern as if it were a fly. "That doesn't matter. The clients can taste the wine for themselves. There is plenty of good wine out there. What they want is to be reassured. And what you have to do is make sure they remember you and the wine you are representing. What are they going to remember, some wine with a pretty label and yet another high *Wine Spectator* rating, or the producer who sent an actual French brand ambassador to meet with them? It won't be just what you say, but how you say it. Your selling point is authenticity. You're a beautiful French girl, your name is Dugas, and you're selling good French wine. What American wouldn't believe in you?"

"Oh," I said, too unsure of myself to point out that this was hardly the definition of authentic.

I didn't know how to feel. It was a relief to know that I had a head start and a cushion in case I floundered, which I was still sure I would. But it was not how I wanted to prove myself, and I worried I would always doubt my own skills if everyone I spoke to saw me first as a Frenchwoman and only second as someone with real knowledge to offer. But then—I *didn't* have any real knowledge to offer, beyond the talking points given to me by my uncle and the practiced tidbits of wine-speak I was picking up from Elise. Wouldn't it be foolish not to accept any advantage I had?

And it wasn't hard to enjoy being Elise's shadow. Just two weeks earlier I'd been having pad Thai at staff meals at L'Éléphant and avoiding the rancid wine. Now, I was eating some of the best food of my life, day after day after day. You might think that in Paris it's fine dining all the time, but that's hardly the case. Like any other kid I mostly ate at home with my family. Now I was having three-course lunches paired with wine I couldn't afford to buy for myself. Warm winter squash salad and a creamy fish stew with a rich Chablis. Grilled quail with a Moulin-à-Vent—one of the ten special "crus" of the Beaujolais region—that was plummy and earthy and so much better than I would have expected based on the reputation of Beaujolais (shows how much I knew). Elise introduced me to a rarified realm of New York that I knew I would only experience because of my job. But that didn't mean I couldn't be seduced by it.

When I was not tailing Elise my own foreignness was largely invisible to me. As long as I could order food and drink, make change at the Laundromat, keep track of my dollar denominations and the different coins, I felt blended in with the melting-pot fabric of New York—especially since my friends were also French. I often ate long meals with Rose, Nico (we were close enough now that I called him by his nickname), Maya, whose front stoop I'd cried on all those weeks ago, and her boyfriend Alex—the French way, until late, after which we'd stand on the sidewalk chatting before finally parting in a flurry of embraces. Once, Nico invited an American friend to dinner, forcing me to do my best to keep up in English. When we were all outside saying goodbye in our usual *dénouement*, the American friend left us to run an errand before a store closed. Half an hour later we saw him approaching from the other direction on his way home; his mouth dropped open and he said, "What? You're still here?"

So there were some moments in which I saw myself through American eyes. But there were also days I spoke basically no English—working with a French rep to sell French wine through a French conglomerate to mostly French restaurants, eating dinner after work with my expatriate friends, coming home to Carl and Shaina, who weren't speaking English or anything else to each other. Then I would Skype with Jules or my family in French and go to sleep, and dream in French. It was enough to make me worry that my English wouldn't be good enough to get by with on the road.

Even with the American-born Luc at Moët I spoke French. I found it strange and funny how he appeared so conspicuously American in the way he stood, the hand gestures he used—but with perfect French coming out of his mouth. And then he would change again, walking the floor of his office as an all-American guy, with a big laugh and grin, patting the staff on the back, teasing everyone. It was uncanny, and I wondered if I could ever approach that sort of duality.

When I was not with Elise in the field, I was with Luc in the office, planning my itinerary, making sure that I would hit both the big markets and the ones with growth potential for my uncle's wines, trying to learn a little about the wholesalers I'd meet. After that, it was up to me to make final arrangements, with the costs split between Moët and Château la Nerthe. When we finally had a calendar set, we went out to lunch at a Japanese restaurant by the office to celebrate. I'd hardly ever eaten Japanese food, except for one mediocre experience with sushi back in Paris. I was nervous about the food, but mostly about the fact that our preparations were complete and my job was about to really begin.

"The owner is a big name," Luc told me in French as we approached the restaurant. "Great food, and he serves your uncle's wine! French wine and Japanese food. Always have a good relationship with your neighbors."

There's nothing like your first taste of excellent sushi, and it put at least some of my nerves at ease. (I'm only sad on behalf of my country that the Japanese discovered and perfected it first.) The tuna seemed to melt with the slightest pressure from my tongue, the rice was perfectly warm and tangy. We drank Château la Nerthe's standard white, called the Châteauneuf-du-Pape white (named after the appellation), which was perhaps a little full-bodied and rich for sushi, but I didn't mind. I would have been a fool to.

Luc was clearly enjoying my reaction, and ordered fish after fish for me to try. Outside of the office he seemed more relaxed. He told me a little about what it had been like growing up speaking French at home and English everywhere else until he started working for Moët, and asked me what I thought of his French. I said it was very good.

"Your English is getting there," he offered. He meant it as a compliment, but my face must have seized up in anxiety, because he quickly apologized.

"I have an idea," he said. "Why don't we switch to English, you and I? From now on, until the six months are over."

"I'd like that," I said.

He nodded. The next words he spoke were in flawless American English, and although there are many moments I could say really launched my wine journey, this is the one I return to most.

"We'll start right now," he said.

## Thinking About Wine

If young wine is often misunderstood, then Beaujolais may be the most misunderstood of all. Some of it is due to marketing; some of it has to do with the lighter gamay grape and a widespread tendency to equate bold wines with better wines. I say it's a small national misfortune.

When you're considering a wine, the grape variety is your first clue about what to expect: cabernet sauvignon, cabernet franc, and merlot in Bordeaux; malbec in Cahors; mourvèdre in the south—these, for example, are grapes made for aging. The tannins—the chemical compounds that come from the skin and stems and that give a wine fullness and that dry sensation on your tongue and gums—are more concentrated. With enough time in the bottle the tannins evolve, growing subtler and bringing out unexpected flavors. The dominant grape in Beaujolais, however, is gamay, which is naturally light on tannins, and so it lends itself to fruity, refreshing wines best drunk young and slightly chilled. Though to many ears this might sound like "unserious" wine, that reputation is wholly undeserved.

The grape alone does not decide flavor. Côtes du Rhône red blends rely on grenache, syrah, mourvèdre, and cinsault, as does the nearby Châteauneuf-du-Pape, but while the former appellation is known for young, inexpensive wines, good wines from the latter can be aged for decades. So what you'll taste also depends on the terroir, the land and climate, which varies dramatically. And much also relies on the skills and strategies of the winemaker. Two producers in the same appellation, working with the same varietals on similar land, can make very different wines.

But back to Beaujolais. If you are even a casual wine drinker, you've likely heard of or drunk Beaujolais nouveau—it's often the only wine that people know from the region. Beaujolais nouveau is actually a particular kind of wine called *vin de primeur*, which is meant to be consumed the same year the grapes are harvested. Plenty of French people dismiss nouveau as undrinkable, saying it tastes and smells like bananas and is a vulgar excuse to party. But just as many French people participate in "Beaujolais Nouveau Day," the third Thursday in November when that year's wine is released at midnight; for many bars and restaurants, their entire stock of nouveau is consumed that night. The truth is a little of both: there is plenty of bad nouveau, but it can also be quite respectable in the hands of the right winemaker.

The real pleasure of Beaujolais, however, is found in its other wines. Officially, there are three "tiers." Nouveau generally comes from the first two: basic Beaujolais, and Beaujolais-Villages, a designation given to villages whose terroir has the potential to yield higher quality wines. Then there is Cru Beaujolais. In France a "cru" can refer to a village or even one specific vineyard—the important thing is that a cru has been certified as producing wines distinct enough to receive special classification. A cru doesn't guarantee quality—nothing can do that—but it's a good sign that the history and geography of a particular place is extraordinary. Beaujolais has ten villages that have earned the cru label (the unshaded sections grouped below):

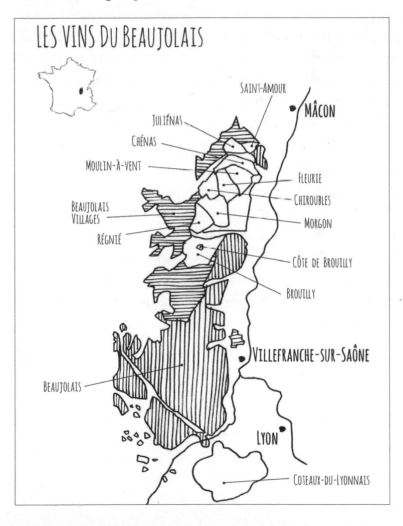

LES VINS DU BEAUJOLAIS

SAINT-AMOUR
MÂCON
JULIÉNAS
CHÉNAS
MOULIN-À-VENT
FLEURIE
CHIROUBLES
BEAUJOLAIS VILLAGES
MORGON
RÉGNIÉ
CÔTE DE BROUILLY
BROUILLY
VILLEFRANCHE-SUR-SAÔNE
BEAUJOLAIS
LYON
COTEAUX-DU-LYONNAIS

There's no magic pattern to the cru geography: Morgon produces fuller-bodied wines with good minerality thanks to its soil composition. Saint-Amour wines, just to the south of Burgundy, are among the lightest of the crus, but intensely fruity. Brouilly, the southernmost of the crus, is also light, yielding juicy wines, while those from Fleurie, true to their name, have floral notes.

Another interesting note about Beaujolais is that its producers are free to make different kinds of wines, which is not always the case. One fine winemaker is Jean-Marc Burgaud, who makes a remarkable nouveau while also producing great wine within the crus Régnié and Morgon. Another producer to look out for is Olivier Merlin, who makes Burgundies as well—his Moulin-à-Vent wines are gloriously perfumed and complex. I also admire Marcel Lapierre, Jean Foillard, Jean-Claude Lapalu, Christophe Pacalet, Jean-Paul Brun—I won't go on endlessly, but you get the point. The Beaujolais crus are real wines.

The only other quirk to note before you start shopping for Cru Beaujolais: the label will list the village name, such as Saint-Amour or Chénas or Brouilly—rather than Beaujolais—meaning there's a good chance the very people who turn up their noses at Beaujolais have actually been drinking it happily all along.

# 3.

............................................................................................

## There's More to Wine Than the Grape

*Le cépage, oui! Mais pas que...*

There are no shortcuts in wine. That is, there is no substitute for simply drinking and paying attention. Ratings and scores can't do it for you—though these days it can feel like a risky proposition to purchase a bottle that doesn't have a big number written on its tag. Well, take that risk!

This is not to say that reviews can't play a useful role. The danger is when they start to influence—or worse, override—your own critical faculties. If you buy a 92-point bottle, how could you not have that number in your head the first time you take a sip? How confident would you feel disagreeing if that particular wine doesn't suit you? What if, horror of horrors, you prefer a wine that received an *80*? Taken alone, scores don't tell you anything about the type of wine, your personal taste, or who you're drinking with.

Scores are convenient shorthand that often say more about the person or institution doing the grading than the wine itself. The accompanying tasting notes are to my mind more valuable. If they say this bottle has some spice to it, think: Do you like a peppery kick? Do you prefer red fruit or dark fruit? Used wisely, the notes help remind you about your own preferences.

Another shortcut is the grape variety. I was surprised to discover that most New World wines are known by a single variety, and are even produced with the goal of achieving some "true form" of that grape. French wines are referred to by region and appellation, *not* grape, since the French place greater value on terroir; some of their most prestigious wines, like Bordeaux, are blends of more than one grape variety. Wines made in the U.S., however, are generally what are called varietal wines, and are almost always purchased that way: *Oh, I'd like a glass of chardonnay/cabernet sauvignon/merlot.* You would never hear someone in France order wine that way. For one, it suggests that all, say, pinot noirs taste roughly the same, when that's not true. Though the grape certainly has specific qualities, a pinot noir from Oregon is different than one from California (or Burgundy!). You might fall in love with a delicate and refreshing Oregon pinot noir and believe you've found your favorite varietal wine. Imagine your surprise then when you drink one from California that is too bold for your tastes.

For a time, chardonnay, the most planted white grape in the world, developed a bad reputation for being overly oaked and bulky. So now you hear people in restaurants and bars murmur, "I don't want chardonnay; it's too oaky." But many chardonnays are steel-aged, or aged only slightly in oak, resulting in a totally different wine. Don't let stereotypes about a certain grape variety make you prejudge wines that include it.

But have no fear. The good news is that there is more excellent wine in the world now than ever before. The bad news is that there is more excellent wine in the world than ever before—more than you can drink in a lifetime. You may think this is reason enough to cheat a little, to outsource your own care and judgment. But in fact the opposite is true. Let the sheer volume of wine set you free; since there's no way you will try it all, take your time with it, and look beyond the label.

My first trip as brand ambassador was by far the longest I'd take during my six months at Château la Nerthe and in many ways the biggest test of the job—three weeks on the West Coast. On my flight to Seattle, all I could think about was just how much I didn't know: not just the new cities and unfamiliar customs, but the very business I was supposed to be an expert in. The distance between what was asked of me and what I knew how to do had never been so great. Would I be able to perform the bare minimum, to come off as anything but an idiot? Would I somehow, in these three weeks, achieve an understanding of the wine I could still only imagine?

Elise's directive to *be French* had stuck with me, but I could now see that her success was due to more than that, that for whatever reason she'd played down her professionalism, savvy, and work ethic. While in her company I'd been able to follow her cues and copy her winning smile as best as I could, but now I was on my own and, with nothing but my Frenchness to save me, would quickly be exposed as a fraud and sent home. There was no way that a foreign accent and a few talking points could cover up for a fundamental lack of experience.

I would turn out to be both right and wrong. Wrong because for the most part I did fine on that trip, and when I faltered, people were—in their American way—forgiving and supportive. I also was able to fool a good number of people. But I was also right, too, because the entire time *I* saw the gap between who I was pretending to be and who I really was. And it bothered me like little else ever has.

I landed in Seattle and took a car to the hotel, and had only an hour to gather myself before a sales rep arrived to pick me up. This would be my routine on the road for the six months ahead: a full day of appointments with restaurants and stores, chaperoned by the rep, capped off by a dinner with our most prized clients in the area. There would be no sitting quietly and listening to others. I was going to have to charm, charm, charm. It was as Elise had said—a personal touch could help a business owner cut through the noise and decide to carry our wines. I'd also overheard Luc on the phone saying, "Ms. Laure Dugas is coming from France to visit only our best sellers and most valuable clients. You'll have her for three days. Select your top reps."

It was a lot to live up to.

My first two days I had two different sales reps take me around, both men. The first, Robert, was very much an old-school salesman, with a big smile, booming voice, and salt-and-pepper hair that must have been premature because his face was still unlined. I don't know if Luc had clued in any of the distributors about my inexperience, but the meetings were so painless that by the end of the day I began to feel a flush of confidence.

The first store was on a tree-lined street just outside of downtown. The owners were a husband and wife who both greeted me with a relaxed warmth. I'd stepped through the jingling door feeling on edge, unsure how I'd ever prove myself to them, but it was immediately clear that *they* felt honored to meet *me*. And as I tried to form an adequate greeting in English, their faces lit up, as if my fumbling was actually charming.

Elise and Luc had been right! It was, as they'd both known, all about the power of expectations. This nice couple had been told they'd be getting a visit from a 92-point expert—why would they ever have suspected that the young Frenchwoman walking through their door had no rating at all? But I also must have somehow managed to keep my cheeks from turning their usual beet red.

And although Robert wasn't as charismatic as Elise, he was a pro; he kept up the small talk and helped move the tastings along so smoothly I wanted to ask if he could accompany me for the next three weeks. During that first sales call we developed a routine we then had no trouble repeating the rest of that day.

"And here I'm very happy to show to you our prize red, the Cuvée des Cadettes," I'd say.

As the client's eyes widened in anticipation, Robert would say, as if for the first time, "Ah, this is from the *vieilles vignes*, is that right, Laure?"

"Yes, that's quite right, Robert. Very old vines. A century, in fact, it's true. The grenache vines my uncle cultivates in this plot are more than a hundred years old. The syrah and mourvèdre vines are a bit younger, but still among the oldest of the estate, and it's from these three that the Cuvée des Cadettes is made. The vines are the lifeblood of the wine. The nineteenth-century owner Joseph Ducos had to replenish his vines from American rootstock after the great phylloxera crisis of 1881."

It sounds good, no? But I was embarrassed by the fact that my job involved repeating these mini-speeches over and over again, and especially that the rep would be there listening each time while I tried to make it sound fresh and new. How do salespeople do it?

But there's nothing like a little success to take the edge off. The first two stores placed their orders right there in front of me, and as we left Robert winked at me. I'd be lying if I said the feeling wasn't a rush.

Robert and I had our first client dinner with six men of around my father's age, one the owner of the restaurant. They all knew one another from the Seattle wine scene, so not only was I the odd person out, I was also the center of attention. I was very conscious of being the only woman—and of being a *young* woman—but there was also a strange comfort in being so obviously an outsider. In fact, they seemed to love the ways in which I was different, not least was the fact that I was the only one to order Pacific salmon amid a roster of steaks. I've noticed that the volume of a man's laugh increases in proportion to the number of other men in the room, and these guys emitted belly laughs while I sat at the head of the table and smiled, toggling between honest curiosity at their industry gossip and an air of forbearance every woman is expected to put on when surrounded by men.

I knew to pay the most attention to the restaurateur who was our host. I asked him about each dish, and received some teasing chuckles when I added, "Egg and plant, what is that?"

The lone French speaker among them explained, "Eggplant. *Aubergine*."

I felt myself turning red, until I remembered to be as Elise-like as I could. "Ah," I said, raising myself up in my seat a little. "Well, eggplant is a stupid name. You should change it."

This got bigger laughs, and my confidence grew. I pointed to the remains of a T-bone steak and said to its owner, "In my country it is customary at the end of a meal to dip the bone in the wine and chew on it." He hesitated, appearing to consider doing it, and his peers around the table started to roar—they wouldn't soon let him forget it.

In many ways the dinners were easier than the sales calls: for one, I could actually *drink* the wine instead of spit it out, and the setting was more convivial and less overtly businesslike. Even a novice like me, though, could sense the transactional undercurrent at every meal. Château la Nerthe and Moët Hennessey were paying for it, and despite the jocularity, the men's faces would turn momentarily serious whenever they sipped my uncle's wine. When we were down to the last of it, the host raised his glass—toward me. "We thank you for coming all this way," he said. I realized he meant from France, not New York.

"*Santé!*" I called out, thinking of Elise's advice. "To your health." And everyone echoed, "*Santé!*"

The waitress returned with the check and scanned the faces of all these accomplished older men. I can still picture the barely restrained look of surprise on her face when it was my hand that rose in the air to receive it.

I would be lying if I didn't admit that as surreal and nerve-racking as the experience was, it was also heady and glamorous. Who wouldn't want to feel like a foreign dignitary there to close a high-profile negotiation by signing a restaurant bill for a couple thousand dollars? I suddenly understood how appropriate the title "ambassador" was for the job. It only further hit home when Robert drove me back to my five-star hotel, the fanciest place I'd ever slept. It boggled my mind that my employers would put me up here, but Luc had explained it this way: my uncle's wine was not cheap, and Moët was a luxury house. It wouldn't have befitted their joint reputations to have me slumming around in roadside motels—which I would have been perfectly happy to do, though I wasn't about to complain. The hotel was unlike anything I had ever seen. I strode past the front gardens, beneath the glittering awning, through the glass doors held open for me by white-gloved men. My room had a silent pristine majesty about it, with floor-to-ceiling draperies and a marshmallow-soft bed wider than it was long. If I had really been a wine princess, maybe I would have felt at home in such extravagance. The day had been very convincing.

With an extra three hours between us, there was no way to get in touch with Jules at this hour, to reorient myself around the compass point of his personality. I fell asleep on that bed without changing my clothes or brushing my teeth, the cool touch of the white bedspread as powerful a sedative as the prick of a spindle.

I woke just before dawn, confused by the darkness. I walked down to the water, only a few blocks away, as the sun was coming up. The air was cool and, though I had been warned about Seattle's weather, dry. Some boats were already on the water, or had been there overnight, their lights still on. Even in the dim sunrise the ocean was an immense and humbling presence. It was the first time I had ever seen the Pacific, and it made me realize just how big the country behind me truly was.

I have a theory about cities with a coastline, as opposed to river cities like Paris and New York. People of the river are traders at heart and are more likely to abuse it the way you end up abusing

any tool. People of the sea, meanwhile, have a broader perspective. You can never trick yourself into believing you own an ocean.
Though I'd been in Seattle for only a day, I felt something in the
locals that reminded me of my time in Spain. I looked at the ocean
and felt suddenly breathless over how many thousands of miles—
with all of America's river people, ocean people, mountain people,
desert people, everyone I hadn't met yet or never would—I'd
crossed to be standing there.

Then it was Friday, and my magic carpet ride of pleasant sales
calls and sociable lunches and dinners was over. It was time for my
presentation to the local sales force. This was the real test—no
small talk, no helpful chaperone at my elbow. Just me and a hundred and fifty reps in person and on the other side of a video
camera.

I woke up that morning laughing. The thought of giving a
presentation to a room full of professionals was so unreal, so hi-
larious, that I kept laughing in the shower, and while salting my
eggs at the hotel breakfast. Then the laughter took a sharp left
turn into nausea. One or two store owners was one thing; a half-
dozen clients at a dinner was another; but a hundred and fifty?
The most people I'd ever spoken in front of was maybe my classmates at school, but that could hardly count. I called Jules in a
half-hiccupping, half-giggling fit, hoping to calm my nerves.

"Do you know what you're going to say?" he asked me.

"Yes, I've practiced it many times, but"—hic—"I'm too anxious."

"Say it to me."

I began to recite my opening, voice shaking.

"No, no, no," he said. "Think about what you are doing. Think
about the wine. Pay attention to what you're saying."

The French, for all their romantic reputation, are a relatively unsentimental and blunt people. But I couldn't tell right away if his advice was helping or hurting. I hadn't been worried about the speech itself, only my nerves, but now thanks to Jules I was worried about both.

"I just need a little reassurance," I bristled.

"I *am* reassuring you. I know you can do this."

I felt a burst of both gratitude and exasperation toward my boyfriend. Angry, frustrated, determined, I spat out the opening of my presentation so quickly—and flawlessly—that Jules couldn't keep up, even though his English was better than mine.

"That was good, you see?" he said, satisfied.

We said our usual affectionate goodbyes, and I hung up with a sigh. I knew, despite my agitation, that he'd helped, and that I wouldn't have gotten so annoyed if we'd been able to stay in as close touch as we normally did when I was in New York. What did this mean for us over the next few months of heavy travel? I didn't know. And I had no time to think about it. At the table where I'd eaten I took a photo of a heart hastily constructed out of sugar packets and texted it to Jules. For the moment, it would have to do.

So there I was, standing on the other side of the door to the tasting room. The two office managers who'd greeted me and helped me get set up didn't need special powers to see how nervous I was. But they were kind enough not to say anything. My lips felt dry, even with gloss on, but I couldn't possibly drink any more water without risking an incident. I paced in a small circle until it was time.

Then I was through the door and in front of a dozen rows of well-dressed men and women. I spotted the camera to one side, which stared at me unblinkingly. I tried to clear my throat but out came a little cough instead, which seemed to echo around the room. Everyone shifted in their seats. I realized that there was no cue—no prompt for me to know when to begin. Walking in was my own cue. I was supposed to start—now. I searched for the words I'd spent so long memorizing.

*Hello, everyone! My name is Laure Dugas, and I'm so happy to be here.*

I took a deep breath as unobtrusively as I could and plowed ahead before my nerves had a chance to catch up.

*I am the niece of Alain Dugas, the winemaker of Château la Nerthe. I'm traveling the U.S. for six months to tell our most important clients about the wine. First, I would like to describe for you Château la Nerthe and what makes it and the Châteauneuf-du-Pape village so special. Châteauneuf-du-Pape is the most prestigious cru from the southern Rhône. I probably don't have to tell you that. Gigondas, Vacqueyras, and Beaumes de Venise all make wonderful wine, but, let's be honest, they cannot compare with Châteauneuf-du-Pape, which is blessed with the superior terroir. And Château la Nerthe is one of the most prestigious châteaux from Châteauneuf-du-Pape. So you might say we have the best of the best.*

*Now, I did not have anything to do with it—I'm just a lucky girl to be representing such quality. My uncle is the one with the flair for wine-making. He was the one who convinced the current owners to acquire the château in 1985 when it was producing good but unexceptional wine, and worked hard to improve the vineyard, expand the cellars, and reno-*

*vate the château. I was just a baby. It was he who on faith introduced a greater percentage of the mourvèdre grape than usual, to complement the all-important grenache base and give the wine great aging potential. He also had high enthusiasm for* counoise, *which provides structure and peppery, spicy aromas characteristic of a good Châteauneuf.*

I garbled a few words here and there, and was nearly derailed by a couple of faces in the crowd whose frowns set off flares of panic in my mind: did no one understand a word I was saying? I could see some pens moving on notepads, but others were still. I quickly scanned for friendlier faces, and located a woman who was smiling enormously at me—but this was distracting, as well, so I ended up fixing my eyes at a point just above their heads.

I finished the introduction and steeled myself for the difficult part, walking them through the tasting. Luc had told me over and over that these reps had at least four hundred wines, or "references," to memorize—it was therefore my job to make sure Château la Nerthe was not a name they'd forget. If I was already having trouble communicating, the tasting would truly expose me. Thankfully, no one asked difficult questions, only the occasional request for me to repeat a few facts, which I did happily. They were busy sipping the four Château la Nerthe wines (two white, two red), and I stood there feeling an inkling of relief, thinking it was a bit surreal to be surrounded by so many people sniffing, swirling, sipping—and spitting—all at once. They wrote things down and nodded as I recited the notes I'd memorized but still didn't understand.

*Here is our flagship Cuvée des Cadettes. My uncle says this release, 2005, is one of the best ever. It's characterized by a dark red color with an intense aromatic expression. It is rich, concentrated, and dense. The tannins are suave, and the wine has a long finish of fruits and spices. It is a wine you can easily age for ten or fifteen years before drinking. But as with all great wines, it can also be appreciated while young if you really can't wait.*

Only once did all the reps pay perfect attention and begin scribbling simultaneously: when I shared the high Robert Parker and *Wine Spectator* scores. So you see, scores are important to everyone, professionals and amateurs alike, even if there's so much the numbers can't capture.

The Cuvée des Cadettes tasting marked the end of the presentation. I wanted to sink into a plush chair and take a nap, but I still had some socializing to do. The reps shook my hand and said brief thank-yous. Their meeting was to continue without me, so I stepped back out to the office area, where the managers patted my arm and said, "Great job!" in a tone that suggested that I hadn't really done a great job at all, or that they hadn't expected me to.

American optimism and cheerfulness are wonderful qualities that aren't celebrated enough. Americans are always lying through their teeth to tell you how nice you look or how wonderful their day is. How could this not make the world a better place, even when reality is in fact a little disappointing?

But sometimes a kind lie is the last thing you want to hear.

I took a car back to the hotel to get my things before my flight to San Francisco, and could barely keep from bursting into tears when Jules called me. The texts I'd been sending him all morning had been alarming enough that he'd stepped away from dinner to use the phone. But as I explained what had happened, down to the office managers' responses, his soothing tone hardened a little, and he said, "You are reading too much into things. It sounds like you did fine. Everyone tasted the right wines, yes? You did not mix anything up, any descriptions?"

"Yes, no. I mean, yes, I got the order right."

"Then that is the most important thing. They will remember you. Who couldn't? You are very charming when you get nervous."

"I hate you."

I wiped my nose with a cocktail napkin I'd taken from the distributor's office, but Jules had managed to thwart any more tears. By the time I landed in San Francisco, I felt better, my mood overwhelmed by the view of the Pacific coastline as we followed it to the nub of land that was our destination. I hadn't known San Francisco was a peninsula, and the sight of the water gave me a little lift. After checking into another luxurious hotel as the sun was setting, I walked up the nearest hill, thinking that would make the return route easier, but the land played a trick on me by falling again, then rising once more, until it was fully dark; and, tired and lost, I took a taxi back and ordered room service.

I ordered room service the entire weekend, and when I wasn't outside I was in the hotel bathrobe. I indulged because I was alone, and because Seattle had worn me out, as new and challenging experiences do. I did touristy things like ride a cable car and take pictures of the sea lions at Fisherman's Wharf for Jules, but otherwise had little opportunity for conversation, which, for the first time since I'd landed in November, I was thankful for. San Francisco felt like a more weathered Seattle, dirtier but also livelier, *almost* Old World (and at the risk of alienating one great city for another, possibly more beautiful). I'd been told it would be cold and windy, but just as I'd lucked out with no rain in Seattle, it was actually warmer in San Francisco, the air crisp and still, with blue skies.

Come Monday I was ready to go again. As I waited in the hotel lobby for my chaperone, the embarrassment I'd felt on Friday was long behind me. The week went by quickly. My visits to the stores and restaurants went well—I was in my element speaking to just one or two people at a time. There was one sales rep who was aloof and uninterested, despite the fact that I was there to help *his* client relationships, but I managed to hold my own, even with the small talk and transitions that I'd been relying on my escorts for. Each night I returned to the hotel and sat for a minute trying to think about how I felt: Was I enjoying myself? Was I improving? Was I comfortable talking about wine? And each night, to my surprise, the answers were yes, yes, yes.

My Friday presentation to the entire sales staff was still a little herky-jerky, but better. I slowed down. I thought about what I was saying, instead of just discharging a rapid-fire barrage of words. I paused and smiled. Once, Luc had given me the strangest advice— somewhat hesitantly, as if he didn't believe it himself—that it could help to picture the audience naked. I didn't even try to follow it. Instead, I pretended the audience was a casual acquaintance I wanted to convert into a good friend—someone I had to win over and flirt with, someone who would bring out, albeit in a temporary, superficial way, the best in me. *Remember me!* was the command I tried to channel. *Remember me!*

There were no pitying pats on the arm from the office managers this time.

Then I was on the plane again, to Los Angeles. I wasn't going to train reps this time, but to represent Château la Nerthe at Moët Hennessey's annual West Coast wine show. (The Midwest and East Coast shows were to follow in Chicago and New York.) My uncle had made it clear how important this was for publicity. As an event it was less about selling wine than about getting the château's name in front of new people in the industry—a rare opportunity to represent ourselves directly to them, instead of relying on wholesalers. It was important enough that my uncle—employer and kin—was flying out himself.

Let me tell you a little about my Uncle Alain. Though he's my father's brother and my grandfather's son, unlike both of them he ended up an expressively happy and positive person. It's possible this is what drew him to the south of France, where there are more people like him. The family members in Paris have more dour demeanors and higher blood pressures—we love one another with little bites and snaps, a tradition Uncle Alain doesn't participate in, instead sitting slightly apart with a big smile on his face. He loves the good things in life, and it's no surprise that his calling was not only to sell wine, but to make it, and make it very well.

Just standing outside the Roosevelt Hotel, right on the Walk of Fame, I felt a sense of déjà vu even though I'd never stepped foot there: this was Hollywood, which to anyone not raised underground needed no introduction. The giant movie theaters along the street, the palm trees, the sunshine, the warmth—like a summer day in Paris but in late January. Los Angeles, more than any other city in the U.S., looked and felt exactly as I'd expected (even if I hadn't yet seen any movie stars in the hour since arriving). After eleven days on my own, I was hungry for a familiar face, and a little nervous: other than the short time before and after my six-week crash course in wine, I'd never spent much time alone with my uncle. As my father's elder brother, he had been a sage if playful presence in my life, someone I'd always felt like a little girl around (after all, I'd *been* a little girl for most of our relationship), but now I had to pretend, every second we were together, to be a competent employee—and an adult.

I dropped my bags off and knocked on the door of his room just down the hall. After a minute he opened the door, a little bleary-eyed—I'd woken him from a nap. I started to apologize but he embraced me. "Here we are! California!" he said, immediately launching into a string of stories—for my uncle, life is a long comedy that it is his job to narrate—about the guy at the airport who almost accidentally walked away with my uncle's luggage; how he was certain he'd seen Julia Roberts on the street but she wouldn't turn around when he called out; the very hip sunglasses he'd bought in the gift shop because he'd forgotten his, and had I noticed how *bright* everything was?—all while changing his shirt, pulling on his shoes, splashing water on his face and bald head. "All right, let's go!" he said, leading the charge.

While the valet went for his rental car, he told me three times to "just wait"—until a silver Mustang convertible appeared. "California!" he said, as if it were the explanation for everything. Laughing, we took a picture in front of the car and sent it to the rest of the family.

"Where are we going?" I asked as we pulled out.

"To the beach, where else?" he said. I protested that I wasn't prepared for the beach, but he waved his hand and explained that we weren't going *on* the beach, just *near* the beach.

I have since confirmed that both Beverly Hills and Venice

Beach are in Los Angeles, but the drive seemed to take forever. The city never ended. We stayed on one road for as far as it took us toward the ocean, and whenever we hit a red light I pushed off my seat a little to look around. My uncle loved driving with the top down, chuckling every so often at nothing I could see, happy behind his new sunglasses. After a while I couldn't hold it any longer and began to ask questions about the business—the new world—I'd entered just a matter of weeks ago.

"Hush, Laure, let's not talk about work today."

But I would not leave him alone. "Sulfites," I said. "Someone asked me how much sulfites you put in the wine and I didn't know the answer!"

"Just a few milligrams a liter," he said with a sigh. "We are trying to reduce the amount. You can say that. But a little bit is important to halt fermentation."

"Do we have to decant the 2005?"

"Oh yes, the 2005 is still so young you must decant it!" He looked over at me with alarm in his face for the first time, as if wondering if he'd made a mistake with me. "Tell me you decanted it."

"We did," I said, and patted his hand.

His brow relaxed, but I would remember that moment of tension—a reminder that this was serious stuff.

We had to speak loudly to be heard over the engine as I asked him more about his wine. He was openly amused, as these were questions I'd never asked before, though I'd had plenty of opportunity to. The top button of his shirt was undone and his collar flapped in the breeze. I'd never seen him quite like this. When we arrived in Venice we walked along the boardwalk and joked about my father, who had never been to California, wondering—as we passed a unicyclist in cutoffs being pulled by a large dog shaved to look like a lion—what he'd think of the place. How remarkable it was, he said, that the two of us were here together, five thousand miles from home. Though I'd always liked my uncle, we now had something else connecting us besides blood.

The sun was setting directly over the water, something I couldn't remember ever seeing before this trip, and I wondered if the daily sight of the sun being extinguished by the ocean had an effect on all the people who live on a western shore. It certainly made an impression on me. We turned around and drove back to the main commercial strip for dinner, where my uncle knew the owner of a popular restaurant called Primitivo, named after an Italian red wine grape. We sat on the rear patio in the warm night and ordered too much: steak, which my aunt doesn't normally let him eat, a goat cheese salad, Spanish-style potatoes. Alain acted as if he didn't want to think about work, but he handed out cards to everyone his friend introduced him to—regulars at the bar, local businesspeople, a family of four.

The next day Alain made even less effort to suppress his networking instinct, stopping at restaurants he thought looked interesting as we drove semi-aimlessly around Beverly Hills and Hollywood and West Hollywood and Santa Monica. We ate tacos for lunch because he had a craving, then stopped at three French restaurants so he could meet the management and tell them about the upcoming trade fair. He stuck with ginger ale while I got a little drunk on cocktails.

"I'll tell you a secret," he said at one point. "This is when I am at my best as a salesman. When I am relaxed and happy. It is infectious."

"It won't work with me," I said, feeling a little sorry for myself.

"My English is still too poor. Everyone speaks too quickly and they understand me even less."

He shook his head slowly and dramatically, and I was afraid for a second I was about to be reprimanded by my uncle and boss.

"That's not it at all. Laure, my dear," he said with a hand on my arm, "everyone understands a smile."

The trade show was not quite what I expected. Moët had rented out a large restaurant and nightclub in which long rows of cloth-covered tables were set up for each of the fifty to sixty producers to be represented. At one end of the room was a temporary stage with a tall metal frame supporting what looked like theater lights. I didn't know what it could possibly be for. We set up early, at eight-thirty in the morning, unpacking the wines, opening them ahead of time to let them breathe and to make sure they weren't corked. We checked before cooling the whites, because, my uncle told me, bad wine is easier to detect at room temperature (this is why cheap wine is often served very cold). Other winemakers were setting up their booths, too, and occasionally my uncle would wander over to someone he knew to say hello.

After an hour or two, people started to file in. They were os-tensibly all folks in the industry who had signed up, with their identification on lanyards as proof, but I suspected that some were friends or dates tagging along for the free wine. A seller or som-melier there on business might taste dozens of wines, hence the spittoons at every booth. There was no way to stay clear-headed if you actually drank every pour.

Let's just say that our spittoon did not get very much use.

Around midday the purpose of the stage became ostentatiously clear: a DJ had set up while I wasn't paying attention and was now playing loud dance music that echoed through the hall. The lights began to shine bright primary colors over the booths, zipping around and spinning, as if it was Friday night on a dance floor, not Monday afternoon at a corporate, industry event. My uncle was in the middle of describing the color of his Clos de Beauvenir to a potential buyer when a green spotlight landed on the glass, turning the golden liquid an unappetizing neon. I watched as two beautiful young women I'd seen drinking at nearly every booth suddenly turned toward each other and started kissing.

I looked at my uncle helplessly, and he seemed to shrug to me with his eyes: *What do you expect? It's Los Angeles!*

If he wasn't annoyed, then why was I? Moët had made the L.A. show fun and sexy, and I took it personally. I'd wanted it to be more serious, because *I* wanted to be more serious. I'd said yes to my uncle's job offer on a lark—free travel! free English!—and had underestimated how much work and care would go into the actual wine. I could see—and my nerves had made crystal clear—that I wasn't going to be able to skate by on my Frenchness. Even if I could fool some people, I'd never fool myself. The bits of knowledge I'd accumulated thus far only made what I still had to learn that much more apparent.

I was also starting to realize how much I missed New York.

## Thinking About Wine

Though a wine label cannot tell you everything, it does convey vital information: where it was made, when it was made, and who made it. French wine labels are among the most complicated, because they must follow strict rules—far more stringent than in the U.S. They're not always artistically designed, the way many American labels are, and are often just-the-facts. What information is allowed or required on the label also varies from region to region, and while we don't have room here to list every combination, the major components of a French wine label are as follows: 1. Region, 2. Sub-region and/or appellation, 3. Producer, 4. Vintage, and, often of interest, some 5. Miscellany.

Notice: no grape varieties! With few exceptions, the type of grape is not listed on a French label (sometimes you'll see it included in an attempt to market a wine internationally). There are several reasons for this. For one, as I've said, wine is more than the grape. Wine can also be more than *one* grape. Bordeaux is the most famous example, as the three grapes found in almost every Bordeaux red are cabernet sauvignon, merlot, and to a lesser extent cabernet franc. That's why it's impossible to be in Bordeaux and order a local "merlot."

The Châteauneuf-du-Pape appellation, meanwhile, allows the blending of up to *thirteen* specified grapes for red wine, the main ones being grenache, syrah, and mourvèdre. This astonishing number comes from the fact that the region has wonderful terroir but harsh (very hot!) conditions. Blending allows the producers flexibility to fine-tune their formulas, so to speak, based on what the land gives them. And the Châteauneuf-du-Pape land gives producers a wide mix of soil types to deal with, including the *galets*, which translates roughly to "pebbles." These stones, which form a natural layer over the sloping mounds of clay and sand rising above the Rhône River, help ripen the grapes by storing heat during the day and warming the vines at night. They also allow water to penetrate the soil, reducing stagnation and disease.

The effects of the features unique to this region are really remarkable. And they've allowed great wine to flourish there since the fourteenth century, when the pope lived in Avignon instead of Rome (hence Châteauneuf-du-Pape, which means "the pope's new castle"), and even long before then.

Here is a reproduction of Château la Nerthe's label for its flagship red, the Cuvée des Cadettes:

From top to bottom, you can see the information clearly conveyed: the producer (Château la Nerthe); the appellation, or geographical region (Châteauneuf-du-Pape); the tier designation of this particular French agricultural product (the highest being *appellation d'origine contrôlée*, AOC, as the apellation name indicates); the house name for this wine (Cuvée des Cadettes); an assurance that the wine was bottled at the estate (*Mis en bouteille au Château*); and the year of harvest, or *millésime*.

It's a lot. And every detail, and the order they're in, changes from wine to wine, region to region. (Right now there are sixteen official wine regions in France, and, gulp, 383 appellations. On the next page is a map of the region most important to this chapter: the Rhône Valley, which you'll see is more complex than Beaujolais.) Not all houses have a special "nickname" for the wine. The estate may call itself a *château*, or a domaine depending on the region—either word, though, is a clue that this is the name of the producer. Sometimes, as with Cru Beaujolais, the cru is named but not the greater region. Sometimes, as with Bordeaux, the subregion is spelled out in big letters. In some places, like Burgundy, the finest crus are their own appellation, and their own vineyard, too. It's complicated. You'll also see official signifiers like *1er cru* (*1er* means "premier"—very good) or grand cru (even better). There are also unofficial, unregulated signifiers that sound fancy but don't mean much, like *réserve* (special collection), *vieilles vignes* (old vines), or *vieillit en fût de chêne* (aged in oak—but what kind of oak?).

Whew. Ready to just go back to ordering single varietal wines? But don't give up quite yet: take heart in that you don't need to know French to read a wine label. In many ways, a label is its own language. And to speak it, you need to know not its grammar, but its context: a little about the different regions, and the character of each and the viticulture there. How much of the story you want to hear is up to you, but once you have a grasp of the bigger picture, your trips to the wine store will become much more interesting.

# 4.

······································································

## Taste the Present

### Savourer le présent

Imagine a beautiful village of several thousand people, each interesting in his or her own way. You want to meet all of them, and
not just *meet* them, but get to know them a little, spend time with
each and every one. Even if you shared every meal of every day
with a new friend, though, it would take years. And how would
you remember Julie as you sat down with Bob? What if you really
liked Lucy and wanted to eat a second meal with her, even if that
meant that everyone else had to wait? Consider also that people
are always changing, so if you miss someone one year, well, they'll
be slightly different by the time you do get around to them. This
is the conundrum when it comes to tasting wines—even just from
Bordeaux, say, a huge region with thousands of producers. Imag-

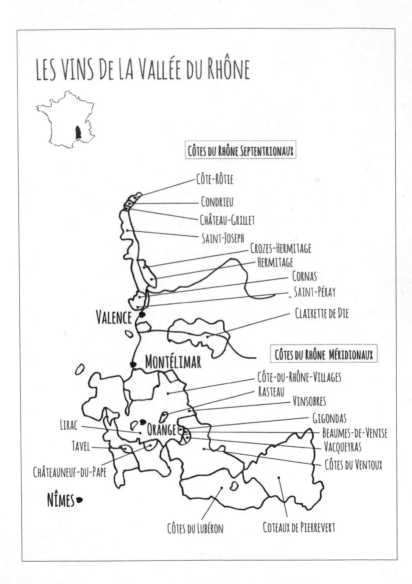

# LES VINS DE LA VALLÉE DU RHÔNE

**CÔTES DU RHÔNE SEPTENTRIONAUX**

- Côte-Rôtie
- Condrieu
- Château-Grillet
- Saint-Joseph
- Crozes-Hermitage
- Hermitage
- Cornas
- Saint-Péray
- Clairette de Die

VALENCE

MONTÉLIMAR

**CÔTES DU RHÔNE MÉRIDIONAUX**

- Côte-du-Rhône-Villages
- Rasteau
- Vinsobres
- Gigondas
- Beaumes-de-Venise
- Vacqueyras
- Côtes du Ventoux

Lirac

ORANGE

Tavel

Châteauneuf-du-Pape

NÎMES

Côtes du Lubéron        Coteaux de Pierrevert

ine the task at hand if you wanted to meet all the wines of France, or all the wines of the world. It's impossible.

Yet it was a task I felt I had to at least attempt in good faith, even while acknowledging its futility. I mentioned this to my uncle on our flight to Chicago. We'd spent one more day in the silver Mustang meeting with clients in San Diego, a beautiful, relaxed city that felt like Los Angeles without Hollywood, and were on our way to the second leg of Moët's wine shows.

"No, no," he said. He leaned back against the headrest and closed his eyes, pursing his lips as he settled in to nap. "You can't think of all the wines out there, like all the books you never got to read. You'll go mad. Think only about the wine in front of you." He smiled to himself as he fell asleep, as if he had a particular wine in mind that very moment—possibly one of his own.

It was good advice ten years ago, and even better today. We are living in a golden age of wine in terms of more information available to the consumer than ever before, and the advancement of viticultural techniques that allow excellent wine to be produced in more places. Don't listen to the voices that say things were better *back then*. It's simply not true. I know an older man who is always nostalgic for the days when French wine mainly meant just Bordeaux and Burgundy. "Laure," he has said with an astonished look on his face. "I just had a wine from the Languedoc that was . . . superb." And he would shake his head, as if disappointed.

You may already know about the American wine boom that began with Napa Valley in the 1980s. But you might be surprised to find out that something similar was happening in Europe—yes, even in France. In the seventies and eighties, Languedoc was little more than a giant wine factory, mass-producing cheap table wine. Even regions as historic as Châteauneuf-du-Pape and the Rhône

Valley were turning out inconsistent products. For a long time, there was even *too much* French wine on the market, which may not have been good for sellers but brought prices down.

In 1985, my uncle saw an opportunity. He loved the terroir of Châteauneuf-du-Pape, and at the time most of the grapes were being sold into trade, not made into wine at the estates. He saw great potential in Château la Nerthe in particular, which was a good value for its terroir, but still too expensive for him to buy. So he convinced the Richard family to buy it and hire him as winemaker. It took a decade for my uncle to prove himself to the wary community. Other producers started to take advantage of opportunities in "up-and-coming" regions like the Rhône, the Languedoc, and up north in the Loire. And now with great wine coming from all corners, the mark of a true enthusiast is no longer determined by who has a bottle of 1947 Château Margaux gathering dust in a dark cellar. That rarified world still thrives, but the truth is that there has never been a better time to fall in love with wine than today.

The West Coast was still shimmering in my mind, golden and bright like an overexposed photograph, when we landed in Chicago, and it remained the most vivid of all the places I would see in my remaining months as brand ambassador. We spent two days in Chicago before returning to New York. Our only full day we spent at the trade show, held in a hotel ballroom and a far more sedate affair than the Los Angeles disco ball. Nearly all the attendants were sober, literally and figuratively.

Chicago itself was beautiful, with a skyline that reminded me of Manhattan, but more manageable. I was charmed by the elevated trains, which made the city seem antiquated to me, but in an admirable way, like an old clock that has been lovingly preserved. The city was also cold. Bone-chillingly, mind-numbingly cold. I'd never been so cold in my entire life, especially having stepped directly out from under the California sun.

Then, nearly three weeks after I'd left, I was back in New York. For someone who had lived in the city for only a couple of months, it was a strange experience, like coming back to someone you'd dated only a short while and weren't sure if you would still be attracted to. It was my third arrival, and my first at night, and my heart lifted when I saw the lights outlining Manhattan in the distance. When I reached the East Village I stood in the hall outside the apartment for a few nervous seconds. I pushed open the door and rolled my suitcase toward my bedroom. Shaina was in the living room watching a sitcom without laughing, and I said hello. She grunted. Carl's door was open, and he was at his desk in nothing but boxers, eating cereal. They weren't acknowledging each other's existence. I smiled to myself.

I was home.

My uncle stayed another few days in New York. He attended the final show of the Moët tour, and a day later he had a black-tie charity event at the gorgeous main branch of the New York Public Library, also sponsored by Moët. He told me to come with him. It felt like a natural extension of the high-altitude schmoozing I'd done with Elise and on the West Coast (would I ever come down?). But I had nothing to wear. Rose and Maya ransacked their closets for me, but everything was too small—in the case of Rose's clothes, comically so. Maya held up a finger and went into her roommate's closet and brought back a beautiful, simple black dress with a dark, shimmering blue lace overlay. I wore my favorite earrings of Rose's (who couldn't be seen without a pair on), shaped like dia-

monds surrounded by tiny black gems, and a simple necklace of
Maya's.

I met my uncle at the foot of the stairs to the library, the stone
lions proudly guarding the entrance. Inside, as I stood awkwardly
by the banquet tables in the main hall, there was no doubt that I
was among the city's wealthy and elite. I couldn't spot anyone else
even close to my age. My uncle seemed unfazed, even if it was not
his natural crowd.

"There are a lot of people here like us," he whispered during
dinner, as though reading my mind, "invited to make the night
more interesting. If you can't tell by the clothes, look here and
here," he said, smiling, touching his neck, his ears, and his wrist.
My skin suddenly still felt bare and underadorned.

The night before Alain left he took me to dinner with a small,
respected importer from upstate, a Québécois man named Mark
Brodeur. It was possibly the most decadent French meal I've ever
had, eaten the most French way—five courses over four hours in
a three-star restaurant overlooking Central Park. It was nearly too
long for me, but the men, intent on catching up with each other,
didn't notice. I enjoyed watching my uncle interact in French with
an old acquaintance, especially someone who had as joyful an air
as he did. They swooned collectively over a white Burgundy,
praising its toastiness and firm acidity, while I remained silent, too
intimidated by the depth of their knowledge to add anything.
When we finally finished, it was late, but they insisted on spending a little more time walking up Broadway smoking cigars and
interrupting each other. I stayed a few steps behind. When he had
to leave to make his train, Mark gave me his card and told me to
call if I needed anything.

"You see," my uncle said as we watched him dash off, "I am
making sure everyone is watching over you." He took me by my

shoulders with a firm grip I had not felt from him before and kissed me loudly on each cheek, then looked at me for several seconds with a big smile, as if to imprint it on me. "You're going to have a great time," he said. "I can guarantee it."

But once he was gone, like a floating feather I slowly descended into a sort of lull. I spent a week in Houston and Dallas, which I hoped would add new exciting dimensions to the map of the U.S. that I was drawing in my head, the way my previous trip had, but I was disappointed. It was nice to have a warm reprieve from the New York winter, my sales calls and client meals all went smoothly, and both cities were impressively large, but I couldn't quite get a grasp on either. I knew Houston was near the gulf, but didn't get to see the water, and the parts of town where I spent my time remained anonymous to me. I was also likely affected by constant texts from Jules, warning me that I was in George W. Bush's home state.

Dallas was a letdown for one other reason. My late grandmother had watched *Dallas* the TV show obsessively, and as a child I'd often sit beside her in the afternoons and watch along. So I wanted above all else to visit a ranch, to see horses and cowboys with big hats, and I thought for some reason it would be a natural part of my business there, though I was too embarrassed to ask Luc to confirm. Instead, I spent my whole time within sight of the downtown skyscrapers and felt cheated, as if I'd gone to San Francisco and been told the Golden Gate Bridge was unavailable for viewing. (Back in New York, Luc asked me if I'd had any trouble with the Texas accent, and, confused, I said, "What accent?")

My next trip was to Boston, which I loved. It felt almost European: I was at home among its narrow, crooked streets, its brick buildings and unmistakable sense of history. One client dinner was at a restaurant in a town house on a tree-lined street that could have been in a quiet London neighborhood, or even a Parisian one. It also made me homesick. The initial thrill of the job was over, it seemed—and so soon. Boston was my third trip, and I was impatient that I hadn't made more progress with my wine education. I was a bit more polished, but I was building expertise solely in Château la Nerthe wine, nothing else.

I was also lonely. Though I'd already spent a school year apart from Jules while in Spain, it turned out that being in the same time zone had kept us feeling much closer (and we were, of course, physically closer). I couldn't get used to the dramatic way our days were now misaligned. By the time I woke up, he'd finished lunch, and our goodnight calls had to happen before I went to dinner while he got ready for bed alone. I'd leave a restaurant with Rose and Nico, and Alex and Maya, the couples wrapped around each other, and grip my phone, knowing it was too late to talk to Jules.

But I loved spending time with the foursome. Even though I had no real alternative, socially, and was lucky to have friends given how much traveling I'd been doing, I genuinely liked them. I liked Rose's compact fierceness, Nico's frank gregariousness, Maya's devil-may-care attitude, and Alex's sense of play. Rose and Nico were Parisians, like me, but Alex and Maya were southerners, she from the coastal town of Marseilles and he from Aix-en-Provence. You could spot the differences immediately when we were together. Rose and Nico—in fashion photography and advertising, respectively—dressed sharply, Rose in sleek shoes and dark colors, Nico in skinny ties and trendy hats. Maya, meanwhile, was a publicist who wore dresses and leggings, and Alex was a Himalayan salt salesman and favored casual shirts with the top buttons unbuttoned. We grew close in the way expatriates are forced to be, but each couple had met and started dating before I'd known them—the southerners in a bar in New York, and the Parisians going back to their freshman year of high school in France—so there was always a secret history and a depth of intimacy among the couples that I couldn't come close to, or experience myself.

The next city on my itinerary was Las Vegas, and even that was hard to get excited about (my friends were excited enough on my behalf). But if many of the cities I saw in the U.S. have since blurred together in my mind, Las Vegas isn't one of them. How could it? From the window of my descending plane I saw the Great Pyramid of Egypt, the Space Needle (hadn't I just been there?), and, of course, the Eiffel Tower, all reconstructed at smaller scale on a single street. I checked into my hotel, but not before watching in amazement as a singing gondolier steered a middle-aged couple down the indoor, too-blue-to-be-real Grand Canal.

"It is like the gift-store version of everything that is wrong with America," Jules said when I called him. It was long after midnight his time. He was a night owl, but he yawned, bored perhaps by the pinnacle of American extravagance.

"I kind of like it," I said. This woke him up.

"How so?"

"Because it's all out there. At least it's not pretending to be anything but entertainment."

He made a scoffing, dismissive noise. "*Je t'aime, mon coeur,*" he said. "I'm going to sleep."

"*Je t'aime, mon loup,*" I said, and hung up. Outside my hotel window, it was as bright as a desert day can be, amplified by all the reflective surfaces up and down the Strip.

The sales rep, one of the few women I'd work with, picked me up in a car, though nearly everywhere we went was within walking distance. The restaurants for our client meetings were inside the hotels, the diners sitting among fine art or looking out on swimming pools made to look like a tropical resort's. Each time we walked across a casino floor and I heard the ringing of slot machines and the cheers of groups huddled around the craps tables, I felt a strumming of excitement—not because of the games themselves, but because I wanted to believe, as everyone else did, that anything could happen.

Dinner that night was on the larger side, with ten clients, so there was less pressure for me to hold court. I spoke a little at the beginning about my uncle's wine and how happy we were for it to be served in such fine establishments, including the one we were sitting in. We toasted to Château la Nerthe, and to partnerships, and of course to lady luck. The sommelier to my right was a handsome brown-haired, blue-eyed man who couldn't have been older than thirty. While he was deep in conversation with the older man on his other side, I tried to remember if the rep had guided people to their seats, or if he'd sat there on purpose.

When he paused and turned to look my way, as if to speak, I said, "I'm sorry, there were so many introductions. Which restaurant do you work at again?"

"This one." He smiled.

I felt the red shoot straight into my cheeks. "Forgive me. You are so young."

"I could say the same about you. So you've come from New York?" he said—not *France*. He'd been paying attention.

"Yes, I live there right now. But I was born in Paris."

"I never would have guessed. Your accent is undetectable."

I snorted, and hated myself for laughing at such a cheap joke. He told me he'd gone to the French Culinary Institute in New York and had wanted to be a chef before switching to wine. I said I lived close by, in the East Village. He asked about a *pommes frites* shop he loved and was relieved and pleased when I told him it was still there.

I don't remember the rest of dinner. At the end I said another thank-you to all the guests, looking each client in the eye during the final toast (another tip from my uncle), and I stood as everyone began to leave, shaking hands all around, exchanging cards, joking that the 2005 vintage was going to be a tough year to beat but we'd ask the weather gods to do their best. When I shook hands with the young sommelier, he said, "Would you like to try some of our other wines? They're not as good as your uncle's, but they're not bad."

The hardest times to say no are when you have more than one reason to say yes. It was too easy to convince myself that the opportunity to taste great wine was the real justification for accompanying him alone to the restaurant's temperature-controlled vestibule, next to the kitchen but tucked away, out of sight. He put two glasses on a narrow shelf and ran his fingers along a row of bottles whose labels I tried to read, then said, "Hang on, there's an open bottle at the station from earlier today. It should have breathed enough by now."

He left me alone for a minute, during which I could feel all my muscles clench and unclench in a slow and steady rhythm. When he returned, I said quickly, "I didn't realize how tired I was. I should go."

He studied my face for a second, and said, "You have to try this, unless you know it already?"

I didn't—it was Californian. "Like me," he said, a little raffishly. "It's a Bordeaux-style blend—cabernet-merlot. I want you to try it and see what you think."

I took in the aroma: fragrant, fruity, with a woodsy edge. I sipped. It was powerful, with a sweet spice that made me think of Moroccan food. I said some of this out loud, and he gave a gentle, appreciative smile and nodded. "I get the nutmeg," he said, and I felt another flush spreading over my body, a more pleasant one this time. "Sandalwood," he added. The wine made him extremely happy—it was all over his face. And I was happy, too, to share it with someone who was affected so openly.

He held eye contact over our glasses, and I could see him hesitate. "I have something else you have to try," he said, and turned back toward the bottles, breaking the spell.

"Thank you," I said, silently instructing my feet to move this time. "This has been really nice, but I have to get back to Venice."

He laughed. We shook hands again, and I left the restaurant, and the bells of the casino floor were like Cinderella's chimes in the seconds before everything turns back the way it was before, her carriage into a pumpkin.

I woke up the next morning in my hotel room feeling nothing but relief. I couldn't stop my mind from flashing to what might have happened, but I knew I hadn't really wanted it to. I sleepwalked through the rest of my Vegas obligations, with only one overriding conscious thought: the hope that I wouldn't see the sommelier again, even though I thought I might around every corner.

*Good morning?* My phone buzzed when I was already with the rep heading to the nicest wine store in town.

*Sorry! Good morning. Bisous,* I wrote back. I always texted right when I woke up, and if he had been the jealous type, some questions might have crept into his head. (I was the jealous one. If he'd ever gone a day without texting me, I probably would have called our friend Vera and demanded that she track him down by any means necessary.)

But my little tête-à-tête with the sommelier had given me an idea. I'd been thrilled by his attention, yes, but also by the wine. I'd felt a real tingle while holding a glass of something I'd never tasted before. The deep red swirling in the bowl and the aromas wafting up at me were a kind of flirtation even more alluring than the interpersonal one happening at the same time. I'd fallen for the wine, and for the experience of encountering it in a moment where all my senses were in tune. It had been nothing like ordering wine in a restaurant, or opening a bottle at home before putting a movie on. At those times my attention had been divided, the wine secondary.

I realized how timid I'd been these last weeks, how little I'd really worked at either my wine appreciation or my English. In between appointments, I texted Rose and Maya: *Let's do a wine tasting. What do you think? I'm back Friday.*

*Yes!* they both wrote back. Maya added: *We can do it at my place. Alex says we should make it a competition between French and American wines.*

Men!

I invited Carl and Shaina, though I wasn't sure they'd come. As soon as I landed at LaGuardia I asked a cab driver to take me straight to a wine shop that Elise had once recommended, not too far from my apartment. With my travel bag in tow, I asked for Jacob, the name she had given me, and a friendly-faced, round little man stepped out from behind the counter. He had extremely hairy arms and a thick beard, and wore a T-shirt that read MEGADETH, a name that meant nothing to me. Was this really the person whose taste Elise trusted above all others?

I told him I was looking for two good but affordable Burgundies, each around twenty dollars, one white and one red. Picking Burgundy was strategic. I knew Alex would choose bold California wines heavy on the fruit—hot-headed, like himself—and I was sure I could beat him with a subtler approach. As soon as I started speaking, Jacob's face lit up. "Ah, *bienvenue! Je parle Francais. Vous êtes au bon endroit.*" I was surprised by the quality of French coming out of his mouth! He told me that most stores didn't carry a lot of Burgundy, but that he personally loved it and bought as much as he could. He helped me pick two bottles. I made a point of writing the names down so I'd remember them, and these were the first entries in my American wine journal: a white Mâcon-Village from the Auvigue brothers, and a red Côte Châlonnaise from François Raquillet.

I must have been tired from my flight, and from my Las Vegas exertions, but I could hardly feel it. I went home and showered and then walked over to Maya's giant three-bedroom apartment, which she shared with two roommates (one of whom had lent me the dress I wore to the library gala). She was the only one of us who had a real kitchen, with counter space and room for a butcher-block island in the middle. I found her in there humming and unwrapping canapés, bread, and cheese from Dean & DeLuca, taking samples for herself as she laid them out.

"You caught me!" she said. She held her food-coated fingers away from her body as we kissed cheeks.

Alex arrived straight from the wine store, too, and began cutting paper bags to tape over the labels. "Don't look!" he said to anyone who approached. I didn't have the heart to tell him you could tell the Burgundy and California wines apart by bottle shape (mine were low-shouldered and wider).

Two of Nico's friends were the next to arrive, Min-Ji and Peter, both of whom were Asian. "Where do you guys live?" I asked, and was about to add, "And how long have you been together?" before Min-Ji firmly but politely mentioned that her boyfriend was coming soon. (Have pity on this naïve Frenchwoman!) It turned out she and Peter were co-workers at a film production company next to Nico's office. To hide my embarrassment and bright red cheeks I went to help Maya in the kitchen just as Rose and Nico arrived with Min-Ji's boyfriend, Derek (who for the record was very tall and very white). Carl showed up, too, but not Shaina, which was just as well, because he immediately and irrevocably fell in love with Rose and could hardly keep his eyes off her.

All together there were ten of us, including one of Maya's roommates. Alex, never forgetting the competitive aspect, tore slips of paper for everyone to use as voting ballots. We gathered around the island and realized we were split exactly: five French expats and five Americans. The four brown-papered bottles stood in the center. Alex raised his empty glass.

"Laure, why don't you get us started?"

All eyes were on me. It was as though I was back in a distributor's tasting room in front of a dozen reps. I picked up one of the bottles of white, and poured a small taste into the ten glasses. I lifted mine. "Color first," I instructed, and they followed my lead. "Then look at the legs; they can give you some indication of the alcohol content—the more alcohol, the more droplets. Now smell it—before swirling. Smell it first, breathe it in deeply."

Everyone breathed in deeply. "Think about what you are smelling. Now swirl just a few times and smell again, and see if it's different this time.

"Remember, you are courting the wine," I said, and everyone laughed. It was not something I had ever said in a presentation to professionals. Something new was expanding inside me. I was already being more adventurous with my English, and with wine I'd never tasted before and did not already have the answers to. "Clear your head. Don't think about where it might be from, what the label might look like, how much it costs. When you're about to kiss someone, you don't think about anything else but the feeling of wanting to kiss them.

"Clear everything away except the color you saw and the aroma you smelled, and then sip. When you sip, don't think to yourself, *Should I like this?* Think, *Do I like this?* Let the wine touch every inch of your mouth."

"Just like a kiss," Maya said, almost with a sigh, and there was more laughter around the table as everyone lifted their glasses.

I took a sip, and it was like a liquid bite of fruit and flower, with balanced richness and minerality. I knew it was mine because of the shape of the bottle, but I was surprised and taken with it no less.

When we had tasted all four wines, Alex tallied up the scores and looked up with a triumphant expression: the French white had beaten the American white, but the French red had lost to the American red, a victory he found more significant. I conceded—but only as far as this test went. I'd quickly realized my mistake: given such small pours, of such young wine, the bold California red with strong undertones of oak and vanilla had overpowered the vibrant but velvety and earthy Burgundy. People are always seduced by big punches in little packages.

We began to have apéritifs every Friday. The regulars, aside from the French couples, were Nico's friends from the first tasting, who were great additions to the group: Peter a somewhat raucous free spirit, Min-Ji sweet and steely with a surprisingly filthy mouth, and Derek, for whom nothing was unworthy of irony. We always tried a few new bottles, from all over, plus at least one French wine—I had decided that I couldn't dive into other countries' wines before learning more about my own. Wherever I was during the week—Charleston or Atlanta or Denver or Portland—by Thursday my mind was on the apéritif and what kind of wine I'd bring.

At the end of March, I went to Miami. My first destination was a private community outside the city whose purpose I couldn't understand when Luc tried to describe it to me at lunch before my flight. We'd nearly resorted to speaking in French before I finally got what he was saying. It was a place established by millionaires who wanted to spend their retirement with other millionaires, living in a private club with its own grocery store, high-end restaurant, and, naturally, security force. They wanted to serve Château la Nerthe at a special dinner, and when they'd heard the brand ambassador was in the country visiting, how could Luc say no?

I gave a simplified version of my usual presentation to a room full of very rich old people and spent the rest of dinner pretending to recognize the names of all the companies and funds they used to run as I met the residents. For all my brushes with extreme glamour and wealth over the previous few months, this was the most surreal. I looked at everyone's wrists, and necks, and ears, and everything glittered.

They put me up in a guest bungalow for the night—two thousand square feet just for me. I slept restlessly, eager to leave but worried there was a chance no one ever did. I sent a message to Luc blaming him for anything bad that had happened to me.

(Now when I tell this story to people, they shake their heads and say only, "Florida," as if it is explanation enough.)

In the morning a driver picked me up and I was finally free from the eerie enclave. Never before had I been so excited for my next destination: South Beach. After being dropped off, the first thing I noticed was that I was severely overdressed in my beige and gray silks. The buildings I could see were beautiful, and blindingly white. I worried I stood out for being just as pale. In the sun-drenched lobby a receptionist in a white uniform gave me a bright pink drink and told me to enjoy my stay. I had high hopes I would.

I took the elevator to my room, where Jules was waiting for me.

Three months was the longest we'd ever gone without seeing each other. Jules had wanted to go somewhere warm and was curious to see if he'd like Miami. (Spoiler: he didn't.) It had been all I could do to keep from thinking about it every day, every hour— I kept telling myself not to live in the future, when I had so much going on. Each time we texted each other *Can't wait to see you in Miami*, I immediately blocked it from my mind. It was the only way I could get on with my day.

So even as I put the key card into the door slot, fingers trembling, half of me believed he wouldn't actually be inside. He was. Suddenly he was enveloping me. And I couldn't think of anything but his smell—a smell that was unlike all the thousands of strange and novel smells I'd sought out the last few months, in my unrelenting pursuit of the new, new, new. His smell surrounded me like everything comfortable and familiar at once. I wanted to drown in it.

When we woke, it was nearly evening. He brought me out to the balcony where he'd had a bottle of champagne waiting on ice. The ice had long since melted. We waited for the wine to cool in fresh ice, and watched the endless ocean crash gently upon the shore, where colorful little dots of people were sunbathing and splashing in the last light of the day.

"So this is it," he said. He'd arrived just an hour before me, bought the champagne at the airport, and had seen nothing beyond the hotel lobby and this view.

I brushed the hair out of my eyes to look at him more clearly. His hair was even and very short—he must have gotten it cut just before leaving.

"What is it?"

"America!" he proclaimed in English, throwing his arms out wide. Some people are just good at languages. I'm not one of them. Even though I'd lived here for months now, his accent was better than mine.

"Well, we are facing the wrong way to see the rest of it, but yes, this is some," I teased.

We ordered room service and drank the champagne and didn't leave the room that night. In the morning we went for an early walk around the neighborhood for tea and croquettes. I kept holding his arm, or touching his shoulder, not only to remind myself of his physical presence, but because I also felt protective. The country, I knew, was something he was on guard against, and I wanted to protect him from it—or it from him.

It was an unconventional slice of America to introduce him to—the sandy streets, Spanish floating through the air, the ocean-lovers in sandals and cutoffs and neon bra tops, their bodies bulked up or otherwise augmented. There was more bare skin in three blocks than you'd find in the entire city of Paris.

Soon it was time to get ready for work—the rep was picking me up in thirty minutes. I hated to leave him so soon, but he said, "I'm fine, I'll be fine."

"What will you do?"

"Oh." He shrugged, and a glint came into his eye as he gave me that tentative smile I'd found so attractive the first time we'd met. "Rob a bank, buy a lot of cocaine."

I spoke a little faster to the customers that day, and the rep must have wondered at my nervous energy. Who comes to Miami and is unable to relax? Between my last sales appointment and the client dinner I stopped by the hotel, but Jules wasn't in our room. I texted him and got no response. I went out onto the balcony and looked up and down the beach, then wandered around the lobby, and was thinking about retracing our steps from that morning when the receptionist told me I might find what I was looking for out back.

There he was, lying on a floating mattress paddling slowly up and down the length of the infinity pool, sunglasses on, with a daiquiri in his hand.

"*Bonsoir, mademoiselle*," he intoned from his lazy perch. He lifted his drink in salute. "This was twenty dollars."

We had the weekend all to ourselves, during which we did very little other than go to the beach and pool, walk a short distance for meals, and spend a lot of time in bed. Saturday night we took a very expensive taxi to the mainland for Cuban food, and on Sunday we went dancing at a club not far from the hotel. I had to twist his arm to get him to go, and had to physically push him toward the door of the club while he kept looking at me accusingly. Once we were inside, though, he suddenly became very passionate, holding me close, spinning me a few times almost roughly—never in sync with the music, mind you—before dipping me and giving me a long kiss that made me forget which side of the Atlantic we were on.

That night in bed, I fought sleep as I lay against him. Even though he was coming back with me to New York for a week, it was so rare for us to have space all to ourselves, even when we were in France, with nobody knocking or calling or needing anything. I was sure Miami would forever be a special place for me, because for a few days it had been our own strange and dazzling planet. Then I made the mistake of asking him if he liked it.

"I think it's a silly place."

"It's beautiful, isn't it?"

I felt him shrug with my head on his chest. That my disappointment also had a hint of fear meant only one thing: I was not only asking him about Miami, but about New York, too, before he'd ever seen it.

His reaction to the city that was currently my home could best be described as *scientific*. It could have been worse. He'd hated Alicante, where I'd studied in Spain—the buildings were old and ugly, the marina an eyesore, the beaches no good. We once drove to the resort community of Benidorm for a weekend, and he hated it there even more. You must understand that Jules was a man for whom his dislike of some things was matched by his extreme passion for others. Viewed as a whole, you could even say he was quite balanced. And I have always been drawn to people with such concrete and articulated judgments—they're appealing to someone like me who operates mainly on instinct and only later can explain my reasoning.

So *scientific* was not so bad. In the cab ride it involved a lot of staring out the window and throaty noises that sounded like curious grunts—*"Huggh"*—and asking forward questions of our Middle Eastern driver about how long he'd lived in New York and what his family did. In Paris, I didn't care whether Jules liked what I ordered, or wanted to walk the direction I did, or felt the same way about a film. But in New York I was suddenly hypersensitive, wanting to defend both him and my temporary home. I was worried that they might be incompatible.

I hid him from the others the first night we were back, but my friends made it clear that I wouldn't be able to do it again. I had to make some sales calls in nearby Westchester, a welcome break from flying, but no client dinner, so Rose and Nico, Maya and Alex, and Jules and I went out. Once we were all seated, for once equally paired, my anxieties melted away. It went even better than I'd hoped: Jules bonded with Nico over their hatred of George W. Bush, Rose over design, Maya over Disney cartoons (one of the things he loved with a true and abiding ardor), and Alex with jokes about Americans.

"So what did you do today while I was gone?" I asked him as we walked home.

"I played basketball with your roommate."

It was the most Jules answer he could have given. I'd left him a guidebook but knew he would ignore it. Playing basketball with Carl was his form of tourism. He ended up doing it every day I had to work.

Friday, I brought him to our apéritif, where he stood a little to the side and smiled warmly at everyone and shook hands with his long, loose arms. Peter had brought a girl he was dating, and Jules spent the most time of everyone interviewing her intently—where she was from, what she did, how she met Peter (whom Jules had just met that same night), and what she thought of Maya's apartment.

I liked her immediately; she admitted how little she knew about wine, but she was fearless. We were trying a Loire Valley red from the Chinon village and appellation, a wine that was fresh and round, perfect with the cured meats we were eating, and she was the first to speak up:

"I taste . . . blackberries," she said, a dawning awareness in her eyes.

"That's great," I encouraged her. "I taste it, too." She beamed at me. Peter looked as if he couldn't decide whether to be proud or embarrassed. (This is the sad mentality of wine drinking today!) His expression became a little clearer at her next question.

"Does that mean there are blackberries in here?"

Jules later repeated this question that night in bed, where we whispered to each other so Carl wouldn't be able hear even if he was hanging around outside the door. "Who asks that?" Jules said, as if she'd had one chance to do right by her entire country, and had failed.

"I think it was a good question," I said. "You don't hear it much."

"Why does that make it good?"

I didn't have an answer right away. I was distracted, distressed: his Sunday flight back to France was approaching. "Tomorrow," I said as we fell asleep. "Tomorrow you will do everything and go everywhere I say."

"*Oui, madame.*"

I knew better than to try to take him to anything touristy. So instead we went to the places I liked best. A morning chai latte at the coffeehouse across the street. Russ & Daughters for bagels and lox. Tompkins Square Park to watch the morning dog run. Union Square Greenmarket for apples and cookies. The Whole Foods café for lentil salad. The early spring day was wonderful, sunny and cool. Jacob's wine store. It was nearly three—time was running out. Bubble tea near NYU. A single skewer of chicken skin on St. Mark's. The footbridge at Tenth Street that went over the FDR to the edge of the East River. A window seat at the Astor Place Starbucks where we could watch people come out of the subway.

In one long tour, I was trying to convince him of how great the city could be. We sat at the counter without speaking for a few minutes, looking out the window and then at each other, smiling. I imagined someone seeing us from the sidewalk as they walked by: me, freckled, red-faced, as readable as an epigraph etched in stone, while Jules was lithe, angular, fine-boned, long-lashed— beautiful.

"I like that you have made a nice nest for yourself here. I like your friends. I like how exciting your job is," he said without being prompted. "I like the passion you are developing for wine. I think that's a really good thing." He paused. "And I feel very reassured knowing you'll be happy here until your job is finished and you come home."

I started to cry, having fully processed now that he was leaving in a matter of hours. And I cried, too, knowing that I'd failed in one week to make him love New York as much as I did, and that come June I was not sure I'd be ready to leave.

## Thinking About Wine

"Why is wine made from grapes?"

This is the other way to phrase the question that Peter's date asked during that apéritif. I'm not qualified to answer it well, although it has to do with the particular combination of tannins, sugars, and acidity of grapes that allow both fermentation and aging. But when she asked, I told her that the first thing to know about French wine is that it's *only* made from grapes. If it tastes like blackberries, it's a chemical effect of the fermentation alone, and has nothing to do with actual blackberries. It's all chemistry. Wine can taste like other fruit, or mushrooms, rocks (minerality), or smoke. It can taste like vanilla or butter, which can come from the oak barrel it's aged in.

The interesting thing to me, though, is that this question is rarely thought of, and never asked. The French either take it for granted or find the whole topic gauche. I'd gone twenty-four years without it popping into my head once. But only five months in the U.S., and there it was! It made me surprisingly happy. We're so lucky to have a strain of grapes that produces the wine we cherish. Here is a fruit that sucks up all the essence of the land and conveys those qualities to you in liquid form. This is terroir. It's important to remind oneself of this miracle once in a while.

Of all the wine regions of France, Burgundy is the most obsessed with terroir, and is most defined by the way even the smallest differences in the terrain—a different side of a hill, receiving different sunlight; being a few miles closer to a river or to a vein of limestone—affects the wine. This, along with its historical ties to the French clergy, is why Burgundy is still one of the two most prestigious regions in France.

It's not a big region, but every patch of it is so meticulously identified and marked that in an area much smaller than Bordeaux, Burgundy has nearly twice the number of appellations (with many more sub-appellations, to boot). You can see this prioritization on its labels, where the appellation figures more prominently, and the producer is smaller and near the bottom. The message: terroir is key.

Within each of those five growing regions are appellations you might recognize, like Nuits-Saint-Georges or Gevrey-Chambertin in the Côte de Nuits region, or Meursault or Pommard in Côtes de Beaune. The premier and grand crus—the best of the best—have their own appellations. Hence a Nuits-Saint-Georges is different (and less expensive to buy) than a Nuits-Saint-Georges 1er cru.

All this famously documented variation in the terroir also helps to explain why Burgundy pretty much runs on two grapes: pinot noir for red and chardonnay for white. Within this narrow strip of land, those two grapes have created a lasting and rich variety. Burgundy wine is generally characterized by a complex minerality and richness, but within that is an entire world. It is not a wine that flexes its muscles, that shouts, that grabs you and says, *Love me!* It seduces and enchants, demands your attention in order to appreciate its delicacy and power. Some would say that because of its subtlety, Burgundy is not a beginner's wine, but why not? For beginners who want to understand the relationship between wine and the land, there is no better place to start.

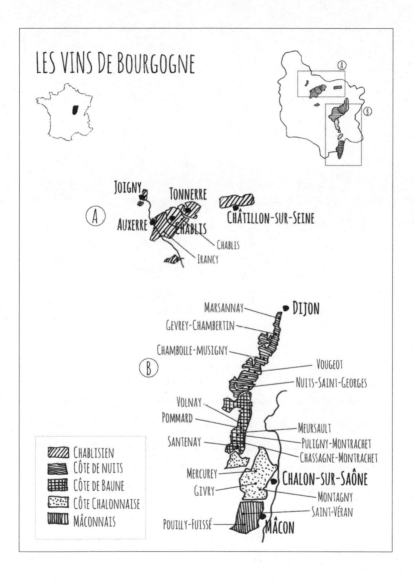

LES VINS DE BOURGOGNE

A
JOIGNY
TONNERRE
AUXERRE
CHABLIS
CHABLIS
IRANCY
CHÂTILLON-SUR-SEINE

B
MARSANNAY
GEVREY-CHAMBERTIN
CHAMBOLLE-MUSIGNY
DIJON
VOUGEOT
NUITS-SAINT-GEORGES
VOLNAY
POMMARD
SANTENAY
MEURSAULT
PULIGNY-MONTRACHET
CHASSAGNE-MONTRACHET
MERCUREY
GIVRY
CHALON-SUR-SAÔNE
MONTAGNY
SAINT-VÉRAN
POUILLY-FUISSÉ
MÂCON

CHABLISIEN
CÔTE DE NUITS
CÔTE DE BAUNE
CÔTE CHALONNAISE
MÂCONNAIS

# 5.

What's Your Vintage?

*De quel millésime es tu?*

Every bottle of wine has a story, and some stories, if we're to be honest, are better than others. It would be nice to be able to love all wine equally, but this would be like loving all people equally. It's too much to ask. Some will have started out closer to your heart. Some will agree perfectly with your palate. Some will taste like vinegar. It can't be helped.

But there are a few ways to get an idea of what a wine will be like before opening it, and one of the most important is the vintage. Without it, you may know *who* produced the wine and *where*, but not *when*. A bottle's vintage is like its calling card—it can tell you whether the wine was born in a good year and how long it has aged before you meet it. If you become an experienced and observant enough drinker, certain years from a certain region will evoke for you the place and time, the start of a season, the strength of the sun and rain, even if you weren't there to see it yourself.

But vintage cannot tell you everything. Just as family and schooling cannot guarantee a person's character, a well-known vintage is not enough to assure a bottle's integrity. You can always find bad wine in good years, and good wine in bad years. You might think this kind of inconsistency would be undesirable, that a wine should taste the same no matter when it was produced.

But that is not what terroir yields. And it is not what nature yields. Real-life stories never follow a straight line and rarely turn out as predicted. Where a wine starts at that moment of capture, the bottle sealed, is not where it ends up at the moment of encounter. Wine changes as it matures, the tannins mellow, flavors deepen and mutate. The same is true for me or you. The me who had just gotten back from Spain with no intention of moving to America—let alone staying there longer than the allotted time— was not the me lying in my Second Avenue bedroom listening to the street traffic. Your personality—your desires and tendencies and traits—is a message in a bottle. To find out what it says, you have to open it.

My time working for my uncle was coming to an end. It was May. I had just a few trips left, including one to Nashville, Tennessee, a city that I knew nothing about. Truth be told, I would have rather skipped it altogether; I would have rather returned to California, as I didn't know when I'd get a chance to see it again.

My job was ending in weeks—and then what? All I had was a

vague sense that my time in the U.S. wasn't finished, a buzzing that grew louder and louder in my inner ear with each passing day. That I had yet to talk to Jules about it was starting to eat away at me. I am not someone who holds on to secrets, but this felt less like a secret I was guarding and more like something I was scared to face. Perhaps I did not know myself as well as I thought I did.

"Do you know anything about Nashville?" Jules asked the night before my flight. We were Skype messaging instead of talking, so that I could step away and keep stuffing things into my luggage.

"Not much," I said, though I knew less than that.

"There is nothing there," he said. "It is surrounded by desert."

"Is that so?"

"Totally barren," he said. "Except for a great fort where America keeps all its gold."

He was teasing me, I sensed, but I was too distracted to play along. Telling him that I wanted to stay here, in this vast and strange country, was on the tips of my fingers that night, on everything I wrote. But I still couldn't say—or type—it out loud. I was afraid that my honeymoon with America might be over, and that we were about to see who each of us really was. I was afraid we would both end up disappointed.

"And not only is it barren, but it is full of *ploucs*." He said. Hicks.

"Stop," I said, not in the mood to be needled.

"It's only one week," he said cheerfully. "Then soon you will be back here and everything will be fine."

I suddenly didn't feel well.

Jules started complaining about one of his classes, and I snapped at him. I regretted it immediately but it was too late. The conversation cooled.

If you have ever been in a long-distance relationship, you recognize this moment, when it suddenly becomes so easy to turn against the person closest to you because of something you feel guilty for.

We made plans to talk again in the morning and logged off. But then I opened my computer again and began to type, "You've been so patient with me. You will not like what I want to say . . ."

But I deleted it without sending.

On the flight the next day, I took a short, fitful nap and woke feeling groggy and airsick and a little put out. I was still in a bad mood, and the only thing that had really started to grate on me about this job was the flying—and the fact that I'd failed to get a good sense of some of the cities I'd visited. My hotel was an elegant, old-fashioned place downtown. The taxi took me right by what must have been an active district at night; looking out the car window at the unlit marquees, I felt a twinge of curiosity, but then went back to being irritable.

I would be accompanying the same sales rep for both days. When I came down from my room at the appointed time I saw a man in a dark blue suit and tie who made no move toward me, though he looked like he was waiting for someone. There was no one else around.

"Jim?" I called.

He looked up, startled.

"Oh," he said, shuffling over. "I'd thought—I'd—the name I had was Lawrence Dugas."

"It's Laure," I said, perhaps a little short.

It didn't stop him from laughing. "Laure! Yes, of course, that makes so much sense. I can see how that might happen." He chuckled to himself. His suit was three sizes too big, and he had a spot of dried mustard in one corner of his mouth. This was one of Nashville's top wine salesmen? "Oh, boy," he said, shaking his head and letting out one last hoot. "Well, you're here now, you made it. We found each other," he said, extending his hand.

"I'm sorry, Jim," I said. "You have a little something," and gestured at my own mouth.

"My," he said, and retrieved a folded napkin from one of his cavernous pockets. He wiped at his face. "Eat and run, you know," and gave another friendly chuckle.

Eating and running is something the French certainly never do. Looking at my disheveled companion through my emotional hangover, I felt a flash of both regret and relief—maybe Jules was right, that I would be home soon.

I gave Jim a tight smile and followed him out to his car.

We headed to our first appointment, a wine store in the West End, a neighborhood Jim made sure to tell me was a nice area. He'd seen the look on my face as I'd lowered myself into his beat-up Nissan—at my feet were a few empty snack bags and candy wrappers that he must have forgotten to throw away before picking me up. At some point, I was fairly sure, this car had seen some very good wine paired with Funyuns and a Baby Ruth.

The sales call was pleasant enough, as was lunch with three other local business owners. Jim was friendly with everyone. He was a likable guy, eager to please, but different than the other chummy, backslapping salesmen I'd worked with—Jim seemed to make his sales more through puppylike endearment than bulldog persistence. Maybe in a place like Nashville it was enough. At one point, as we drove along a particularly green stretch of road, I

asked, "How far out of the city is the desert? I haven't seen it yet."
He paused only briefly before responding, but it was just long
enough to cause a rush of red to flood my cheeks. I remembered
now that Jules had only been teasing me about the desert.

"I don't think there are any too close," was all Jim said. I
thought about explaining, but then realized how silly it would
sound, and kept my embarrassment to myself.

We pulled up to our last call of the afternoon. In retrospect,
there were a number of red flags from the start: my own poor
mood, the store's dim interior, the dark gray walls and black metal
racks making the labels hard to read unless you were standing directly beneath one of the lights hanging from the ceiling. A tall
man in a suit that matched the walls stepped out from the back.
"That you in here, Jim?" He reached over to pump Jim's hand
without acknowledging me. "What have you brought for me
today?"

"Humphrey, we've got a treat for you today. This is Laure
Dugas, from Château la Nerthe. She has some very nice—"

"Don't know it."

"It is an estate in Châteauneuf-du-Pape," I began.

"I love a bold Burgundy," he said.

"Rhône Valley," I corrected, bristling somewhat.

He blinked at me. It was already obvious that this man knew
nothing about wine. I'd encountered one or two others like him in
my travels, people who owned a store as a business but had no love
for their product. Most of the time, the distributors did a thor-
ough job culling them from the list of people we were to meet,
even if they were good clients.

"Do you have a price list?" he asked before I'd even started my
presentation. It was his right to ask, of course, but the clients gen-

erally knew this was an informational visit first and a sales visit second. I never turned down any sales, naturally, but my priority was educating and building a relationship. Selling a couple of cases was just a sign that I'd succeeded at my main job.

"Maybe we should try some first," I deflected. Humphrey turned and repeated the question to Jim, who said, "Let's talk about that in a bit, Humphrey. We've got some great wine here to introduce you to. You're going to love it."

"I have four stores from here to Knoxville, and they'd close in an instant"—Humphrey snapped his fingers—"if I didn't know every single number associated with my business." But he added, "All right then. Let me get some cups."

I could feel the heat radiating from my chest and only hoped it wouldn't reach my face. The store owner returned with a stack of red Solo cups, peeled off three and set them up on the counter with the edges touching, as if he expected me to pour into all three without lifting the bottle.

"Do you have any glassware?" I said through tightened lips. "I believe glass would allow the wine to express itself better."

"Tennessee China," he said, waving a hand over the cups and giving a dry laugh that made my spine tingle.

Jim—clearly sensing that things were about to go very wrong—tried to call a truce by jumping in to say he thought he had a couple of glasses in the car. While he was gone, I didn't move a muscle, standing with both hands on the countertop, trying to look as placidly as possible to one side while Humphrey studied me with overt disdain.

Jim returned, huffing a little as though he had sprinted the fifty yards to the car and back, and looked relieved to have found things no worse than he'd left them. "Got 'em!" he said. "Just got to give them a little rinse first."

As Jim prepared the glasses, I opened with a shortened version of my normal presentation. It calmed me down to settle into the well-worn words about Châteauneuf-du-Pape, the galets, the château, the vineyards. Humphrey was a little perfunctory as he tasted the first white, but seemed satisfied. "My customers will like this?" he asked Jim—not me. I pretended not to notice the slight.

"They'll love it, Humph. It's a real winner."

I cleared my throat. "But most important, what do *you* think?"

He replied too quickly for me to understand, and I asked him to repeat himself. He cleared his throat and said, "I'm just trying to do business, sweetheart."

Something in me snapped. "Men have been saying that for a long time," I said. "It's grown quite stale by now."

As I turned to leave, my elbow tipped one of Jim's glasses off the bar, but by the time I heard it shatter I was halfway to the door. I didn't look back. I'd had it with Humphrey, four stores or no, but also with myself, for being so combustible, hasty, and unsure. For being too Obelix. (Though I was admittedly a little proud I'd been able to express my anger so precisely in English.) I thought about my uncle's advice in Los Angeles, about how the best salesman is a happy salesman, and felt a pang of despair at having failed him.

When Jim finally returned to the car, I'd managed to stop crying. With the windows up and the late spring sun pounding down, I had a sense of what it must have been like to be one of his candy bars melting on the seat.

"Oh, Jim," I said, hot with shame, when he opened the door. We may not have been friends, but at least by the nature of the partnership, we were on the same side, and I'd let him down in addition to myself. "I'm so sorry. I'm sorry about the glass. I'm sorry about my behavior."

Looking a bit weary, he put the tasting bag in the backseat and told me he had to make a call. Through the hazy window, I watched him pace the perimeter of the parking lot but couldn't hear what he was saying. Then he got in and started the car. My mind was racing. *Had he just gotten me blacklisted? Would Luc cancel the rest of my trip?* In a perverse way, that would have made the decision I was facing much easier.

But Jim said only, "I've worked with Humphrey for years now but didn't know he could be such an idiot. I don't know how that happened back there. I'm sorry." We pulled out onto the street. "You know what's funny?" he continued. "I think he's going to buy the wine. He doesn't know it yet, but I do."

"I don't want my uncle's wine in that store," I said.

Jim made a sympathetic but noncommittal sound—which was, all things considered, generous of him.

There was only one thing to do when I reached my hotel room, and that was fall facedown on the bed in self-pity. Eventually the self-pity gave way to self-recrimination as it began to dawn on me how intolerable I'd been all day. Even worse—as I'd been so busy reducing everything in Nashville to a stereotype (*ploucs!*), I'd become a stereotype myself: the snotty French girl.

I passed out where I lay on the still-covered bed, and slipped into a dream in which Jules and I were living in Nashville, in a house attached to the restaurant where I'd eaten a mediocre salad niçoise at lunch. There was no separation between the home and the restaurant and only a single shared entrance, and every time we wanted to sleep I would see and hear the diners just a few feet away. But they wouldn't acknowledge me even as we were lying there, completely open to them.

I woke to a knock on my door. In the way that dreams can run straight into reality, I was certain it was Jules. I first thought he'd just come home to our restaurant/house. I then realized it had been only a dream, but still believed he'd flown in to surprise me. I lunged for the door and threw it wide open, nearly scaring the life out of the woman who had come to turn down my bed.

Jim was early picking me up for the client dinner, and I was late coming down. He was still his polite, smiling self—making me feel relieved and guilty at the same time. "You look lovely," he said when I got in the car, yet another kindness. It was still light out, but the sun was dipping in and out of the tree line. Soon the stores fell away, and the houses started to grow farther and farther apart, separated by wide swaths of land. One side of the road was walled off by trees. For the second time that day, faint alarms began to go off in my head. "Are we not going to a restaurant?" I finally asked.

He looked over with a wide smile and it was suddenly clear that he was holding back a surprise. "Nope!" he said. My heart sped up. When you start to feel a little frightened, smiles can actually make things worse. The French fairy tales I grew up with are similar to the ones American children hear, but with bloodier consequences (we are Catholic, after all). If Jim turned out to be a wine salesman and serial killer, I knew there'd be no woodsman to save me, and that if these really were my final moments, I'd probably done something to deserve it (again, Catholic).

"We're almost there, don't worry," Jim added, but somehow I wasn't reassured. "And no, it's not a restaurant. It's the home of a collector. And a very good client. I wanted to surprise you."

*A collector!* I thought with relief. And then, because I could not help myself, said out loud, "Of wine?"

Jim laughed.

The driveway we pulled into took us past the longest, largest lawn I'd ever seen, short of Versailles. The house was nearly as big. Before we reached the end, I saw the front door open between enormous white columns, and a tall, trim man appeared, wearing a cardigan and no tie or jacket. He came down to the car and offered to help with the tasting case, and I wondered if he was a servant of some kind.

"Paul, this is Laure Dugas," Jim said, "the grande ambassadrice from Château la Nerthe."

The tall man reached out his hand. "Just last week I had the pleasure of opening a bottle of your uncle's 1995 Clos de Beauvenir and it was tremendous."

I didn't know what impressed me more, Jim's French—not bad at all!—or Paul's familiarity with Château la Nerthe. Clos de Beauvenir is the white grand cuvée of Château la Nerthe, a blend of the best rousette and clairette grapes of the estate. And 1995 was one of the finest years in recent memory, with flavors of marmalade and honeysuckle, spice and nougat. I felt Paul's words starting to charm me, and I had to work to maintain my wariness.

I moved to follow the men toward the house but felt something catch and pull me down to the asphalt. I'd caught my skirt in the car door. The men rushed back to me and looked even more concerned when I only laughed a little. *What else could possibly happen?* This trip had quite literally brought me to my knees. There was a long tear in my skirt, and I spent more time trying to keep myself covered than paying attention to my skinned knee. I told Jim I thought I should go back to the hotel, but Paul insisted that I stay, taking off his cardigan for me to wrap around my waist.

"Stay," he said again, his gray eyes leveling on me in a polite but firm way that made me think he was someone not used to hearing no. "My friends have been waiting for you, and I understand this is your only night in Nashville. Please. We shouldn't waste any time."

Against my better judgment, I followed him, still dazed by the fall. I expected to end up in some reception room with a couple dozen of his closest associates, like a smaller version of the millionaire commune outside Miami. But instead he led us to a kitchen the size of my entire apartment, where to my surprise there were only three people: an older man with a white beard and a cane hooked on one forearm, and two women standing close together, one about Paul's age and one much older. Everyone was hovering around the kitchen island.

The man, I learned, was Vernon, an old friend of Paul's, and the younger woman was Paul's sister, Jessica. Everyone laughed when he introduced the older woman, Judy, as Jessica's twin. Paul asked the women to help me find the bathroom to address my skinned knee. To my surprise they entered the room with me, where they fought over the peroxide as Julia, the older woman, repeated, "This house, it's just too big!" as if it were to blame for my fall.

After I was patched up, we wasted no time in going through a tasting of all four of my uncle's wines. I was very informal with the presentation—I had to be, with a sweater tied around my waist—and it felt easy and comfortable, like one of my apéritifs at home (but better, with more expensive cheese). The older man, Vernon, was chatty throughout, the first to react to a wine and the first to say something. The women sipped, murmuring about the aromas and flavors and nodding to each other. Only Paul stayed silent, with a look of concentration as he pinched the stem of his glass, swirled the wine with three quick motions of his wrist, and immediately brought the rim up to his nose. When he sipped he closed his eyes, and sometimes kept them closed when the others spoke. After the Cuvée des Cadettes, he paused for a little longer, and a small, private smile crept across his face.

When he opened his eyes again, it was as if from a deep, refreshing sleep. "That was marvelous," he said. "Simply marvelous. But you know I'm already a fan. Now that you have so kindly shared some of your wine with us, we should try some of mine." The smiles on the twins' faces could not have been bigger. I looked over at Jim with confusion and he only gave me a reassuring lift of his eyebrows. Paul reached down to open a cooler built into the kitchen island and pulled out a bottle of champagne.

"Is that . . . ?"

He pretended to squint at the label.

"I believe it's a 1985 Krug."

I've told you that even though I was raised on champagne, we drank only my family's. We were makers, not collectors—it was like drinking our local water. But Champagne is not a very large place, and the famous houses are well known by the French people, who are as proud of good champagne as of anything else in our history. And Krug is one of the most illustrious of them all. I knew that 1985 had been a very good year for champagne. The bottle had been aging for twenty-two years, which sounded obscenely long to me but could have been just right for a barrel-aged wine of Krug's stature.

I watched Paul carefully divide it among the glasses. The liquid was a deep straw gold, not the bright transparent yellow of the young champagne I was used to. We toasted, and, without further ado, sipped.

How do you choose the right moment to taste a wine that has

been waiting for twenty-two years? In this case, the moment had chosen me, and I wasn't about to question it. I let the wine sparkle on my tongue, taking in its depths. It was rich and elegant—aristocratic—powerful but still fresh, deeper and more expansive than a young champagne, tasting of apples and toast and light citrus. It was a wonderful encounter, and one that would have been different a year before, or a year after that night, but always distinguished by the complexity that Krug is known for.

After that first sip, any remaining jitters were gone. My embarrassment, my fears—all of it disappeared. Not because of the alcohol. It was the pure pleasure flowing through my body. I glanced around the island and everyone had the same beatific smile, like in a Renaissance painting. Even Vernon was quiet.

"Can I finish this whole glass?" I asked no one in particular.

Paul laughed. "I'm not going to finish it for you."

I don't need to say again how shallow the depth of my knowledge was, how everything I knew about the great producers and vintages was simply from family conversations I'd overheard. But I didn't need any special knowledge tonight.

It was getting late, and I was ready to say thank-you and goodbye when Paul reached once again into his cooler—the way a magician reaches into his hat—and pulled out a red wine, turning the label to face me. I leaned in.

It was a 1961 Cheval Blanc.

Let me explain briefly how wild this was. Cheval Blanc is one of only four premier grand cru classé A producers in Bordeaux's Saint-Émilion region. And 1961 is considered perhaps the finest vintage of the twentieth century, a year in which even the spring frost and the summer rainstorms were perfectly timed to produce a smaller, more concentrated yield.

First a 1985 Krug. Now a 1961 Cheval Blanc.

I can hardly describe it. Drinking the Cheval Blanc was one of the most overwhelming sensory experiences in my life. I tasted cherry, plum, tobacco, chocolate, damp earth, and more I couldn't even name, rising and falling and merging and separating all within seconds, drawing out into a velvety sweetness like a long violin note.

I lost track of time. It felt like hours went by between sips, each one spreading through every nerve ending of my body. Paul brought out steak tartare and salad, which I nibbled on before I turned back to my glass, taking only tiny sips. Then, to my surprise, he tied an apron around his waist and in ten minutes produced a simple pasta with tomatoes and basil—a perfectly light dish to complement the spectacular wine without trying to dominate it. Judy had finished her glass of Cheval Blanc and was reclining in a reading chair at one end of the kitchen, singing to herself.

"I think she's ready," Jessica said, nodding in my direction.

"Ready for what?" I said. At that point I would have been game for almost anything, as long as I didn't have to stop drinking the Cheval Blanc.

"Paul has a tradition with new friends."

"I do," Paul agreed. "Come with me, Laure."

I followed him down a hallway I hadn't noticed, sweater still tied around my waist and apron still tied around his, and glanced nervously back at Jim, who waved me on ahead. My host entered a code into a keypad that opened a door, and we went down a set of stairs that glowed from within. At the bottom, there was another door with thick glass panels through which I could faintly see the outline of wine racks. He unlocked this door as well and we stepped inside to the climate-controlled room, also as big as my apartment, filled with wine racks containing hundreds of bottles. I turned toward him, wonderment on my face.

"It's custom-made," he said. "It didn't have to be underground but I liked the tradition."

"How do you decide what to put in here?" I said, a little breathlessly.

"What to collect? A lot of it is by reputation," he said, almost sadly. "I wish every decision were personal. I have a penchant for the Rhône Valley. But I have learned that once you know your taste, you are made even happier by what you like. And it also makes you more forgiving of what you don't like, strange as it sounds." It felt true to me, if a little cryptic. "I'm lucky to like a lot of things," he continued.

"You can afford to," I blurted out before I could stop myself.

He laughed. "That was a lot of luck, too," he said. He'd been scanning his collection proudly, but now turned to face me. "Tell me what year you were born."

"*Non*," I said, mostly out of surprise.

"Tell me."

"1983."

"1983," he repeated, and his eyes widened as an idea came to him. "A fine year, though I'll bet you wish you were a year older," he teased. Some believe 1982 was an even better year than 1961 for French wine, so he was not the first to make that joke—my family had always needled me about it.

"It's not something I had a lot of say in."

"This one," he said, and gently pulled a bottle from its resting place.

It was a Château de Beaucastel, one of the largest and most storied estates of Châteauneuf-du-Pape, just a few miles from

Château la Nerthe. He handed the bottle to me, and I cradled it with two hands, afraid I would drop it. No, the vintage wasn't as renowned, but at that moment I wouldn't have traded the 1983 for a 1982 or anything else. This was my year. I was holding a piece of my homeland as it had been at the time of my birth.

When the others saw the bottle Paul had picked out, the twins exclaimed cheerfully, Vernon mumbled approvingly, and Jim just smiled. Paul opened it carefully and decanted the wine before pouring. The '83 Rhônes are known to be muscular and rustic, and this one was, despite its slightly faded color. It had a palate of dark fruit and pepper, as well as a meatiness, and the harsher edges it might have had earlier in its life had rounded out. I could see that it didn't compare to the Cheval Blanc in overall complexity and refinement, but I loved it all the more.

Even after all this, there was still an encore. And what else but a Sauternes, France's most celebrated sweet wine? The night had been such a string of unbelievable wines I was almost—almost—unsurprised when Paul held up a bottle of Château d'Yquem. My first sip of this storied wine conveyed tropical fruit, light oak, a marmalade finish. It cast a buttery glow on the evening, which now felt both endlessly long and far too short.

I could not give a warm enough farewell to the ebullient twins, to the dignified gentleman, and to Paul, whom I embraced at the bottom of his front steps under the warm Nashville night. All the pretense of my ambassadorship was long gone, evaporated with that first sip of the Krug champagne. He hadn't even needed to taste la Nerthe; I saw plenty of my uncle's wine in his cellar. He'd poured thousands of dollars' worth of wine tonight, much of it going to someone he'd just met.

"Why me?" I asked him.

"Your uncle has given me so much joy," he said. "Please tell him."

"I will," I promised.

Back in the car, Jim said, "I used to pick on that boy in high school. Can you believe it?"

"Where did he make his money?"

"Computers," he said, and shook his head in disbelief.

We were a few miles away when I cried out, "The sweater!" which was still around my waist. Jim told me not to worry; I could give it to him tomorrow. He'd mostly stopped drinking after the Cheval Blanc to be sure he could drive, but had tasted everything. We talked about the Beaucastel, and I found myself stumbling over my inadequate English trying to articulate its gamey, leathery flavor. But I kept going. Something had changed—the cautiousness with which I'd always talked about wine, the measured, practiced, almost guarded way I'd approached it, was gone. I was—there was no other way to describe it—giddy.

"Do you have a Southern accent?" I said, the thought just occurring to me.

"I guess you could say I do," Jim said.

I started to giggle softly, and then laugh outright. "I can't hear it," I said. "I can't tell. Americans all sound the same to me. Isn't that awful?"

Jim chuckled, too, and leaned down to retrieve something from the floor. "Listen to this," he said. He inserted a cassette, of all things, into the stereo, and out came the warbling high voice of a man accompanied only by a guitar.

"I don't know what he's saying!" I started to giggle again, but then, as I began to catch words here and there, I heard a sadness that conflicted with his jaunty strumming.

"This is strange music," I said.

"The greatest of all time, Laure," said Jim. The headlights ran over the trees along the side of the road.

"Elvis?"

He laughed. "I'll tell you this: that voice helped make this town, though he didn't live to see it. His name was Hank Williams and he was a better artist than a salesman. And I'm a salesman, not an artist. He had a bad back and a drinking problem and died before he was thirty. But you can hear what he knew. And this town sells what it learned from him. Nashville is full of salesmen, Laure, not just the wine sort. Everybody's selling."

"That's terrible."

"Naw, it's not bad. It's only bad if you're selling bad things. This is a good thing, music. Country music. Real country music. Wine is a good thing. You can't just give things away in this world. People have got to live."

It was the most philosophical I'd heard him get. It was the most philosophical I'd heard any sales rep get. I still felt ashamed for behaving so poorly that morning, but his kindness—and the great wine—had started to ease my guilt.

Then we were downtown again, passing the neon signs. "These places, they play music?"

"Sure do."

"Let me out, Jim. I can walk from here."

He studied me for a few seconds as if waiting for me to change my mind. "I'd go with you, but my family's going to be up early. If you need anything, go here and ask for Lois." He scribbled something on a scrap of paper and handed it to me.

"You have children?" I asked him.

"Two girls."

"I could have guessed," I said, and he smiled.

"If the boys don't leave you alone," he said, "pretend you don't speak English." He thought about it for a second. "Or give 'em a good kick. That works, too."

I was feeling brave, brave enough, at least, to go into two honky-tonks, sweater-skirt and all, order a root beer, sit at the end of the bar, and listen to the bands play. I didn't learn to love the music that night, I'm sorry to say. But I was happy to hear it.

I walked down Broadway beneath the bright marquees, music drifting out every door. When I reached the hotel it was past midnight. The doorman seemed surprised to see me walk up alone, but my face must have reassured him that everything was all right. It was more than all right.

My room was eerily quiet. I thought about turning the television on for company, but then realized I didn't really want any. I sat for a minute on the edge of the bed, then made a call to France, where it was now after seven in the morning.

"*Tonton Alain*," I said.

"Yes, Laure, is everything all right?" my uncle said, a rare strain of concern in his voice.

I told him about the night, stumbling over my words, this time from excitement. I told him about Paul and the wine we'd had. He was impressed with the Krug and started to say, "That's very good," but I cut him off to explain about the Cheval Blanc. He let out a low whistle. Then I told him about the Beaucastel, and he murmured an appreciative, "Ah!" When I got to the Yquem, he emphatically demanded, "What year?"

"1947," I said. I only later learned that 1947 is the most famous year for Sauternes.

There was a long pause, as if he was trying to imagine the experience for himself. Finally he said, "Laure, even after you've worked in this business a long time, as long as me, you will have only a few nights like that. It is not just the wine—though that was very good wine. It's the generosity."

"I understand."

"Remember this night. This quality, the passion and enjoyment you're feeling, it will have a positive effect on the rest of your career."

*My career.* I didn't even think to contradict him. There was nothing to contradict.

Then we hung up, and I counted to ten before calling Jules.

## Thinking About Wine

The wine I drank that night in Nashville (not including the Château la Nerthe) had aged more than a hundred and fifty years combined. It's an impressive number, but on its own means nothing. I've said before that older wine is not always better wine. Wine can become *too* old and start to fall apart—its fruit fades and its complexity thins out into flatness. Some experts even say we're reaching the end of the era of aging wines for decades. In the old days, young wine was often extremely tannic and acidic, and needed many years to soften and round out. But viticulture has changed, and now wines aren't as harsh in their youth. In fact, the best window for opening most bottles is somewhere between now and ten to fifteen years from now—that's it.

Knowing this, you may start thinking about creating a little collection. It's not so hard! We can't all be like Paul. Keeping even half a dozen nice wines, each bought for what you'd spend on an inexpensive bottle at a restaurant, is a completely reasonable goal. If you drink one, that's simply a great opportunity to buy another.

To make a simple wine collection, there are only two things you really need to pay attention to: how you'll maintain the climate in your home, and the reputations of recent vintages for each region you're interested in. The easiest solution for the former is to buy a small wine cooler set to fifty-five degrees (your refrigerator is too cold—it's not just heat that can damage wine). For the latter, you first need to know what kind of wine you enjoy, and, assuming you don't have tons of spare cash lying around, the best value for that type of wine. Don't think you have to start your collection with a Cheval Blanc that you'll hang on to for decades, taking it out only once every five years to stare at it longingly. For you and me, there's very little point. Of the places I've already discussed, Cru Beaujolais wines are often more than worth their cost, as are some of the southern subregions of Burgundy, like Mâcon. If you can wait even a year before opening that 2013 Burgundy, you may get a lot more out of it—it's as simple as that. Which is why being able to store wines in your home for more than a short time may be valuable to you. And while you let your wines age longer, you can continue to enjoy the numerous young, drinkable wines that are out there, and open one of your older, more special bottles when the right meal calls for it, or the right occasion, or just on a whim. Overall it won't cost much more than just sticking with whatever you're used to drinking. It's more a matter of timing.

Another reason to have a few wines aging at the house, even

just for one or two years, is that while it's true young wines are more balanced and more elegant now than in the past, they are still frequently sold too young. If you stop by the store for a dinner party you're hosting tonight, most of what's being sold will be one, two, three years old. That's because the pressures of the market have decreased the time between bottling at the estate to arriving at your home. Whereas in the past winemakers may have aged the bottles longer before releasing them to the distributors, they now get them to the stores as quickly as possible, in order to keep the cash flowing. And stores aren't going to age their inventory—that would be a waste of retail space—so they sell wine quickly, too. That last bit of helpful aging, then, falls on you. Short of finding that unicorn of a store that sells wine from 2011 and before (they are out there!), you will benefit from keeping your own wine around a little longer.

There is one alternative to putting the time and effort into storing wine for over a year: have a decanter at home, and use it liberally. If you open a bottle and pour a small bit to smell and taste, and find that the wine is tight, not very expressive, or gives off a limited bouquet, decant it! Just pouring a wine into a decanter will open it up, but an hour there will often do wonders.

As with all the other aspects of wine, millésime (vintage) is not everything. A great vintage from one place is not always great from another. Weather can cause similar patterns all over France, or influence one region very differently (or even an area within a region). And while a lot depends on the weather and terroir, yes, you also need a dedicated and expert winemaker.

With those caveats, here are some well-reputed French vintages. You can see that while there is some overlap from region to region, there are many dissimilarities. And as always, memorizing these years won't be enough to find the perfect glass; you must drink them!

### GOOD YEARS IN BURGUNDY:

2010, 2009, 2005, 1999, 1996, 1995

### GOOD YEARS IN THE RHÔNE VALLEY:

2010, 2009, 2007, 2005, 2004, 1998, 1995

### GOOD YEARS IN CHAMPAGNE:

2012, 2004, 2002, 1996, 1995

### GOOD YEARS IN BORDEAUX:

2010, 2009, 2005, 2001, 2000, 1996, 1995

### GOOD YEARS IN ALSACE:

2007, 2005, 1996, 1995

### GOOD YEARS IN LANGUEDOC:

2011, 2007, 2000, 1998

### GOOD YEARS IN BEAUJOLAIS:

2011, 2010, 2009, 2005, 2000, 1999, 1995

PART II

Cultivation / Culture

# 6.

There's Always Occasion for Champagne

*Toutes les excuses sont bonnes pour faire sauter le bouchon*

My mother has never been one to wait for the perfect moment. After all, how often does such a moment come around? There are no prizes in this life for denying yourself pleasure for an ideal that may never materialize, and this is why the worst bottle of wine is one that is never opened. My mother does not have this problem. The wine that most people save for special occasions is exactly the wine she had too much of around the house: champagne. To come home from school on a Tuesday afternoon and see her cooking, a glass of bubbly in one hand, was an education in how to enjoy life.

"Why are you drinking champagne, Maman?"

"Why on earth not?"

Now, we don't *need* champagne to appreciate the great luck of our very lives, but it certainly doesn't hurt. Like everything else, champagne as we know it is a product of chance and environment. The Champagne region has produced wine for hundreds of years (and developed its celebratory reputation because it was used to consecrate the Franc kings in the Middle Ages), but the wine was still, not sparkling. In the 17th century, when the extra fermentation that produces carbon dioxide became well known, it was considered an imperfection! Dom Pérignon himself had tried first to eliminate the bubbles, not refine them. Sparkling wine only grew popular in the 1800s, and that's when Champagne became synonymous with effervescent wine.

So you see, what is taken as fact now was not so obvious at one time, and was the product of a happy accident or two. I moved to the U.S. because my uncle overheard me say I wanted to go to England. I wanted to go to England because I'd loved my time in Spain. I went to Spain because while at university in Paris someone came to tell us about the EU's student exchange program, and that they were accepting only two spots from our school. I knew that all my classmates would consider it carefully and take their time in their French way; if I wanted to go, my advantage would be in filling out the forms immediately, without even telling my mother. I made a friend do it with me. We were the first to turn in our applications, and we were the ones selected. I didn't even look up what Alicante was like, or I might not have done it at all. I might have waited until I could go somewhere prettier, more famous.

And so on. Each decision leading to another. If I had stayed in France, I would have gotten my economics degree and gone into NGO or social work. Would I still have fallen in love with wine? Or would I have felt oppressed by it, surrounded by the family business? Who knows! All I know is what happened. I went to the U.S., to my own surprise. And there, the love snuck up on me.

Now the job was over. Like a whirlwind romance, it had left me wanting more—of wine and of New York. I'd found something that suited me in this city, its energy and its feeling both old and constantly new. And it was full of people, brave and adventurous, who were at least a little like Obelix, fellow members of a tribe I hadn't known existed.

But just because I wanted to stay didn't mean I could. The expatriate life is full of goodbye parties. Getting a work visa is no easy task—my first had been as a French employee working temporarily in the U.S.—and it's even harder for people whose fields fall under the broad category of "business," as sales, advertising, and marketing jobs do. Maya and Alex, whose positions were ending a month after mine, were having trouble finding work, and Nico's contract was almost up, too.

I was the last to arrive, and it was increasingly looking like I would be the first to go. I had some interest from a mid-sized firm called Pringent, which like Moët owned a champagne house and also imported wine to the States. I was a nervous wreck waiting for them to call. I took a second sales trip to Boston, a city I'd really liked the first time, but wasn't able to enjoy it. I got back to New York just in time for Pringent to tell me they didn't have the budget to create the position they'd wanted to, and just like that, my last chance to stay was gone.

It seemed everyone I had met in New York came to the party Rose and Nico hosted for me. Even Carl and Shaina arrived together and politely stood side by side with their drinks. I felt fondness for them both. We had never been friends, but roommates do the important work of staving off the nightly loneliness that can haunt new arrivals in New York. A few glasses in, I threw my arms around them and demanded that they make up—they only had each other now, I said, and shouldn't take each other for granted. I don't think my speech worked—I heard Shaina moved out of the apartment not long after—but my intentions were good.

There was beer and liquor for the Americans, but I insisted on sparkling wine. We couldn't afford champagne for everyone, so we bought prosecco instead, which is far more affordable, though less complex and generally sweeter, its bubbles closer to fizzy soda bubbles than the fine, long-lasting bubbles of champagne. But prosecco is perfectly pleasant and celebratory, which is what I wanted. I refused to even call it a goodbye party. But I could only hold the tears back so long. By the end of the night Rose and I were hugging and crying and promising to visit, wherever we ended up. I would never have expected the reserved, birdlike woman I'd found so cool and intimidating eight months ago to have become one of my closest friends.

Maya and Alex were among the last to leave. They embraced me for a long time. "Goodbye," they said.

"Don't say goodbye!" Rose commanded.

"No, no, it's okay," I said. "There's no point denying it now."

I was embarrassed. To have spent all that time agonizing over whether to stay in New York, and now not to even have the option! When I'd called Jules after Nashville just a few weeks earlier he'd been supportive, but I knew he hadn't been happy. Now he was.

Everything I owned besides the clothes I could fit into my two suitcases was gone: my bed and dresser, the little typewriter stand I'd found with Rose at a flea market, a stone vase where I'd kept pussy willow branches I wouldn't have to water while traveling. I had one bottle of my mother's champagne that my Uncle Alain had brought me as a token from home. I'd saved it since February, waiting for the right moment, hoping that moment would be when I found a permanent job in the U.S. Now I gave it to Rose. "Drink it the next time you're happy," I said as we embraced.

And only hours later, I was on board a flight back to France.

Jules met me at Charles de Gaulle, his face, when I spotted it, an endearing mix of joy, relief, and sympathy. I was lucky not to be stopped by security as I ran like a crazed woman into his embrace.

"If you're not happy to be home, don't tell me, I won't be able to take it," he said.

"No, of course I am," I said into his neck. And it was true. Rose had once told me that she always felt like she no longer belonged when she returned to Paris, but though I'd felt a little strange on my last visit, everything had still been comfortable and easy. What I felt now was disappointment; once I'd acknowledged my desire to stay in New York, I wanted it more than anything I could remember—and I had failed.

I planned to reregister for university in September and finish my economics degree. After that, Jules and I would see who found a job first; no matter where it was, the other would follow. We'd spent so much time apart in the past year and a half, making a promise seemed like the best way to create a life together. I wanted to go back to New York; he knew and accepted that. He surprised me by saying he'd been entertaining thoughts of finding graphic design work in China once he finished his degree that summer.

"You, China?" I said. I had trouble picturing him living any-where besides France.

"It's the future," he said solemnly. "Why not see the future?"

By Julesian logic, it was a very practical answer. I laughed, and for a few nights lay awake trying to picture myself in Shanghai.

I mostly spent time with my mother and riding on the back of Jules's Mobylette to dinner or a movie or a party. When I'd been back for Christmas I'd felt déjà vu everywhere I went, as if my first two months in America had been a dream. But now there was no ignoring the impact the experience had on me. My friends all said I was the same, but I knew it wasn't quite true. They were most curious about what Americans were really like, how the cities I'd visited differed from Paris, and if the food was bad. No one asked how I actually felt about my time there, perhaps assuming they knew the answer or not wanting to hear anything that would contradict their preexisting notions. The few times I said that I would love to go back, I was met with surprise and exclamations. But the biggest change was simply having Jules always near—I could reach for his face and touch warm skin, not a laptop screen. It was not so bad to be back, no. In nearly every way it was wonderful.

My mother knew better, though. "I see you here but your brain is somewhere else," she said over breakfast one morning.

"I'm just getting used to things again." I smiled at her. But she didn't smile back, instead examining me skeptically over her glasses.

Then late one night Jules and I were at a house party when I heard my phone ring. It's still a mystery how, because I never hear my phone ring, even when it's in my pocket—this drove Jules crazy—and that night my purse was buried in a pile of coats on a chair ten feet away. I hurried to retrieve it, my stomach in my shoes. The number was American. I ducked into the bathroom, the nearest place I might find some privacy, pressing "answer" just as I swung the door shut. "Hello?" I said as I crouched low in the bathtub to block as much noise as possible. It was in this dignified position that I learned Pringent had changed its mind and wanted me to start as soon as possible.

"How long will it take for you to come back?" asked Rachel, the head of marketing and my new boss.

"I don't know, with the visa paperwork . . . maybe a few weeks?" I said, hardly able to believe what I was hearing.

"Do it as quickly as you can," she said. "We're excited to have you."

"Yes, yes, of course," I said. At that moment, all I could think to say was *yes*. It was not unlike the conversation I'd had with my uncle nearly a year before.

Someone knocked on the door. I threw my hand over the phone and shouted, "One minute, I'm sorry!" If my future employer heard anything untoward, she said nothing.

When I left the bathroom the woman outside said, "*Enfin!*" and slammed the door behind her. I wandered the party, stunned. I must have been pale, because my friends stopped what they were doing and called my name. "Laure? Are you all right?" I spotted Jules in the back of the room just as he saw me, and from the look on his face, the small but worried smile on his lips, I could tell he knew exactly what had just happened.

Jules skipped his classes the next day so we could meet at his favorite bar, in Ménilmontant. When I got there he was already chatting with the owner, who smiled at me and moved away.

"This is great news," he opened.

"For me, or for us?" I asked, taking one of his hands in both of mine. So far every major choice we'd made as a couple had been to accommodate my ambitions. It had seemed, just two weeks ago, that we finally had a fifty-fifty chance at focusing on his instead, and I wouldn't have blamed him if he was now having second thoughts about our pact. Once again, the coin had landed in my favor.

"What's good for you is good for us," he said. I didn't think he was lying, but I knew there was more.

"You must be angry."

"Why would I be angry? I want to be where you are. That's all that matters."

"That's not *all* that matters," I said to prod him. "You don't like New York."

For the first time, he didn't have an immediate response. My heart began to sink.

"I have to finish school, then I have that project in the south"— a one-off design job he'd taken on—"so it's a difficult time . . ." he trailed off. I braced myself for something along the lines of *So, good luck without me. It's been a nice ride*. "I won't be able to come until September," he finished.

I nearly tipped the table over throwing my arms around him.

My mother had said very little that morning when I'd told her of my change in fortune. She didn't say anything when I got home that evening, either. She'd always been supportive, always believed my blundering ahead was ultimately for the better. But I knew it couldn't be easy for her.

"I will still be here for a few weeks," I said, smiling weakly. She turned back to her book. I told her Jules was going to move in a couple of months, too. Her frown grew slightly deeper. Then she walked over to the cooler for a bottle of our champagne.

"We should toast, at least for you," she said, popping the cork with a wry smile. "I personally have nothing to celebrate."

Later that week I stopped by Pringent headquarters to meet my new counterparts, even though I didn't expect to work directly with the Paris office. Everyone was welcoming and kind. It was still a family business—three generations of Pringents—and tiny compared to the giants of champagne like Moët. This seemed comforting.

Then my mother and I drove to Champagne to see her family. When I was growing up we made regular visits to Ambonnay, within the subregion of Montagne de Reims—the city of Reims being the heart of Champagne.

Here's the thing about Champagne: it makes great wine, but it is a terrible place to live. Of the great winemaking regions of France it's the closest to Paris, only a hundred miles to the east, but you can leave a sunny day in Paris and arrive to clouds and chills in Champagne. The region is a network of small villages each about the size of a Parisian city block, in which you have one florist, one baker, one school, et cetera. There is something admirable about old towns that owe their existence to a single craft, where the traditions have changed only slightly over several generations, but they can also be stultifying.

We ate a long lunch in the garden of my uncle Charles, the oldest of the brothers and just a little younger than my mother. My other uncles came by to say hello, embracing me in the cool manner of my mother's side of the family. My uncles have some conflicts with one another, mainly about the land, but everyone likes my mother. The three men sat across from me, mostly silent, like the land itself—a bit rough in manner, but proud and candid. Whenever they reached for a glass or a piece of cheese I was reminded of how large and callused their hands were. They rarely spent more than a few days a year outside Champagne, even for the holidays. The one time we convinced them to vacation in Paris for a week, Charles grew so antsy we had to let him leave early and return home. Now we ate bread and cheese and meat and drank—what else—champagne, while my mother and her middle brother jokingly traded barbs. "You're looking old, Vincent." "Is that a slight limp you have, Marie-Brigitte?"

We said little about my past year and future plans—if Paris was a foreign land to them, you can imagine how New York seemed. If I talked about how quickly things changed in New York, how fast everyone walked, how many restaurants were on every block, I might have given them a headache. I did tell them I'd be working for Pringent, thinking they might be intrigued or have some local gossip. Uncle Charles shrugged. "I have never worked with them." Only my cousin Charles-Henri, the son and heir, seemed interested, telling me he once knew someone who worked there and would send me her name.

The vineyards of Montagne de Reims are mostly pinot noir. My family's wine, especially the *brut*, meaning dry, is nearly all pinot noir, which lends a hint of red fruit and a fuller body to the wine while still being as refreshing as you would expect from champagne. That afternoon I walked out among the vines that rose up with the slope of the land behind the house. At the beginning of June is the blossoming, when flowers appear on the vines to indicate that the fruit is soon to follow. Thus the timing of the bloom gives the winemaker an important hint as to when the harvest will be. The flower clusters were out now, but I didn't have the skill to decipher what they meant.

This was Charles's plot. My mother's was near the village entrance, tended by her brothers, with most of the grapes sold to other producers for blending. My mother and her sister had both left Champagne as soon as they could, deciding that winemaking was not for them, and my uncles' daughters had done the same. So only the men were left, with their wives, caring for the land. All of them sons of sons.

My uncle Charles did little work in the field anymore—most of that was left to Charles-Henri. Every September the family would hire a dozen people to help with the harvest and my aunt and my cousin's wife would make everyone lunch and dinner while the men worked. It was the same at the vineyards cared for by my mother's youngest brother, François, and his son Pierre-Emmanuel. (Vincent, the middle brother, had no sons and had retired from wine production, selling his grapes instead.) I'd come here nearly every year around the harvest growing up, but it had always felt like just another holiday. I'd never really understood how important those days were to my family's business—and as a girl I wasn't expected to have much curiosity about what went on with the land.

I did now.

I returned to New York in July, dropped off by taxi once again in front of the apartment on Eleventh Street. More than eight months ago I'd stood on this very spot, with these very suitcases—but so much had changed since then! For one, the woman now walking quickly toward me was no stranger, but my friend and new roommate. Rose and I embraced warmly, and she helped wrestle my luggage into the apartment she had once politely kicked me out of. This time, the second bedroom would be mine for real.

Everything looked the same, but I immediately felt an absence—Nico was gone. Generous, gregarious Nicolas had been unable to find a new position in New York before his visa expired and had flown back to Paris just days earlier to continue the search from there. Rose was unhappy but not distraught—after all, she kept saying like a mantra, it had worked out for me. Until he came back, though, it would be just us girls.

When I finished showering and rejoined Rose in the living room, she brought out the bottle of my family's champagne I'd left with her.

"You still have it! You were supposed to drink it with the first good news."

"You're looking at it," she said. I knew what she meant: Maya and Alex were gone, too. Unable to find new jobs, they'd flown back to France just over a week before, unlikely to return. In the span of one month, our little social circle had scattered. There didn't seem to be a reason for a celebration. But it's nearly impossible to drink champagne and stay sad; it always does its best to lift you up. So we drank it with ambivalence, happy to be reunited in New York, and in honor of the friends we were missing.

I slept restlessly that first night. In the morning I called Jules, and we sighed together—here we were again, an ocean apart, but at least this time we knew we would be together in two months, this time for good.

My first day at Pringent, I decided on a conservative gray skirt and white shirt that I hoped projected seriousness and efficiency—

and adulthood. This was my first real job that I'd applied and interviewed for. An office! A commute! I took the elevator up to the top and was surprised when it opened not onto a hallway but directly onto the floor. I felt exposed—I'd planned to at least smooth my hair and take a deep breath before opening the door, and yet here I was. The executives' doors were clustered by the front, and beyond them the space opened up to the cubicles. The tasting room lay in the center of the office, enclosed by glass so that wherever you were you could see all the bottles and glasses lined up, waiting to be opened and used. Thankfully, everyone was on the phone or typing away and paid me no attention.

I might have stood there all morning if the office manager, Allison, who was also the CEO's assistant, hadn't come and found me, greeted me warmly, and showed me to my desk.

I sat there—at my first desk—and fiddled with my hands until my boss, Rachel, the head of marketing, called me into her office. I noticed she was wearing a similar outfit to mine; from the way her eyes widened a little when we shook hands, I could tell she'd noticed, too, and wasn't pleased about it. Though I'd met her once before, at my interview, I'd forgotten how beautiful she was. She was, you could say, All-American—blond, thin but athletic, in her early thirties. On her desk, angled so I could see it, was a photo of her with a man nearly as good-looking as she. No children.

"Is that your husband?" I asked.

She held up a finger while she finished an email. Finally she said, "And . . . *send*," and turned to me with a wide smile as if I'd just walked in. "It's so good you're finally here!" she said. "We've been waiting in excitement. Yes, that's my husband. Isn't he a cutie?"

She paused, as if I should jump in. So I said, "I'm very happy to be here. Pringent is a very respected champagne. But there's always room to grow," aiming for something that was least likely to be wrong.

"I like that attitude!"

My title was marketing assistant. I'd be running campaigns to expand brand awareness of our champagne, but the truth was, I knew nothing about marketing. Pringent had more or less hired me because of the contacts I'd made during my quick tour of the U.S., and because I was French. I had no illusions about that. But I also wasn't sure how exactly they planned to make use of those things—or, really, what I was supposed to do at all. But I couldn't bring myself to ask this rather basic question.

"I . . . can't wait to get going," I said.

"Neither can I!" she said. "I'll let you get geared up then. If you have any questions, don't hesitate to ask Marianne. Talk again soon!"

I left her office with no more direction than I'd come in with and went back to my new desk. The girl sitting at the desk next to mine was Marianne, the other marketing assistant. I introduced myself and was delighted to find out she was French, but as soon as I began to speak to her in our shared tongue she made a sharp cutting motion at her neck and hissed, "Speak English." Before I could respond she handed me a giant binder titled "Champagne"—an endless, haphazardly organized scrapbook of old campaigns and design standards, like the size of a banner, the logo, a list of everything needed to man a table at an event, how many bottles were needed for $x$ number of people, and dress codes for conducting the event. I started to understand her cool attitude—the way she talked about the portfolio made it clear she'd previously worked on both the still wine and sparkling wine accounts, but now they'd split up the business and given the more "glamorous" half to me. "The next big one is Fashion Week," she was saying. "Since I've already put a lot of work into it, you have a good head start."

I sat down with the binder until it was nearly one. "Have you eaten?" I asked Marianne. "I was thinking of going out for food."

"Not yet," she said without taking her eyes from the computer screen.

I lingered for another minute, uncertain how to interpret what she said, then left the office alone. Our building was in the Flatiron District, a neighborhood that I hadn't spent much time in. I wandered a few blocks until I happened on a bakery that made sandwiches, and I also bought myself a cookie for good luck.

When I returned, Marianne was gone. I asked the man sitting two desks away if he knew where she was. "She and some others went out for lunch just after you left," he said, and went back to whatever it was he was doing.

I spent the next few days trying to pinpoint the exact number of the questions I could ask Marianne or Rachel before their answers became clipped and annoyed. I wasn't doing much more than making sure the right number of cases of champagne arrived from Paris and then went to the right places. I had to follow up with the printers, the vendors. It wasn't very interesting work, but I couldn't help but feel a smile creep across my face every morning. It was all still new to me.

The office itself was beautiful. There were only about fifteen of us, so the space felt open and uncrowded. Arched Beaux-Arts windows lined the walls, and from a couple of them you could see the Empire State Building ten blocks to the north. The real draw was the tasting room, a see-through bank vault that featured every bottle in Pringent's current portfolio, tucked into floor-to-ceiling shelves. In the center was a huge, austere tasting bench, loaded up with wine glasses hanging upside down.

But smiles seemed hard to come by, so I kept mine to myself as much as possible.

Without my noticing, New York had taken on a different character. It had grown smaller in some ways, because I was there every day instead of traveling during the week, and bigger in others, because without my friends the neighborhoods felt less accessible. Rose and I were an odd but inseparable pair. One short, one tall; one blond, one brunette; one quiet and one loud. We occasionally saw our American friends from the apéritifs, but those weekly nights had ended with my departure and we hadn't started them back up again.

Because Rose couldn't talk to Nico at night, when it was late in France, I tried to get her out of the house. She wasn't used to long-distance relationships, and I could tell she was having trouble handling it. Sometimes we would just walk around, ending up at a Japanese place on St. Mark's, or try to meet our few acquaintances at bars or parties. When she wasn't in a social mood I would pick up a bottle of wine from Jacob, who was always clad in a different T-shirt and always greeted me happily, and bring it home for us to share.

What Rose really wanted to do, however, was go dancing. I know I've described her as guarded, even a little uptight—in every way my opposite. But on the dance floor she was totally free and natural. I may be bold and outgoing most of the time, but I am a stilted, spasmodic dancer, like a marionette whose strings have come loose. Rose, however, danced like smoke in glass. She closed her eyes but never made an awkward move or bumped into anyone, even though everyone nearby was inexorably drawn toward her. I always wanted to stop and watch. How could a woman who cut her food into a hundred little pieces dance like that?

Those two months, when all we had was each other, we went out at least twice a week. Rose could get us in anywhere. Not only was she stunning, wearing tops that threatened to slip off her shoulders but never did, she could also charm any bouncer in perfectly clear English laced with just enough sultry French. Inside, if we were approached by men (women, too, sometimes), we'd say that we had boyfriends—Rose with a touch of melancholy that only I noticed—and most would move on, but a few stayed and talked to us anyway. These were the people I loved meeting, the ones who genuinely seemed to want to get to know us. Every time, it felt like we were on the cusp of making friends. We'd exchange email addresses or phone numbers, dance in a group, and talk until it was time to go home.

"You are so nice!" we'd shout.

"We should get brunch!" they'd say. "Have you been to such-and-such?"

"No! We would love to go!"

"It's always crowded. You have to get there by eleven. But we never get up before eleven."

"We would do it!"

"We know this guy who would love you. Don't worry, he's gay. We'll bring him!"

"Bring him! Bring anyone! We love to meet people!"

"You guys are so funny!"

But they never emailed or texted. This was perhaps the thing that surprised me most about Americans (New Yorkers, at least): how earnestly they seemed to want to befriend me, and how rarely they followed through. For all of the failings of the French, the one thing we would never do is not call you for brunch if we promised to. Is it the price of American outgoingness? Too many friendly people and not enough free time?

But it is to their credit—and purity of intentions, I hope—that even after months of these broken dates, Rose and I still believed them, every time.

I had only slightly better luck with my officemates, most of whom I suspected believed I'd come to take Marianne's job. It was weeks before she eventually caved and had lunch with me but she spent the entire time chewing. (This is the French way of not being friends.) I thought once we were out of the building she would deign to speak French with me, which she did, but only in brief mutters—and when I switched back to English, to see if I got a better response, she looked at me as if I were insane.

There were still plenty of small pleasures. Whenever a sales rep came to the office with samples, I would find a time near the end of the day when Rachel was gone to slip into the tasting room and pour myself a tiny glass. Never before had I such easy access to such a wide array of wines, and been able to compare them in such close proximity: the colors, ranging from light red to deep purple, pale yellow to dark gold. Red fruits, black fruits, stone fruits, citrus, spice, white and black pepper, smoke, tobacco, lico-rice, other herbs and plants, and, most intriguingly, the earth—

clay, chalk, dirt, hay, mud. Once or twice, when I was the last to leave the office (not often, because Marianne gave me dirty looks if it seemed like I was going to stay much later than her), I just stood in the middle of the room for a while, surrounded.

I wanted to take advantage of my first summer in New York. It seemed a shame to go underground for the subway, where it was hot, sticky, and full of grumpy people, so I bought a blue bicycle for twenty bucks at one of the flea markets Rose was always dragging me around to. It was a rusty, squeaky cruiser with a basket, too heavy to carry up and down stairs. I rode it to work every day, locked it up on the sidewalk, and stored it by the recycling on the first floor of our apartment building (the super loved Rose). It was a tank, but I loved its wide handlebars, its fat pedals, its wheel guards. I took photos to send to Jules as if it were a new pet.

*Here is the front!* (Click click.)

*Very nice.*

*Here is the side!* (Click click.)

*Also nice.*

One evening a week I went up to Morningside Heights for English lessons with a retired Columbia music professor. They were ten times more useful than that first horrible class I'd taken by Madison Square Garden. My English was far better now, but since I was no longer touring on behalf of a single estate the amount of memorized and repeatable phrases in my daily conversation had shrunk greatly. I felt that there was no excuse for me not to be able to hold a long, confident, improvised conversation with anyone, so once a week I would leave work, ride the subway as far uptown as I'd ever been, and take a tiny elevator to the fifth floor of a cavernous old apartment building close to campus, where the professor would be waiting for me at the entrance to a four-bedroom apartment he had likely paid a paltry sum for decades before. His wife still taught music, and sometimes while he and I chatted in one room, I heard the muffled sounds of a student plucking out chords on a violin.

There was no lesson plan. We just talked. Each lesson would begin once he lowered himself into his upholstered reading chair, pushed his bifocals to the crown of his white-haired head, rubbed his eyes for a moment, and spoke. He asked me questions about my day, and then broader questions about my life, and as I answered he gently corrected my word choice, tense, and conjugation, without disrupting my train of thought. It was not only instructional, but therapeutic. After a few weeks I felt he knew more about me than all my friends, in Paris or here. He knew about my family, my relationship, my job, my childhood. He didn't know much about wine but saw how excited it made me to talk about it.

I learned only a little about him, although I tried to pry once or twice. There were books everywhere in the apartment, shelves overflowing with them. His children were grown. One day in August he let slip that it was his forty-fifth wedding anniversary, so at our next appointment I brought a bottle of Drappier champagne. It was a little extravagant—it had cost me about as much as the lesson itself—but he and his wife were a lovely couple, a couple I aspired to be like, though I would never have said that out loud. I had no idea if they were champagne drinkers and chose a dry one that would be aromatic and rich and easy to like. They thanked me warmly, but I worried they wouldn't enjoy it.

But at our next lesson my teacher told me they had managed to get through most of the bottle in one sitting, and it had been quite a romantic evening. Forty-five years—I felt myself tearing up.

He cleared his throat. "And how is Jules?" he said softly. "He's supposed to arrive in two weeks, right?"

"Two weeks, yes," I said, realizing I'd been trying to block the exact day out of my mind, so I wouldn't obsess over it. It couldn't come soon enough.

The next day I biked to work as usual, made my calls, suffered Marianne's silence, and responded to Rachel, who exclusively communicated over email even though she sat twenty feet away. As soon as the clock hit five, I packed up and walked out as if a bell had rung. It was a gorgeous day. The sun was high, but there had been a break in the humidity, and the sky was a watery blue and cloudless. I thought about going to the park and staying there until sunset, perhaps even leaving my bike for the night and walking all the way home. At the last second I decided to bring it with me, just in case someone chose this night to steal a rickety old cruiser. As I unchained it, something in the basket caught the sunlight. I leaned closer. It was a plain white card that said "Je t'aime" in block letters.

My heart stopped. My first thought was that I had a stalker, and that I was possibly in danger at that very moment. I didn't know whether to stand still or start to slowly walk away. I had no idea who it could be—maybe one of those American "friends" I'd foolishly given my email address to! *What if they were watching me now? What if they were—*

There was writing on the back of the paper. I flipped it over: "Turn around." And then from across the avenue Jules was running to me, picking me up before I could even scream.

"Surprise!" he said, being a man unable to speak anything but the truth.

## Thinking About Wine

My great-grandmother, Léona, was a family legend who lived up to her name. All she ever thought about was the family and the land. She and her husband Charles came to Ambonnay at the start of the twentieth century and expected their descendants to be farmers, not winemakers. The Montagne de Reims was always more valuable as farmland, even when my mother was a girl. It wasn't until the 1960s and 1970s, when the demand for wine grapes from the region—which has forested, chalky slopes that are perfect for growing pinot noir—skyrocketed, that the farms all turned into vineyards. Of the nearly four hundred villages in Champagne, seventeen are designated grand cru, and eleven of those are in Montagne de Reims. Ambonnay is one.

Besides pinot noir, there are two other grapes that are used in Champagne: chardonnay and pinot meunier. Each gives a specific character to the wine. Pinot noir lends body and complexity, chardonnay elegance and freshness, pinot meunier—the reliable little brother of pinot noir—fruitiness. The average champagne will use more pinot noir than the other two, but you can find combinations using two of the three, or chardonnay alone (which you'll recognize on the label as blanc de blancs), or pinot noir alone (blanc de noirs), or, in a real feat for the underdog, the rare solo by pinot meunier. Blanc de blancs have a lighter golden color and a bouquet not unlike chardonnay—rich and delicate, fruitful, finely structured. Blanc de noirs are a more yellow gold, and reflect the black grape characteristics you'd expect: red fruit, flowers, toast, and a creamy texture.

But wait! There's another variable to champagne, and that's the level of sweetness, or the *dosage;* that is how much sugar is added to the wine. The most common level is *brut,* which is your standard very dry champagne, to which only a little sugar is added to smooth out the acidity and any harshness. In my grandparents' day most champagne was on the sweeter side—*sec* or *demi-sec*— but tastes have changed, and sweeter champagnes are harder to find now. In fact you're more likely to see wine that's even drier than dry: *extra brut,* or the suddenly fashionable *brut nature,* which has zero added sweetness and can be bracing to drink. Why champagnes used to be so much sweeter I can't say, although one reason is surely that poor quality is more easily masked with sugar. Standards are higher now—as they are for all wine—and quality has risen correspondingly, so it's possible to make a well-balanced, very dry champagne with the complexity of still wine that doesn't make you pucker up.

And what about vintage? In fact, 90 percent of champagnes do not have a millésime and are generally marked NV, for non-vintage. This doesn't mean you can't age NV champagne. But it does mean the non-vintage wines won't be as "representative" of the year you purchase it. Because the northern weather can be less than cooperative from year to year, most producers blend grapes from different harvests in order to maintain a consistent house style. This is an exception to the standards for still wine, made out of necessity. If a house feels confident in that year's harvest, it may produce vintage champagne, meaning it all comes from that year's harvest—a risky proposition. It takes more effort and time to produce, and is no guarantee of quality. But when it pays off, you're left with a richer, deeper wine. It also costs a lot more.

But you don't have to go broke buying champagne. The average person can't afford to drink it every day, but that doesn't mean you should write it off completely in favor of less expensive sparkling wines. (As a Frenchwoman it is my duty to mention that yes, only wine from Champagne can correctly be called champagne.) You've likely heard of the biggest names in the game, so here are a few smaller houses that are worth your time to seek out. None are cheap, but at $40 to $50 they all strike a good balance between price and quality.

*Champagne Jacquesson*—From the Vallée de la Marne, the largest of the major Champagne regions. Many champagne houses buy a lot of their grapes from other vineyards, but Jacquesson grows most of its own. These are elegant champagnes.

*Champagne Gonet-Médeville*—From Montagne de Reims and Côte des Blancs, they use grapes from both premier cru and grand cru vineyards. I especially like their blanc de noirs for their vinosity—the way the wines' complexity is reminiscent of regular wine. They also have a charming light pink color.

*Champagne Drappier*—From L'Aube, a smaller, southern region that has only recently started to come into its own. The house is well known for its brut nature, or zero-sugar wine. They also produce a cuvée without added sulfites, a difficult feat since sulfites help keep a wine from spoiling.

*Champagne Legras*—From Chouilly in the Côte des Blancs region of Champagne. This grand cru vineyard specializes in blanc de blancs, which I adore for their bright apple taste and their minerality.

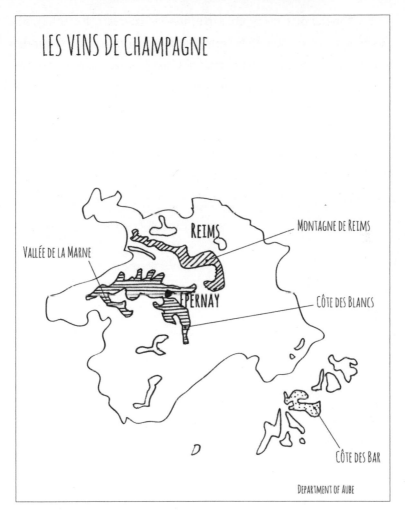

LES VINS DE CHAMPAGNE

VALLÉE DE LA MARNE

REIMS

MONTAGNE DE REIMS

ÉPERNAY

CÔTE DES BLANCS

CÔTE DES BAR

DEPARTMENT OF AUBE

*Champagne Charles Hubert*—From Ambonnay, in the Montagne de Reims. I would be remiss if I didn't at least mention the wine dearest to my heart: my family's. A fruity and rich grand cru champagne that is still fresh and elegant. You sadly may not be able to purchase it in the U.S., but that will make it even more rewarding to find. It is, without a doubt, my favorite wine in the world.

So don't shortchange champagne—or yourself. Few things in this world can do so much with so little. Just one glass is enough to turn any night into a celebration. Champagne appeals to all the senses: the sight of bubbles suspended in golden transparency, the scent of freshness, the taste of fruit, the feel of sparkling foam on your tongue, and not least, the sound of the cork being removed. What other beverage has a built-in starter pistol for festivity? You just need to let the occasion choose you.

*Santé!*

## 7.

# Even the Best Wine Can Go Bad

*Même les meilleurs vins peuvent avoir un défaut*


Wine is an unsentimental teacher for those who, like me, would prefer to be in control all the time. Trying to impose your will on everything doesn't work with people, and it certainly doesn't work with wine. Someone can be described to you a hundred different ways and still surprise you when you finally meet face-to-face—as can wine. A winemaker's power is limited by the land and the weather that comes. For a wine drinker, the notes, the scores, the recommendations, all of it means nothing as soon as you open that bottle. The wine might not only be different than you expect—it might have gone bad.

New York is not a shabby teacher either. Just when I'd settled into the prewar tenement in the East Village I was sharing with

Rose, the landlady told us she was selling the apartment. We would have to move by month's end.

It was nearly too much for Rose, who was unsettled enough as it was without Nico. Now we had to find a new home. We had no luck until with one week left we found a top-floor two-bedroom in a town house just a few blocks away on the same street. The new landlord was sympathetic to our situation, but firm about needing a guarantor since neither of us were permanent residents. I called our only American friends—Peter, Min-Ji, Derek—and they generously offered to act as a combined guarantor, but he still declined. At the last minute, through a network of phone calls, an old friend of my uncle's agreed to help. We were saved. (I later found out that these kinds of high-wire acts involving a deadline, confusion over bank hours, and a lot of awkward running down the sidewalk are extremely common for New Yorkers.)

Those same friends helped us shuttle our furniture in the smallest U-Haul available. We didn't want to pay movers for a three-block move, but we quickly learned our lesson. It took several trips, three pizzas, and a few tears before I finally flopped down on our couch in the new space, among the boxes holding all of our possessions (mostly hers), with lamps and frames and shirt sleeves hanging over the sides.

Only then did Rose go from box to box and say, "I don't need this. I don't need this, either." I wanted to kill her, until I realized what she was doing.

"Nico chose this," she said, taking out a creamer shaped like a cow. "It's useless. I don't need it." She stood up and put her hands on her hips, gazing over the piles. "Let's get rid of it all. I want us to start new."

This new apartment was the one I brought Jules to after he arrived in the U.S. early to surprise me at the end of August. Rose was in France to see her family and Nico (a trip she'd agonized over, worrying that it might make her feel worse in the end), so for a few days, the apartment was ours alone.

Jules and I had never lived together before. In the mornings we moved from room to room separately, one person making breakfast and the other taking a shower as if we were playing house, and when we found each other again we smiled stunned little smiles. It was so sweet and so simple to wake up in the same place every day. We were both acutely aware of having received this gift, and we didn't want to take it for granted.

I don't know what I had expected. For two years I hadn't thought much about the details—I'd just tried to imagine being in the same *country* again, to start. I was blissfully unprepared, and surprised by how wonderful the actuality of his presence in my New York life was. It was as though he'd been my secret diary, to which I confided everything I thought about and cared about but kept in a private drawer, never seen by the people around me. Suddenly, instead of walking down Broadway and texting him about a water pitcher I really liked in a store window, I could just take him by the hand and pull him into the store with me.

I wanted to show him everything. The coffee shop servers (who made my chai lattes) and the lady at the Laundromat all greeted him with some version of "So, you *are* real!" while I blushed. I even made a point of introducing him to Jacob, the wine seller, who jumped at the chance to show off his French.

"*Et qui-est-ce? Est-ce ton petit-copain?*"

"*Oui, Jacob,*" I said, humoring him with a faire-la-bise, a cheek kiss. "*Il s'appelle Jules.*"

And Jacob shook Jules's hand vigorously while Jules looked over at me with a bemused expression.

"Is this what you have been doing?" he asked as we walked out with a bottle. I'd been making a point of buying wine regularly, so I could continue to teach myself about it, and because our new apartment was too hot to store bottles for very long—too hot in the summer because we didn't have air-conditioning, and too hot in the winter when the heat was on full blast (another condition of living in New York). I'd been drinking my way through the Loire Valley but was having a hard time getting to know it well, as its wines are in general lighter and grassier than the wines I grew up with. Like Burgundies, they can confound the senses more used to full-bodied and richer wines. Jacob had turned me on to one of the more affordable Pouilly-Fumé wines from the Loire called Petit Fumé, made by Michel Redde—a fresh and fruity little white cuvée for which I'd broken my rule of not buying the same wine twice in a month. I wanted to share all my good finds with Jules.

"Is this what you've been doing? Making poor American men fall in love with you?"

"They always promise to call," I teased, "but they never do."

The idea that we were always within walking distance of each other, even on workdays, was so novel that we met for lunch every afternoon at Whole Foods. I was happy to have a regular dining partner, since my attempts to ingratiate myself with my colleagues had stalled. I loved spotting him on the sidewalk, tall and long-limbed, with a neutral, slightly glazed look on his face. When he saw me his eyes would come alive, as though he'd just been switched on. In the store he was curious and tentative, stunned by the crowds even after we'd been there several days in a row—almost paralyzed, actually, if I didn't urge him to keep moving. He poked at the mountains of quinoa and chard at the salad bar, looked critically at the cheese selection, and expressed wonderment at the color-coded, talking checkout lines.

"This place," he murmured. "Is it the only grocery store in the city? I don't understand how it can be so crowded."

If we had been in France, we could have carried a bottle of wine to Union Square and taken time with our lunch. Instead we ate quickly in the seating area upstairs—I spent half the time watching him chew the American food carefully, his eyes lowered in concentration—and then I had to get back before Rachel's emails piled up. But Jules's presence meant I was no longer lingering in the Pringent tasting room at the end of the day; I had better places to be.

Though it took some persuading to get Jules to come along, I finally got to act like a tourist in some ways. At the Statue of Liberty, his hair glistening from the salt water from the ferry ride, he looked up and joked, "Much bigger than ours"—on a little island called Île aux Cygnes in Paris, there's a replica only sixty feet tall. At the top of the Empire State Building he zipped his windbreaker up to the chin and made an obligatory loop of the observation deck, impervious to the sort of vertigo I was susceptible to. I could tell he thought it was a nice view, but my mind raced to think of something that would really wow him.

I stamped an Empire State Building penny on one of the machines for him, and we took the long elevator ride back down to street level, where we spent a few minutes watching a man play a drum between his legs for the passing tourists. I thought Jules just wanted a moment to recover from the observation deck, but it was the most excited I'd seen him.

"You," he asked pointedly. "What are you playing?"

"This is a drum, my friend."

"What is it called?"

"It is called a *djembe* drum."

"It's very pretty. Where did you learn this?"

"From my country."

"Where is your country?"

"Trinidad."

"Ah, Trinidad."

Jules listened for another moment. Then the musician took a break and considered this Frenchman watching him so intently. "If you like this music, my friends play in Brooklyn on Sundays after church. Just for fun. All different drummers, my country, Jamaica, Barbados, Saint Lucia. In Prospect Park. You know where this is?"

"No, tell me, I will come," Jules said.

That was Jules: a man who barely lifted an eyebrow at two iconic landmarks, making fast friends with a street musician. That Sunday we were on the subway to Brooklyn. I'd been to Williamsburg, but this would be a new part of the borough for me. The train rose out of the tunnel and we were crossing a bridge, the river below us, and outside the window, downtown Manhattan on one side, and on the other, the Brooklyn piers. Jules and I pressed up against the glass until we dipped back below the surface. When we reached our station I held Jules's hand tightly and followed his lead across the street into the park and up the path. I didn't think he knew where he was going, but then we heard the sounds of the drums, a rhythmic clattering and booming. At a clearing we saw perhaps fifty people standing in a semicircle playing drums. That was it—no other instruments. Just drums, most of them like the one Jules's new friend had played—wood, with leather tops, but of all different sizes and tones, from short and high-pitched to low and resonant. Two men in the back were playing steel drums, and in the front, a small group of children were banging away at instruments their own size.

We spotted our friend somewhere in the middle, and eventually he noticed us and smiled and waved but didn't stop drumming. Most parkgoers stopped for a minute and then walked on, but a small audience stood just outside the circle. It wasn't long before I realized the music had hypnotized me. We watched without speaking. Jules's face was rapt. There didn't seem to be anyone directing the music, but somehow everyone followed the same basic beat. After several minutes the tempo would slow, and some of the drummers would drop off and rest, eventually leaving just two or three still going steady. Gradually they'd all join in again, this time creating a different song altogether.

We stayed for an hour, then walked through the park to a different subway station. When the train rose up again on the bridge over the river, Jules said quietly, "This is actually something good about New York."

"What's good?" I said. His words sparked a hope deep inside my stomach.

"The different people," he said. "It's a good place to learn about other people."

"I couldn't agree more."

And then we taught the Americans in our subway car a thing or two about French public displays of affection.

The more you want things to be a certain way, the more likely you are to believe them to be true. Your mind is always happy to play a trick or two on you. I'd desperately wanted Jules to settle in without a hitch. And the first few weeks were enough to convince me that he had, despite everything I'd learned about his personality in our years together.

And I'd wanted the same for myself and Pringent. When I'd applied for the job, it had seemed on paper exactly what I wanted. I didn't have much of a choice, it's true, but I believed that I would love any position that involved wine and kept me in New York. It even involved making the wine more attractive to others—perfect! Had I been more self-aware I might also have noticed the pleasant tingling I felt at the glamourous prospect of working for the New York arm of a champagne house. That sort of thing can get under your skin quicker than you think. Going all the way back to my first lunch with Elise, I'd become a little spoiled by the five-star hotels, the nonstop schmoozing, the pricey meals.

Then there was Rachel, one of the prettiest and most stylish women I'd ever met, even more than Elise. She emitted a kind of charismatic sparkle that affected everyone within a certain radius. Walking down the sidewalk with her it was impossible not to notice the lingering glances, from both men and women. In short: she was born to convince people to buy things, and thus it was no surprise that she had been able to reach such a high position so young. I liked her for her style and her accomplishments, even if so much of what she did remained a mystery to me. I knew she spent a lot of time outside the office at meetings and lunches. She was admittedly not a warm person, and though she emailed a lot of piecemeal instructions, I'd yet to get a real sense of direction from her. But she was genteel and refined, and had a quick-draw smile, in that particularly American way, that accentuated her high cheekbones. After I'd been there a few weeks, I'd catch myself imitating the way she spoke, her calm, delicate enunciation, or trying to stifle my laugh so that it would come out as a quiet puff of air, the way hers did. We hadn't yet developed a close working relationship or started to brainstorm campaigns together, but it seemed only a matter of time.

It was this hope that made me continue to say hello to Marianne each morning, even though she appeared to seethe more and more as the weeks went by. And whenever I'd start to feel a prick of doubt, there would be an event at the Soho House or on the roof of a Meatpacking District hotel where I'd pour champagne and chat with A-list guests, feeling fortunate just to be there. There's nothing like handing a glass of wine to Christy Turlington and being rewarded with her thousand-watt smile to make you feel decent about life. And just in case I wasn't feeling lucky enough, there would be Marianne's bitterly jealous look to greet me the next morning.

But everything always looks better in the summer, and people hold on to it for as long as possible, until the day they can no longer deny that the sun is setting earlier and it's starting to get cooler at night. This was my first September in New York, and it brought a clearer, sobering view into focus, along with the crisp air. The month was also marked by my first corked bottle in New York.

The wine was from Jacob's store, though it wasn't Jacob's fault. Corked wine can't really be blamed on anyone other than the winemaker, and even she can only take some measures to reduce the chance of it happening. I'd started to shift with the season from the Loire's fresher wines to Burgundies, and it was one of these bottles that had spoiled.

I could tell something was off as soon as I opened it. The cork had a musty, woodsy odor. I poured a small amount into a glass, and when I brought it up to my nose for a whiff, any fruit had been replaced by a dank odor. Just to be sure, I took a tiny sip, and it was like I'd put a sweaty sock in my mouth.

"*Tant pis,*" Jules said, just as he had with the mistaken Monbazillac all those years ago. Only now it was less charming, because I had no other wine in the house and Jacob had closed his store for the night. Jules shrugged.

I won't say it was an omen, but it did come at the same time that there were other signs our New York honeymoon had come to a close. Rose returned from Paris after Labor Day, refreshed but heartbroken again to be separated from Nico. Now there were three of us in the apartment, and my roommates, though both near and dear to me, were little more than strangers to each other. Rose had left behind her boyfriend, with whom she'd once shared a home filled with her carefully selected furniture (and his impulsively selected knickknacks), and come back to New York to find another man in that space. It must have been odd for her, however much she tried to hide it.

It was less odd for Jules, but still odd. "Everything has flipped," he observed one night when we were talking quietly in bed—with Rose back, everything had to be quieter in bed now.

"What do you mean?"

"I mean you were once the third wheel to Rose and Nicolas, and now she's the third wheel to us. Nicolas had to move back to France, and I had to move here." Perhaps it was unintentional, but I noticed that he described the move as an obligation.

We became a common sight as a trio. Whenever we ran into Peter, he'd say, "Look, it's *Three's Company*!" which made no sense to us until late one night Jules pulled up a few old episodes of the show online and we were entranced by the number of misunderstandings three people were capable of having. (But we were nothing like them!) On the nights I brought home a new bottle of wine, we'd pour three glasses, sit at the kitchen counter, and patter on in French about our jobs, and Jules's job search, while trying to find the words to discuss the surprising depth of a Corbières from Languedoc, or the underwhelming fruit of a Bordeaux. Rose was a delicate and patient sipper. Jules was an avid smeller, regularly lifting the glass to his long nose and inhaling for the pleasure of it.

Rose still liked to go out to distract herself, and Jules and I often accompanied her, but I preferred the nights we all stayed in and I could enjoy both the company and the wine. You usually think of a bottle of wine as perfect for two to share, and I would tend to agree (when I'm not hogging it all for myself). But I grew to love sharing a bottle among three. True, we didn't have much of a choice—wine in the U.S. is much more expensive than it is in Europe, and we were young, and one of us didn't even have a job. But I also noticed that two people tend to agree on their response to a wine, maybe just out of habit, whereas a third has the potential to make things interesting.

And even though Jules was a good sport for Rose's sake, the nights we did go out he usually lasted less than an hour before saying, "It's too loud, I have to go home." Once or twice he said nothing at all and just left, and I later found him snoring in bed. It drove me crazy, but I liked his advance warnings only a little more. It was the noise he couldn't stand, and not just in bars and clubs. His most frequent observation was just how loud New York was, everywhere—its stores, its sidewalks, its restaurants. You couldn't get away from it, he said, whereas in Paris, even the bars are quiet. The French talk so much, we consider it a crime against our nature to play loud music (unless it's in a dance club), or to raise our voices in public, forcing everyone else to raise their voices, too. To have to shout over your dinner is about as un-French as you can imagine but a normal New York experience. Jules couldn't get over it. "How can it count as a conversation when you are just asking each other 'what?' all the time?" he said incredulously. "This is why Americans don't listen to each other. They are too busy yelling!"

Once, he even left the theater in the middle of a movie. It was an action film, so not exactly something you needed perfect silence to appreciate, but less than halfway through he leaned over, whispered, "I have to leave," and was gone. I fumed for a few minutes, trying to keep watching, before following him out to the sidewalk, where he was standing with his hands in his pockets and staring at nothing in particular. He gave me a sheepish smile.

"Why did you leave?"

"The people are so loud in there! How can anyone concentrate on the movie?"

I tried to remember who was sitting around us. One woman eating popcorn (the French eat popcorn, too, but not as much), and some audible gasps with every explosion and fight sequence. How could the same man who followed a Trinidadian drummer all the way to Brooklyn be so skittish?

"You didn't have to leave," he said apologetically. "I was just going to wait for you."

"How am I supposed to know," I said through clenched teeth, "if you don't tell me?"

Part of it was just Jules being Jules. It had taken me time to adjust to the city's noise, but I'd never been as allergic to it as he was. But he wasn't stubborn about just his dislikes: once he did actually like something, there was no going back. In Paris he had one favorite bar and could go there four or five times a week, even by himself. If I had no idea where he was and couldn't reach him (he had an infuriating tendency to turn off his phone), I could find him there. He was not just obsessive, he was repetitively obsessive. He had watched every Disney animated film a dozen times with a designer's eye and memorized nearly every one, and he could listen to the same song thirty times in a row (especially Manu Chao), which I still found charming on paper, if less so in practice. And, in what I found a truly ironic twist, his biggest sports obsession since childhood was American in origin.

Basketball.

Jules had always liked basketball, but now that he lived in the country of its birth, his fandom reached new heights. Once the season began in the fall, his life changed; for the first time he was able to go into any bar with a television and watch his favorite sport being played at its highest level. I like sports just fine—I love tennis and appreciate soccer—but his fixation became too much for me. One day I returned home during lunch to pick up something I'd forgotten, and found him in the bedroom with a conspicuously sweaty T-shirt. He had his hands behind his back.

"What were you just doing?" I said, suddenly suspicious.

"*Rien*," he said sheepishly. *Nothing*.

"Tell me," I said.

"Really, it's nothing."

"Show me your hands!" I cried.

Reluctantly, he showed them to me. He was holding photographs of professional basketball players.

"They are cards," he explained. "Collector's cards. There is a photograph on the front and statistics on the back, you see, look. They'll be worth a lot of money one day."

"You are buying these?"

"Not so many," he said, avoiding my eyes.

"And why are you so sweaty? Tell me?"

His long face grew even longer. "I was . . . playing basketball."

"You were supposed to be working on your résumé today! You were playing with who?"

"With . . . Carl."

"Carl? My old roommate?"

Jules shrugged in a quintessentially French way. "He has nothing to do all day."

"But you do!" I said, hitting him with a pillow. "You have two months left to find a job before you are kicked out! And then what happens to us!"

He ran away from me around the apartment.

"Admit it," I said, "you hate it here!"

"No, that's not it," he said, but now that I'd said it out loud I knew it was obviously true. The realization made me even more incensed because it meant he was lying, to me or to himself.

"You have no right to make me feel guilty," I said. "We made a pact. You were supportive."

"I'm sorry," he said, dodging my blows. "I'm sorry."

If you've been in love long-distance, you know the mantra that keeps you from abandoning all hope: *Everything will be better once*

*we're in the same place.* You say it together out loud and in silence
every single day until hopefully it comes true. Even though I knew
that New York wasn't Jules's ideal city, I'd told myself that our
being together would make up for it.

Did I have any inkling that things would get tougher instead of
easier? Is that why I had been nervous to tell him how much I'd
fallen for New York in the first place? Either way, what made it
worse was the fact that I was the one who'd brought him here, and
now I both felt bad and resented that he hadn't been fully honest,
either. The truth was that neither of us had known what would
happen once we were here. Once we were together.

If Jules were a wine, he'd be a red with a lot of character and
depth, intimidating on the outside but soft on the tongue, smooth
and supple and a little sweet. The furthest thing from an easy-to-
drink, flexible Beaujolais. He'd be a wine that takes time to open
up, that isn't easy to understand when it's young. I can think of the
perfect example: a Bandol from Provence, on the southern coast
of France, made from 100 percent mourvèdre—the same moody
grape used in Châteauneuf that my uncle likes to highlight (Jules,
all-or-nothing to the end, would never be a blend). Mourvèdre
can be a hard grape to love, but it blooms with dark fruit, earth,
game, and leather. You have to come to a Bandol on its terms, give
it space to express itself, but when you do, the rewards are immense.

I'm not very good at giving space, though. Now that Jules was
here I wanted and expected to stay in easy reach, like any other
couple. For the first couple of weeks at the end of August, when
he had no cell phone, it was easy enough to just make a date and
show up, but I assumed he would eventually get an American
phone and was surprised when he refused.

"What do I need it for? Nobody needs to contact me but you, and you know where I am."

"I know where you are in general, but not where you are at any given minute."

"Don't worry about it. Everything's fine."

"What about job interviews?"

I learned the answer to that question the first time a strange number showed up on my phone—he'd given it out as his contact, even though I was at work all day. Sometimes he'd be up early in the morning and on my phone in the bathroom, talking to family or potential employers (who never panned out). Then I began to lose track of him in the evenings. He was spending a lot of his free time with Peter, partially to get away from me and my various frustrations, but also because they had a lot in common I hadn't recognized until now: fiercely independent streaks above all. When Rose and I went dancing, instead of putting in his usual hour accompanying us he started to go directly to Peter's place uptown or to meet him for a late-night hamburger. (Yes, hamburgers! This Frenchest of Frenchmen, who could barely walk down the streets of New York without holding his hands over his ears—not only was this man collecting basketball cards, he ate every hamburger he laid eyes on.) If when I got home there was no sign of Jules, I learned to text Peter first: *Do you have him?* and nine times out of ten he replied, *Right here.* A couple of times he wrote back, *Left a while ago!* which meant Jules was now completely off the grid, like an untagged animal in the wild, and the best I could do was stick my head out the window and look up and down the street. Once, he walked home from the Upper East Side, and expected me to be happy that he'd enjoyed himself on the quiet late-night sidewalks, rather than angry I'd lost track of him hours before.

But I didn't like being angry with him. The very things that frustrated me were some of his most endearing traits. Once, about a month after he arrived, I woke to strange whispers in the living room. I bolted up right away, but all I could think to do was pull my sheets up to my neck. I was preparing to scream at the top of my lungs when a man's head appeared in the doorway. "Hi," Jules said. "Don't worry, but there are people here."

"Who is here?"

"Two guys," he said, smiling, as if that would reassure me. "Two guys from North Carolina. They hitchhiked here to go to Ground Zero to protest George Bush. They have nowhere to sleep tonight."

"You just met them?"

"Yeah, I just met them on the street. They are really nice guys."

How could you not love someone like that, as long as he didn't get you murdered in your sleep? (And they *did* turn out to be nice guys, who ate breakfast with us, exchanged numbers—mine, of course—and left to continue their hitchhiking tour of protest.) No, I wasn't in any danger of falling out of love with him. Rather, I worried constantly that the love wasn't enough to keep him with me. By October he had no good leads and only six weeks left on his tourist visa.

"What are you going to do if you don't find a job?" I asked him.

"I'll find a job," he said. "Don't worry."

"Jules," I said. "But what if you *don't?*"

He was sitting on the bed and I was standing in the doorway, upset enough that I had to maintain some distance in order not to break down.

"I'll find one."

"You can't talk as if it is a sure thing. It's not a sure thing. You have to be honest with me. What will we do if you don't find one?"

He spread his hands out on his knees, a sign he didn't want to have this conversation.

"If I really don't?" he said, his voice softer. "What choice do I have then? I'd have to leave. But I'd come back and try again."

I began to cry, but screwed up my face to try to keep the tears in. Something important had just been said and I had to make sure I had understood. "So you wouldn't rather just go back and stay there? That wouldn't make you happier?"

He shook his head vigorously, as if surprised I would even ask. "No, I wouldn't be happier at all."

I was still crying, but now in relief. He stood, and he came to me or I went to him, I can't remember which. More than likely, we met in the middle.

## Thinking About Wine

There is always an element of risk when it comes to opening a bottle of wine. It may not taste the way you expect; that's a given. But it may also just stink. Ninety-nine percent of the time, your sense of smell is all you need to tell if a bottle is corked. A damp cork is not actually a sign of corked wine—it just means the bottle was stored too hot, forcing the wine to expand and push against the stopper and become oxidized. These wines are often flawed, but not always corked.

No, to be corked means a specific chemical called trichloroanisole (TCA) has made it to the wine, most often from the cork, corrupting its flavor. TCA isn't toxic, but it is unpleasant, and humans are particularly sensitive to it. It's what gives that musty, damp-sock odor; the more TCA, the mustier. TCA comes from natural cork only—if there were traces of a particular fungus in the cork when it was harvested, the cork sterilization actually triggers the creation of TCA. This happens in 1 to 5 percent of bottles stopped with natural cork. It's a cruel irony that the most common method we use to seal the bottle, allowing the wine to age and become sublime, can also be the source of its undoing. (It's a common misconception that at restaurants the standard practice is to pour you a small taste to see if you like the wine. They're actually giving you the chance to see if the wine has gone bad.)

But don't let this talk of bad wine dampen the mood. Corking happens infrequently enough that you shouldn't be too concerned. One piece of advice I like to give on this matter: if you like a certain wine that will benefit from aging, and you can afford it, consider buying three bottles. Then you can open one bottle at some point down the road and see how it tastes. If it's still too young, you have two bottles left for another few years down the road, almost ensuring that even if one is corked, you'll be able to enjoy the other. You can never plan for a corked bottle, but you can do your best to be prepared.

If you're just buying a bottle for tonight and discover it's corked, however, all you can do is laugh it off—*tant pis!*—and return it. A store should always refund you for a corked wine (as long as you bring it back).

It's also possible you are reading this twenty years from now and corked wine has become a thing of the past, in which case I'm sorry for wasting your time! As I mentioned, corked wine comes solely from natural cork: plastic corks and screw caps don't produce TCA. Plastic corks are often frowned upon because they don't allow any exchange of air (it's believed that wine ages well because natural corks let in minuscule amounts of oxygen), and are favored by mass producers churning out huge amounts of uninteresting wine. They're also just a total pain to remove.

The screw cap is a more interesting case. It has none of the inconvenience of a plastic cork and is just as resistant to spoilage. And most important, depending on the type and quality of the screw cap, there can be a tiny bit of air exchange, meaning that it might be the best option to replace natural cork. Every year that goes by, more and more winemakers are using them.

The place that seems the most reluctant to give the screw cap a decent shot, though, is (surprise!) France. You do see them, but rarely. Patrice Rion, who makes marvelous Burgundy wines in the prestigious Nuits-Saint-Georges, is a vocal advocate of the screw cap. He's so confident about their performance that he once showed me how he sealed some of his 2005 white Burgundy, the Nuits-Saint-Georges premier cru he calls Les Terres Blanches, using both methods—some bottles with natural cork, and some with screw caps, and stored them side by side. He had us conduct a blind taste test right there.

One was clearly fresher, more pure tasting. You've already heard my thoughts on taste tests, but the results were indisputable: everyone preferred it. And, as you may have already guessed, it came from the screw-capped bottle. The natural-cork bottle was also good, but just the slightest bit duller in comparison. Everyone was shocked. Rion explained that he'd done many tests to find the best cap available, as not just any will do, just as not every natural cork is of the same quality.

I'd perceived the difference with my own nose and tongue, but when I told my father, he refused to believe me. I explained the blind test and that there had been others present. I repeated Rion's explanation. *Non, non, non,* my father said, shaking his head. He wouldn't hear of it. "Why do all the grand crus of Bordeaux use a natural cork then?" he asked.

I had one word for him: "Tradition!"

What I was too angry to tell him then was that the prospect of forgoing natural corks altogether saddens me—not for any practical reason, if the success of screw caps bears out over further years of testing. And not for tradition's sake, either. I just find corks beautiful. Their texture is pleasing. They require a tool to remove, giving the act of opening a bottle a bit of pomp and ceremony. Twisting off a screw cap makes an unattractive cracking sound, a poor replacement for the gentle satisfying pop of a cork being pulled from the mouth of the bottle. It's like opening a gift—a gift the cork can outlast, a piece of memory remaining long after the wine is gone.

# 8.

You're Better Than the Cheapest Bottle

*Le bon marché est toujours trop cher*

Few things sadden me more than when someone comes into my wine store and doesn't want to talk about wine. "Can I help you?" I ask, and with a shake of their head, or a polite refusal, they go back to scanning the labels and squinting at the prices, and then make a purchase, all without exchanging a single word. If that customer comes back, it's less likely I'll remember them than if we'd had even a brief conversation, and I'm always left wondering, Why *that* wine? What's the occasion? Will they like it, based on their preferences? Was it a random choice? Even in the U.S., where people are generally unafraid to say they don't know much about wine, if you offer advice they'll still shrug and demur, "Oh, I can't tell the difference anyway." Isn't that more of a reason to ask a question, not less? If it turns out that you don't like the bottle a store recommends, it's always possible the place doesn't know its wine, and you don't have to go back. But, even better, give them another chance—tell them why you didn't like the wine, and they may find something that works for you.

It's no different with restaurants. Instead of scanning the wine list and settling on one randomly—or worse, picking simply based on price—ask for help. (I know that some people always choose the second-least-expensive bottle on the list, so that they don't *appear* to be deciding based on cost alone. Don't do it!) You don't need to have a tête-a-tête with a master sommelier to find a match—all waitstaff should at least know the general flavor profiles and tasting notes of the bottles on the list. But more often than not, you'll find that a good answer to your questions is another question: "What do you like?" Answer truthfully, and from your own experience. "I like anything" is perfectly valid, if not super helpful. "I like reds" at least cuts down the possibilities, and "I like full-bodied reds" is enough to receive a recommendation. "I don't know" is an honest, admirable answer. And whatever wine arrives, approach it with openness and curiosity. It may not be the perfect match. But it may be an unexpected one. Just remember: drink the wine that you have, not the wine you imagined. Most important, whether you are satisfied or not, preserve your reaction by writing it down, or taking a picture, or just concentrating, so that the next time someone asks you what you like your answer will be a little better informed.

One last thing: don't be afraid to spend a few extra dollars. I don't mean your life savings; I really mean a few extra dollars, a difference in price that we generally tolerate in a food entrée but which makes us hesitate when it comes to ordering a drink. This is even truer in stores than in restaurants—the difference in quality between a fifteen-dollar bottle and a ten-dollar bottle can be significant. Consider skipping your morning latte and get a nicer wine for dinner instead! I'm not saying that more expensive wine is always better—that's definitely not the case. Depending on the region, vintage, and state of the market, the relationship between price and quality varies widely, and there are wonderful wines to be had at a good value. But *value* is different than *cheap*. Small, conscientious growers (as opposed to the mass producers) often produce excellent wine at a relatively low cost, and you'll find that little step up is worth it. It's time to expect more from the establishments that sell you wine, and from yourself.

Until the end of summer I held out hope that Rachel would warm to me, and that even if she didn't become the mentor I wanted, she would at least start giving me more direction, enabling me to grow as a businesswoman and wine enthusiast. In person, she was always nice and never fumbled for her words, but the emails she sent me were often incomplete thoughts, or terse demands with no deadline attached, or sometimes, most unnervingly, just "Can you come here?" I always knew when Marianne got those, because in the middle of typing she would pause, puff a sigh from her nose, like steam from an iron, and walk over to Rachel's office.

But once I accepted that Rachel was a bad manager, I started to view her various charms as a smokescreen. Everyone besides me and Marianne was still fooled. The clients were always a little sad to find themselves talking to me instead of her. "She's such an amazing woman. It must be so great to work for her," they said, as if reminiscing about a lover who had broken their hearts years ago. "You have no idea," I'd reply. Even Paris headquarters would ask after her in an awestruck manner. *Rachel est trop charmante!* She was beautiful and flatteringly dressed, always sporting an impeccable ivory manicure. She was also articulate, even when I didn't understand exactly what she was saying. It still *sounded good.*

When she asked me to go over a marketing plan, I learned to expect one of two reactions. Sometimes, she said little as I went down my checklist, except to repeat certain key phrases. I would tell her the signage for a certain event had to be made from nylon, not paper, since it would be outdoors. And she would tell me to make sure the sign was made of nylon, not paper. She punctuated her comments with nods and ambiguous grunts, and when I left her office she looked lost in thought, dreaming up some strategy, it seemed, that I could hardly imagine.

Once, she asked me to order pens inscribed with "Pringent USA" for the goodie bags. But when I brought her the sample, she said, "Who wants a pen? Nobody uses pens anymore. Whose idea was it to use pens?" I was too stunned to say it had been her idea. Only by chance had I waited to place the final order, assuming that getting Rachel's approval would be straightforward. Now I realized how close I'd been to screwing up by doing exactly what she'd asked.

"We should do something cooler. What's cooler than pens? More *current?* Can we do bracelets? You know, the rubber bracelets for charitable causes."

"But what would our cause be?"

She looked at me as if I was stupid, but her voice was as pleasant and even as always. "It's not a real cause, Laure. Why would *we* need a cause? We just need to pick a color."

I took a deep mental breath.

"What color then?"

She looked down at her own thin wrists. "I don't know. What color hasn't been taken? White? Let's do white," she said.

But the next day she stopped by my desk and said, "Laure, forget about the bracelets. Let's get those pens. The pens are fine." And she turned and walked back to her office without another word.

There's an English expression that captures perfectly how I felt at Pringent after my too-brief grace period: "Rearranging the deck chairs on the *Titanic*." I didn't know if or when the iceberg would show up to tear the whole thing apart, so in the meantime it felt like our ship's fate was to sail onward, disaster on the horizon. Every so often the crew would say to one another, "Are we going in circles?" but no one could tell. We were all busy ordering pens.

I knew I deserved better than what had turned out to be the bare minimum of a real job, but was trapped because of my visa and the knowledge that I was lucky to have it.

Also, despite the glamour of champagne, I began to miss working with still wine, with luscious reds and creamy whites, and knew I'd have to make up for it on my own, after work. The apartment I shared with Rose was too small for hosting apéritifs (we'd been spoiled by Maya's huge kitchen). But one night near the end of September when the weather was still pleasant, we saw the super coming down the emergency stairs connecting our top-floor hall to the roof. The door had a big red push-bar to open it and a sign that read, ALARM WILL SOUND. We'd been too scared to go near it.

"Izzy," we said. "You were on the roof? The alarm didn't go off?"

He glanced back at where he'd come from and said, "Nah. There hasn't been an alarm on the door for years."

After he went back downstairs, Rose and I immediately went over to the door and gave it a shove. It opened without complaint, and then we were outside on top of the East Village, on a clear night. The entire surface of the roof was coated in a silver, reflective material. We approached the edge, where the wall was just thigh high and easy to trip over and plunge six stories. Down below was Eleventh Street, the tops of people's heads bobbing by, and on the other side, the unruly garden space squeezed between the back of our building and one on Tenth. We could see the taller buildings on Third Avenue, and farther up, the colored tip of the Empire State Building. The ambient light of the city made a glowing horizon, even late at night. It was the perfect perspective on New York—not so high that it becomes abstract, but high enough that you feel you've escaped the bustle below.

Izzy told us we couldn't have parties there, but that we could bring a couple of people up once in a while. He might have wished he could take it back after we brought up beach chairs and ran extension cords from a utility outlet to put up a string of lights. We had no table, so we laid out a towel between the chairs, like a picnic blanket.

Our first guest was Peter. It was a pleasantly warm evening, but he seemed uncharacteristically sullen. I'd gotten two bottles of a festive Beaujolais-Villages to inaugurate the rooftop, a deep, fruity natural wine from Marcel Lapierre that I'd chilled slightly. Halfway through the night, though, I realized that Peter wasn't sulking—he was pensive, mesmerized by the sights and sounds of the city, like someone standing before the grandeur of nature, only instead of the Grand Canyon it was the East Village.

The next night he was himself again, joking, laughing twice as loud as anyone else, standing up to do small hip-shaking dances to prove a point. He chose the music on his iPod, plugged into portable speakers, and every twenty minutes took out a pack of cigarettes and considered it, usually but not always lighting one. Our other friends from the apéritifs, Min-Ji and Derek—Peter's colleagues from the film production company—had joined, too, so there were six of us, which is about as perfect a number as there is when it comes to company. When we toasted I made everyone make eye contact with everyone else.

"If you don't meet eyes it's bad luck," I said. "And not just any bad luck. Seven years of bad sex." You've never seen six people look so intently at one another while clinking glasses. We were all low and close to the ground in our beach chairs. Only Jules perched in a taller lawn chair with cup-holders in the arms, and we teasingly toasted him as our king. As it grew later Min moved to Derek's lap to stay warm.

Min and Derek had been dating since they'd first started working together a couple of years earlier—he was a lanky soft-spoken computer animator, and she was a lighting specialist who'd grown up in Korea and moved here for college. English was her second language but she had no problem finding him funny. She would smile with her entire face. Some humor translates easily, for the right people. He was funny to us, too—there was something a little French about his dry, gently sarcastic delivery. He especially liked to shut down any of our complaints by saying, "Baguette about it," which would send Jules into fits of giggling.

"I'm serious," Derek would press on sternly. "Let it go. Baguette about it."

I was happy to be among friends in our own space, and Americans, too, which changed the tenor from when it was just three French people sitting around talking about home and all the things we couldn't understand about the U.S. Even Rose, who loved New York intensely, couldn't always avoid comparing it with Paris. When you live in a country that's not your own, every other thought, especially at first, has to do with that strangeness. Being around the Americans relaxed my brain. We talked about movies, or restaurants, or our childhoods in a way that felt less like comparing notes and more like an introduction, an explanation. *This is who I am.*

It was a conversation, and a game—trying to make everyone laugh, although half of us were more comfortable in a different language—that we played over a nearly consecutive string of nights after we found the roof and before it got cold. Deep into October, three, four, sometimes five nights a week some combination of our group was up there. Peter moved to Fourteenth Street, close to Rose's old apartment, and with Min and Derek in NoHo, everyone was within walking distance. If anyone could help Jules feel more relaxed in New York, it was this group.

I was so afraid of disturbing the fun that I didn't complain about work for the first week or two of roof nights. When I finally did, no one really had any advice, because they all wanted to leave their jobs, too. Rose was tired of doing all the busywork for her photographer boss and wanted more control of her time. Peter didn't want to be a middle manager; he wanted to lead his own projects. It was the same with Derek. Min liked her job but felt overworked. It was the blind leading the blind, all of us sure we wanted more but less sure of how to get it.

Then Benji arrived. Benji was a freelance photo retoucher who'd been doing work for Rose's boss, and he and Rose had become friends. He was a one-man shop—the only one among us to work for himself—so his words had a little extra weight when, the second or third time he stopped by the roof, he finally spoke up and said something that might as well have been directed at me alone: "Here's how I see it: nobody can really be happy working for someone else. No one likes to be told what to do. Some people just put up with it better than others. Some bosses are better than others. You just have to know your tolerance level. Otherwise you have to work for yourself."

Benji was generally quiet, but he sometimes gave long, surprising monologues that made everyone pay attention. He was striking to look at, too, with a full beard and ponytail, his broad shoulders filling out his leather jacket. We eventually learned to recognize the growl of his Ducati motorcycle pulling up on the street below. In comparison to him, we must have seemed to be a ragtag group of misfits and outsiders. But he seemed to genuinely enjoy our company and antics, even though he was really Rose's guest, and (it quickly became clear) was there only for her.

After a few nights during which he'd taken her out to fancy bars and restaurants we'd normally never go to, I asked her about it. "You know he has a crush on you, right?"

"*Non!*" She was adamant. "He knows I have had the same boyfriend since I was fifteen years old."

"Just because he is respectful about it doesn't mean he doesn't have feelings for you."

"No," she said. "It doesn't work like that. He knows nothing can happen. He wouldn't waste his time."

I knew better than to argue. I could tell she missed Nico terribly, and none of us brought him up too often for fear of ruining the mood. Whatever Benji's intentions, I was glad she had someone else to spend time with. One night he called while we were on the roof and I heard her say, "No, I haven't. That sounds fun."

"Where are you going?" I asked her when she hung up.

"Benji's going to take me to Coney Island."

"Is it still open?"

"He says there's stuff to do. I've never been!"

I heard his motorcycle pull up below, but this time he waited for her instead of coming upstairs. I went to the edge and watched her climb on the back of his motorcycle and put her arms around his waist as they rumbled away, like a movie—or like me and Jules when we'd first met, if you replaced a delicately boned French-man on a Mobylette in Paris with a big American guy on a powerful Ducati in New York. They were spending so much time together that Jules and I found ourselves alone more often than we had since he'd first arrived. It was good for us, but it also meant I was more constantly reminded of what was at stake: he had just one month left to find a job. The chances were getting slimmer by the day.

At work I'd thought that once Marianne saw that I shared her view of Rachel, she would start to treat me like an ally. It didn't happen. I asked her about the trinkets on her desk and she only grunted in response. I still hoped we would at least bond over our shared nationality, the way we were the only ones in the office who didn't keep snacks at our desks. *Why do Americans do this, rather than just wait for mealtime?* We would laugh together. Or how Rachel forbade us from speaking French. As Rachel put it, "I just want to let you know this is an English-only office, Laure. We have to maintain our identity as the American division, servicing American clients."

"Sure, this will help me improve my English!" I'd said cheerily at the time.

I slipped up here and there, but couldn't understand why it was such a serious offense. If I was on the phone with Paris, checking on a shipment, or asking their sales department for tips about a common client, it made little sense to spend twenty minutes in English what would take five in French. If my counterpart slipped back into French (there was a wide range of English competence over there), it seemed only polite for me to speak in kind. But suddenly there'd be Rachel, standing in the doorway of her office, smiling at me with raised eyebrows and a very slight shake to her head.

"Oh, *désolée*, sorry," I'd stammer. She'd disappear back into her office while Marianne glowered at me. Marianne obviously thought I was making things worse for both of us.

It wasn't until weeks later that I wondered why Rachel was so adamant about English. Wouldn't it have been better for us to be as efficient, correct, and natural as possible? There was only one possible explanation. She didn't like me to speak French because *she couldn't understand what I was saying*. She worried I was talking about her, or making deals she didn't know about, or doing something, anything, however improbable, that might threaten her position. Me, a twenty-four-year-old she'd saved from deportation. It sounded like the silliest thing in the world, and yet as soon as I thought of it, I knew it was true, even though I had no way to confirm it.

Until, that is, I made friends with Allison, the office manager and executive assistant, a spectacularly well-organized girl slightly older than me with horn-rimmed glasses and an accent she said was unmistakably from New Jersey, although I couldn't hear it. I hadn't had much to say to her, since she worked on the other side of the tasting room and mainly with the CEO. She'd been very patient helping me figure out my insurance. But one day out of the blue she asked me to lunch. Why she chose that day, three months into my job, I still don't know. Either she'd taken pity on me as the odd woman out or, perhaps, she had something she wanted to get off her chest.

She started with harmless banter. "I would love to go to Paris," she told me over soup and salad. "I went once, for a junior-high band trip, but that doesn't count. You don't know what you're seeing when you're in junior high. You probably wouldn't even be able to pick yourself out of a lineup in junior high!"

She drank Diet Coke like it was water. I ordered a glass of house white.

"Do you have wine with every meal?"

"Never for breakfast," I lightly joked. "But when I was growing up I had wine with most lunches and dinners. You can't do that here. It's too expensive."

"But weren't you just drunk all the time?"

"No," I said. "One glass at lunch is fine for me. It's for the pleasure."

As she contemplated her Diet Coke, I mentioned how much I liked her skirt.

"I get everything from Forever 21," she said, "but only the good stuff." She laughed to herself. "I'm Italian-Jewish, which means I'm cheap and have to celebrate a lot of holidays. That's all you need to know."

I realized I liked her immensely.

"So how has it been? You have a fun job, doing champagne. Fancy."

"It's not bad. I like being in the business."

"You like working with Rachel?"

I was surprised by her bluntness. For a second I wondered if Rachel had sent her to spy on me. But she was waiting for my answer with such an open face I decided to take a chance.

"No. She doesn't give me much responsibility. I don't agree with her all the time, and yet she doesn't spend much time in the office, and when she's here she . . . how do you say this, she watches everything I do."

"Micromanages."

"Yes, that's it. It makes things harder. But you know, she's always at meetings, all the time."

Allison took a sip from her Diet Coke without responding and watched the bubbles for a second before looking up with a slightly forced smile. I could tell she was holding something back, something she wished she didn't know.

"What about Eric?" I said, referring to the CEO and her boss, to change the subject. She flinched, just briefly enough that I thought I might have imagined it.

"Eric's great," she said. "Great boss. I really admire him. I feel like he's one of those guys who can be taken advantage of, though. Sometimes I worry about him." It sounded as if she was trying to tell me something, but before I could ask, she cleared her throat and asked for the check.

The new girl is always the last to find out. The clues were there in plain sight, and it took just the gentlest push from Allison to start seeing them everywhere. The meetings, the long lunches. The times Rachel hurriedly but in a strange hush left the office early. I noticed that Eric often would leave the office just a minute before her—sometimes just seconds.

When it hit me, I nearly dropped to the floor. Rachel had called her husband a "cutie" on my first day, and Eric had two children whose photographs smiled out from his desk. I didn't know how long it had been going on or if they'd been more careful about it in the beginning—they must have. But at some point they'd started to get reckless, and by the time I picked up on everything, they were hardly bothering to get in the elevator at different times.

It went a long way toward explaining the tension around the office. It sounds entertainingly scandalous, but the entire balance of the company was thrown off by an affair between two of its top three executives (if the CFO was also involved somehow, I didn't want to know). Business was slow, sales were low, marketing deals were thin and spread out. Whenever the two of them came in the door, red-cheeked and with collars just recently adjusted, we would all glance at one another with withering looks in our eyes before turning back to our computer screens.

Allison and I had lunch a few more times before I dared to bring it up. I knew I had to do it as soon as we sat down or I would put it off again.

"Allison. I know."

She smiled, sipped her Diet Coke, and innocently asked, "What do you know?" When I didn't respond, she said, "Thank God. I couldn't stand you not knowing. But I couldn't just say it, you know?"

"I know," I said.

The next time the waiter came around, she switched from soda to wine.

"What can we do?" I asked.

"What can *we* do? Nothing that I know of. Way over my pay grade. She's bleeding him dry," she said, looking a little angry, and I wondered if she wasn't a little in love with Eric herself.

I lowered my voice. "How long has it been?"

She didn't hesitate. "Six months? Could be longer."

"Well, I wish something could be done. It's poisoning the office. You said so yourself."

"Don't do anything rash, Laure." She gave me a look, like someone who had known me much longer than she had. Was I that transparent?

"I won't," I promised. "Something will happen. It can't go on like this forever."

But I wasn't as sure of my words as I'd sounded.

"Isn't it none of your business?" Derek said on the roof that night, in his contrarian way, after I told them that a co-worker had confirmed my suspicions. "It's at work, sure, but it's still their personal lives."

"But it is making my job worse!"

Only Rose was on my side, but for the wrong reasons. She didn't seem to care whether it was making my job harder (however ill-defined it may have been). Suddenly more Catholic than ever, she said what they were doing was immoral, even worse because they were our leaders. She thought I should take a public stand.

"What, you mean confront them?"

"If you must. Otherwise you could send a letter to Paris."

Everyone looked a little surprised by her vehemence. Back in the apartment, I told her, "I don't know who would believe me. And if I have to leave the job, what then?"

"We'll find you another job. Benji knows a lot of people."

Jules waited until we were in bed to say, "This is not something you can fix, *mon coeur*. It is, what do you call it, *un mauvais bouchon*"—a bad cork.

"But nobody forces you to drink bad wine. I'm forced to go to work. It's not like I have an alternative," I said.

For a second I thought he might say the alternative would be for us to return to France together, especially now that he was down to his last weeks, but to his credit he didn't.

That weekend, Jules and I walked to Chinatown for breakfast and talked more about his own looming job crisis, without reaching a solution. When we returned, Rose greeted us excitedly at the door and said, "What are you doing for dinner? Benji is asking."

"We're having dinner with Benji?" I was confused. "What will you be doing?"

"I'll be there, too," she said.

"Oh!" I said, relieved—and then alarmed. I looked over at Jules, standing uselessly with his hands in his pockets. What could we say but yes, even though it made me uncomfortable? Jules was not as close to Nico as I'd been, and he didn't know Rose as well as I did. She wouldn't accept it if I tried again to tell her that Benji was playing a game of chess against an opponent who was an ocean away.

That night, my stomach was in knots as we walked over to the restaurant, and Rose commented on my stiffness. "Oh, just work stress," I said. In fact, I was dead set against being pleasant. When we sat down I gave Benji a long stare so he would know I was on to him. He didn't seem to notice, though, and was as affable as ever. He even ordered the wine (something that very few people did in my presence these days), explaining it was a bottle he'd had there before and liked—even though, he was sure to make clear, he was no expert. It was such a charmingly American thing to say that I almost forgot to be angry at him.

After the appetizers he cleared his throat and ran his fingers through his beard, and I knew it was coming: he was going to ask for our blessing to date Rose. And she had no idea what was about to hit her! I steeled myself to cut him off, and was so focused on Rose and Nico's relationship that I almost didn't grasp what he was saying.

"So there are these guys I've worked with, great guys." He turned toward Jules. "They started a graphic design firm. They're really small still, but have a good client list."

I suddenly understood. My grip on Jules's thigh tightened so dramatically he gasped and pried my hand off. The food came right then, but everyone waited for Benji to complete his thought.

"So if it's okay with you," he said, looking at Jules, "I'd like to put in a good word. I know how talented you are. I think it'd be a great fit."

And then, having said his bit, he dug into his coq au vin, leaving Rose beaming beside him, and Jules and me still speechless.

The design firm wanted Jules to do a trial run before they'd agree to hire him, so nothing was settled. But even the chance it presented completely changed the energy in the apartment. Jules put his basketball cards away and began to plan for the projects he'd be working on for the next three weeks. It was all he thought about.

I, on the other hand, felt myself start to relax. If Jules didn't get the job, it would be crushing, but I was both confident in him and happy he had any chance at all. The next morning I sat down next to Marianne and told her about a man I'd seen on Broadway carrying a huge python around his neck—and even when it was clear she wished I would stop talking, I kept going until I reached the end (the man got in a cab). If I was trapped at Pringent, I was at least going to make the best of it.

Right around this time, Rachel began to ask me to attend more parties, launches, and shows, and even to present directly to stores and restaurants in the city. The duties were almost like the old days working for my uncle and Moët. Soon I was traveling with a tasting bag all around the city three or four days of the week, sometimes without even stepping foot in the office. Had I been savvier, I might have taken the change as a warning instead of a blessing—that Rachel was trying to keep me away. I'd never actually argued with her, but it's possible she saw something new on my face, perhaps even some incriminating knowledge. I've always been a terrible poker player.

But ultimately, I didn't care what she thought. I felt strangely free, thanks to a combination of Benji's advice, Jules's opportunity, and the knowledge that Rachel and the CEO were sleeping together. I wasn't going to be hasty, as my visa was at stake. But I decided to look for a new job in the spring. I wanted more than this. I deserved more. And to be honest, there's only so much champagne you can drink.

Forgive me, Mother!

## Thinking About Wine

One thing I would never expect the casual hobbyist to fully understand is the French system of wine classification. The term AOC, for *appellation d'origine contrôlée*, is used not only for wine, but for cheese, butter, honey, and other agricultural products. Getting an AOC stamp is a bureaucratic maze, but it does confer a distinct advantage to producers: the ability to charge more. This is both good and bad.

First, appellations are extremely useful and aren't going away anytime soon. They contain an incredible amount of information: the land where the wine is from, the grapes that can be used, even (if you care about this sort of thing) the style of pruning allowed. The appellation can tell you if the grapes are blended from within the region, *villages* style—as in Beaujolais-Villages—or if they come from a single vineyard. There are around 350 appellations in France, each one with its own set of rules and regulations. Generally speaking, when you pay for an AOC wine, you are also paying for a seal of approval—to be able to trust the quality. (Whether the quality-to-price ratio is always worth it is another matter.)

There are also lower tiers of classification with less demanding restrictions. They are generally less expensive, but it's not a given they are lower in quality. Immediately below AOC is Vin de Pays, or "country wine" (you may also see the equivalent term *indication géographique protégée*). These regional categories are much broader: the largest is the Vin de Pays d'Oc, which covers the entire Languedoc region along the southern coast. Vin de Pays de l'Atlantique covers all of Bordeaux, along the southwest. This classification will still give you a general sense of geography and terroir, as well as the millésime—Vin de Pays is still vintage wine.

But while Vin de Pays still has a say over what grapes can be used in the region (no one would try to make a pinot noir wine in the brutally hot south, for example), its regulations are far less strict. You'll see varietal Vin de Pays—single-grape wines—from regions otherwise known for their patented blends; they're easier to market internationally, especially in the New World, where as I've said consumers are much more used to thinking of wines as "chardonnay" or "merlot." The varietal wine Fat Bastard, for example, is one of the biggest success stories out of Vin de Pays d'Oc.

Below Vin de Pays is Vin de France, a category formed in 2009 for wines that were once just called table wines and were nearly unmarketable. Within Vin de France, you can use whatever grapes you want, from whatever regions, mixed from whatever vintages. You won't see a year on these labels, and the wine is usually pretty bad, although there are exceptions.

That's the important thing to remember: that there are exceptions to everything. AOC wine is, on paper, the best you can buy, because the classification is difficult to obtain if you aren't producing from a legacy vineyard or château, and because the rules are so comprehensive. But there's a lot of crappy AOC wine out there. It makes sense: if the AOC stamp alone is enough to keep up sales, some producers will do the bare minimum to keep that wine drinkable.

Meanwhile, a small producer who wants to make a good Vin de Pays or Vin de France, who really cares about putting fantastic wine out there, not only has to ensure that the wine is of high quality, but also to hope that people will hear about it. Big companies use their marketing muscle to push well-known brands, but finding the real prizes within these less regulated classifications takes a little work. You might look for a recommendation on an oenophile's blog or a wine store's website or in a magazine. Price, too, can be an indication—table wine in the traditional sense will be just a few bucks, but quality Vin de Pays or Vin de France will be priced similarly to AOC wine. If you're in a store, you have to ask.

And you may have to pay a little more for a classification that otherwise wouldn't grab your attention. The lesson here is not that you should *always* pay more; when I say to avoid "cheap wine," I don't just mean the price. I mean a more insidious kind of cheapness, that is sloppy or indifferent or, at worst, trades on a name or label to appear more expensive than it's really worth.

Discovering the gems that don't lean on AOC and are good for the sake of being good is incredibly rewarding because no one is resting on their laurels. I'm lucky to be able to sell a few fantastic cuvées in my store, but because there's almost no information allowed on the label, customers usually only find them by talking to me. Here are a few I would recommend:

*Domaine Henri Milan, in Saint-Rémy-de-Provence.* Milan makes one red, Le Vallon, and one white, Le Grand Blanc. The white is a standout, floral and creamy with a hint of the famous Provençal lavender.

*Domaine Claire Naudin-Ferrand, in Burgundy.* An aromatic and complex white she calls Le Clou 34, made in Bourgogne Aligoté.

*Château Revelette, in Jouques, near Aix-en-Provence.* Le Grand Blanc is a Vin de Pays des Bouches du Rhône made from 100 percent chardonnay. It's firm and ripe with good acidity.

I also carry wine made by my cousin Guillaume, the son of Alain. He manages a vineyard in Tavel called Prieuré de Montézargues, known for its rosé. In fact, under AOC rules all Tavel wines have to be rosé, made from a minimum of 50 percent grenache. But my cousin also has a wonderful little red cuvée of pure syrah, deep and spicy, that he has to bottle as Vin de France. He makes only eight hundred bottles each year. The wines are vintage, but he's not allowed to put the year on the bottle, so he stamps it on the cork instead. It's his little way of getting around the regulations, and a secret code passed from him to his customers. The good winemakers find a way.

You just have to find *them*.

# 9.

## Trust Your Palate

### *Faites confiance à votre palais*

Ultimately, in wine as in life, only you can know what you like. You may find the perfect moment, ask advice from others, drink with an open mind—but none of it will matter if you don't know your own taste. When you meet someone new, even if you only speak for a minute, a voice in your head murmurs, "I like her!" or "He gives me the creeps." This voice, if asked, would probably even be able to explain why. Only rarely does it have no opinion at all.

One advantage our instincts about people have over our instincts about wine is exposure. You meet far more people in your life than you do wines (one hopes!). But that doesn't mean it's too late to become a connoisseur, starting right now. With some practice and concentration, you'll be able to tell—from a look, a sniff, a taste—whether a wine is the right one for you. Just as a musician strengthens her ear like a muscle, learning about wine is a mix of experience, memorization, and attention. You must try a lot of wine. You must remember those you try and what you thought of them. You must focus as you drink. *It doesn't happen by accident.* Very little that is good does.

It takes work. It takes desire. It takes commitment. Any world that you are determined to explore seems intimidatingly wide before you start to map it the hard way, on foot.

In December, Marianne was fired. Though by then I was out of the office most days, I happened to be there to see it—or at least the end of it. It had started harmlessly enough, with a regular meeting in Rachel's office. But after several minutes, the volume behind the closed door rose enough that the rest of us glanced at one another with question marks on our faces. The door opened, and Marianne walked out. Whatever the conflict was, it appeared to be over—until, halfway between the office and our desks, she stopped, turned back, and said, loud enough for everyone to hear, "You want to know your real problem? You can't make a good decision to save your life."

We held our collective breath. If Marianne had just sat down, whatever this was would probably have blown over and everything would have returned to its normal level of tension and discomfort. Instead, Rachel appeared in her doorway just as Marianne reached her desk. After a moment, she walked right up to Marianne—that is, right next to me—and said, "Here's one good decision: you're fired. Pack your stuff."

I'd never seen someone fired before, let alone so dramatically.

Rachel remained there, with her rear end against my desk, arms crossed, gaze eerily placid, as it took Marianne a few seconds to process what had just happened. Marianne then began to pack up. I tried to look away but couldn't. Her stunned expression slowly tightened up into one of anger. Her clenched jaw quivered as she threw items into her purse, which was in no way big enough to fit all of her stuff—the little toys, her collection of Japanese pens, all the things we scatter around to make ourselves feel at home.

"Are you sure that's yours?" Rachel said at one point, making everyone go so quiet I swore I could hear several hearts beating. Instead of combusting once and for all, as I might have expected, Marianne just replied, firmly but at a normal volume, "I'm sure." This triggered the final stage of her reaction: her face became dominated by a crazy, crooked grin that only grew wider when Ben, the chatty doorman from downstairs who always had a high-five ready, suddenly appeared from the elevator to escort Marianne out. I still have no idea who called him, and he seemed uncomfortable at having to play the heavy with one of our own.

I didn't know what Marianne's expression meant, though I knew I would remember it forever. It might have been a nervous reaction, or it might have been something else: relief. The kind of instant relief that comes when you achieve the escape you always wanted but were too scared to go after. Clarity and horror at the same time. Marianne's eyes, just before the elevator doors closed, were bright and unblinking, and the grin had faded into a wan smile. Then she was gone, and I never spoke to her again.

I also don't know to this day what became of Marianne's duties. It's not as though Pringent USA closed its normal wine business, but Rachel didn't give it to me either. In the days that followed, I kept waiting for her to call me into her office to discuss new arrangements, but the next time we were alone, she said only, "Well, the holidays are coming, let's try to make it through the rest of the year without any surprises."

"Let's hope!" I said with as much cheer as I could without veering into obvious sarcasm.

The truth was that even though my job was fine—especially since I'd started to spend most of my days out of the office—whatever tiny shred of respect I may have still had for Rachel had utterly disintegrated. Not that it was unreasonable for her to fire Marianne after such open defiance, but no one in the office had been on her side to begin with, and the public execution turned everyone even more against her while breeding an atmosphere of fear. The result was that everyone was outwardly more polite and accommodating to Rachel and the other executives, but inwardly mutinous. If nothing else, it taught me that most corporations survive by the grace of a peaceful society.

But if there was one thing Rachel was good at, it was having a bead on how people saw her. For a few weeks, she and Eric were more discreet, and every few days when I was in the office I'd watch her make a point of touring the floor desks, smiling her brilliant smile and pretending to care about the lives of everyone she said hello to. The bloodletting had also inspired her to new heights of efficiency. Her emails, sent from twenty feet away, were no longer signed with "Thanks, dear," or "Merci!" There were no niceties at all anymore, just her initials: "RM." Without compromising her genteel manners, every efficient motion and gesture said one thing: *I've done it before, and I'll do it again.* I requested a week of vacation between Christmas and New Year's to return to Paris, and she pretended to think about it before telling me, "I'm sorry, but we've got to keep the engine running. You can have two days." Two extra days for an international trip—for Christmas! But just when I'd gathered my senses and opened my mouth to protest, she said, "Please close the door behind you when you leave."

Jules was in France to get his American work visa—he'd gotten the job, to no one's greater relief than mine. It was the happiest possible reason for us to be apart, but it would take a month to process, and he wouldn't be back until after New Year's. Rose and I spent nearly every evening drinking a bottle between us and laughing, cathartically, deep into the night. It was like old times. She was angry at Nico for being unable to find a new position in New York, especially now that Jules had done it. She was bored and frustrated by her current job. Once, in the interest of trying something different, we went to a sake bar in the East Village and ordered a tasting of six sakes of different flavor profiles and opacities. (Japanese cuisine, including sushi, was only just starting to become popular in Paris at the time. Parisians don't like admitting this, but the city is always behind New York when it comes to trends.) The sake was delicious—fragrant and complex—though at home later that night we each had a glass of a Richaud Côtes du Rhône before bed. What can I say? I'm a loyalist.

Each night I'd text Jules something for him to see when he woke up, as I'd done for months and months, and I'd wake in the morning to a text from him. The distance, ironically, returned a simple sweetness to our relationship.

But back in November, during his trial with Benji's friends' design firm, tensions had been high. He worked late into the night, and every morning I would wake instinctively ten minutes before the alarm and stare at his wide, fluttering nostrils. I've never known a deeper sleeper, and I constantly worried about his ability to get up. With one minute left I would shake his shoulder, gently at first, and then rougher. "Jules, Jules, Jules, *attention.*"

"*Quoi?*"

"Jules, don't be late."

"I won't be late."

"Get up, right now!"

What did he need an alarm for? He had me, throwing socks at the sleepy, silly half-smile on his face and pulling the shirt down over his head like a boy.

"You have to get this job!"

"I'll get it, don't worry," he said. "I'm the best designer there."

He only made me more anxious. "Don't get cocky," I said, "it'll make you screw up!" and I would push him out the door with his shoes in his hand and his belt unbuckled.

But he was right. He was the best designer there, and just before Thanksgiving, with days to spare before his visa expired, the owners told him he had the job. It was exactly the kind of good news he would normally play a prank on me with, but he knew how lucky he was to get a full sponsored work visa in New York City, given how many friends and acquaintances had been unable to do it. He called me right away. When she heard me scream in joy, Rose came running into the room, and even she, whose boyfriend had spent months in employment limbo, teared up with happiness.

Before he left, we hosted Thanksgiving. Benji had gone home to Maine, Derek to Georgia, Peter to California, so it was Jules, Rose, Min, and me. Of the four of us, only Min had experience roasting a turkey. We purchased one with a built-in pop-up thermometer and spent the afternoon being scolded by Min for opening the oven every twenty minutes to look; when dinner came around, only the deepest of the thigh meat had any moisture left at all.

I love many, many things about the U.S., but turkey is not one of them. I spent that Thanksgiving feeling sorry for us all. Mashed potatoes, baked sweet potatoes, string beans, roasted root vegetables—all of these I like. But that turkey, the very center-piece of the entire meal: do Americans eat it as a form of punishment? For a dish so proudly void of fat and flavor, there can be no other explanation—an *homage* to the early American struggle, perhaps, or the country's Puritan roots.

But I wouldn't dare suggest a major change to the holiday tra-dition. The only modification I'd propose—just a small one, I promise—is one we adopted that night. Your next Thanksgiving, don't think red or white: think champagne or rosé. As bland as turkey is, you don't have to worry too much about matching a wine. For once the meat will accompany your wine, rather than the other way around. (I've even heard of champagne-basted tur-key, but that's a waste. You're better off drinking it.) We shared one good bottle of champagne, a Drappier brut nature, dry as can be, citrusy and floral, to toast Jules and our New York lives. And then we opened three bottles of Tavel rosé, deep-colored and peachy. Jules sat sheepishly at the head of the table, unused to the attention but red-faced and happy. I've heard my American friends describe Christmas as the holiday you spend with the family you're given, and Thanksgiving as the holiday you spend with the family you choose. This was the family I'd chosen.

As I looked around the table, feeling light-headed and appre-ciative, I thought that everyone reminded me of some wine or other that I had recently gotten to know. This game is more flattering to the wine—people contain far more contradictions and complexities, and bring more pleasure, than any bottle of wine. But the comparisons still worked.

Rose loved champagne above all, but when I think of her I think of a red Burgundy in the Côte de Nuits, say from the Gevrey-Chambertin appellation: elegant, deep, with a personality that needs breathing room to be properly appreciated. But if you take your time with it, you're in for an unforgettable glass.

Min gave us a hard time for ruining her turkey but never lost her good cheer. I knew she preferred full-bodied reds like Bordeaux, but I thought she was more like a Jurançon from the Sud-Ouest, an appellation where you can find both a wonderfully sweet golden wine, tropical-fruit-flavored and easy to drink, and a drier version that is subtle and complex, both honeyed and nutty. The main grapes, not as well known, are gros manseng and petit manseng.

And while Jules might have reminded me of a tempestuous Bandol, like Min he preferred fuller reds (there's a lot to love!). And not just any red; he asked for Château la Nerthe every time we were in a restaurant. He didn't drink much wine before meeting me, but once he found out that Château la Nerthe was a part of my family, he never asked for anything else. If the waitstaff said they didn't serve it (which was usually the answer, and even if they did we generally couldn't afford it anyway), Jules would say, "You should carry it. It's a very good wine. Her family makes it," and point at me. The server would feign interest, while I tried not to dive under the table. Then Jules would ask, "Well, do you have anything at all from Châteauneuf-du-Pape?"

As for me, my friends might say I am a northern Rhône, a syrah, with its spice and bold nature. The truth is that I like all wine—a bit of a cheat, I know—but the northern Rhône does have a special appeal. Given a choice I would be a Côte-Rôtie, my favorite red wine from the region. Elegant, but not as subtle as Burgundy, it's full-bodied and well-structured, and forces you to wait before drinking it, giving the pepper time to soften. It's a wine that rewards patience, without hiding anything.

But enough about me.

The last half of December, Nico flew in to see Rose, so they could have a head start together before they both returned to France for the holidays. With Jules gone, our new apartment fell into a configuration that was familiar—but different in important ways. While I was once again the tentative third wheel, not wanting to intrude, they were anything but the stable, easygoing couple I'd first met. There was an intensity to their interactions—the same way Jules and I must have appeared to others after months of not seeing each other. Hungry, almost malnourished, as if the other person were the only source of food. This was how they looked at each other, how they locked fingers even sitting on the couch doing nothing. And in the fights I heard through two closed doors late at night.

If they weren't arguing in the apartment, they were arguing outside on the sidewalk and then filing into the apartment under a glaring, unmistakable silence. For the first week Rose and I never found ourselves alone so I couldn't ask her about it. Nico wasn't going to ask Rose to come back to France—I didn't think he would, knowing how much she loved it in New York. But he also had to ask her for patience and assure her he was doing his best to return. It was the holidays—no one was hiring now. If I'd had a moment with Rose I would have advised her to relax and just enjoy their time together until the new year. In the days before they flew back to Paris she seemed calmer, as if she had reached the same conclusion herself—or had somehow discharged the bulk of her pent-up frustrations.

To give them space I went for long walks through the Village, something I hadn't done since Jules first arrived. It was dark before five o'clock, leaving long nights to fill. It had been a wet December, raining on and off for the whole month, and the sidewalks glistened from the constant drizzle. New York achieves another kind of beauty when it rains. The lights of the buildings appear in puddles, and while darkness usually makes the city contract, the water makes it expand, the way mirrors make a room look bigger.

For the first time, things were slow enough for me to look back on the year I'd had. What was I doing this very moment one year ago? Walking to my dinner shift at L'Éléphant, probably, dressed all in black beneath my coat buttoned up to the neck, having left the apartment I was sharing with Carl and Shaina (where were they now?). I still looked up into its windows whenever I passed on Second Avenue, but never saw anyone in them.

The decision I'd previously arrived at, to persevere at Pringent until the spring, had loosened me up in other ways. For one, though my budding friendship with Allison at work could have fallen by the wayside after the big reveal about Rachel and the CEO, I made an effort not to let that happen. And when Marianne was fired, we had more than enough material to talk about.

I said I wouldn't have put up with Rachel's treatment if I had been Marianne. "She'd been brainwashed," I said, "working with Rachel too long. I would have made an even bigger scene, trust

me!" We were two cocktails in and I may have felt a little bel-
ligerent.

Allison squinted at me affectionately, and said, "You're really
French."

"What do you mean? Are you insulting me?"

"No! I don't know what it is, it's a lot of little things."

"My mother says I'm so American, because I'm always rude at
home!" I said, laughing. "But I want to be even more American.
Teach me to be more American."

"I promise," she nodded seriously. "Just do as I do."

Eventually she even invited me to her place in Hoboken.
"You'll never be a true American unless you step foot in Jersey at
least once," she said, teasing. I didn't have the standing to argue.
We walked after work to a train station that I'd never noticed before, with a sign that read PATH, and I looked around in awe as
though only a select few of us could even see it. "Like *Harry Pot-
ter*!" I whispered. Minutes later, Allison informed me that we were
in Jersey. We'd gone under the river and I hadn't even noticed.

Allison's street at first didn't look so different to me from some
parts of Manhattan: row houses with apartments stacked over
stores and restaurants. But then I started to notice the clean sidewalks, the concentration of chain restaurants, the seeming scarcity
of non-white people. She lived above a tanning salon on a quiet
side street. Her living space was on one floor and her tiny bedroom half a flight up, where the roof sloped. The bed was neatly
made, a threadbare stuffed donkey propped on one of the two
pillows. For some reason I'd expected girlish décor; instead, her
living room was furnished with a brown leather couch and beaded
throw blanket, a worn reading chair, and, most surprisingly, a
small animal skull on the end table—like that of a squirrel or wea-
sel.

Allison saw where I was looking. "Oh that thing. It's my test. If a guy sits next to that thing for an hour and still wants to make out . . ."

She didn't have any wine in the house. "My secret," Allison said. "Working for a wine company and knowing nothing about wine."

"I'm sure you know more than you think you do," I said, but she shook her head emphatically. "Well, let's go shopping."

The wine store was a block away and we were the only customers dressed to stay in for the night. "What do you feel like?" I asked.

"I don't know."

"White? Red?"

"Red, I guess."

"I hope you aren't this indecisive when it comes to men," I said as a joke, but her eyes widened, as if I'd stumbled upon the truth.

We settled on a Bourgueil from the Loire Valley. I usually associate the Loire with white wine, like Sancerre or Pouilly-Fumé, but I knew the region also had well-balanced reds that could be enjoyed without food or with a small snack. The wine needed to have enough body to stand on its own but be supple enough that we wouldn't have to fight through the tannins. You can get this balance from cabernet franc grapes.

"Let's try it," I said, "and you tell me if you like it. If you don't, we'll pick something else next time."

"Deal," she said. She was normally so confident, but the talk of wine and men had clearly hit a soft spot. She told me she hadn't had a boyfriend in over a year, but I didn't know whether that meant she wasn't dating at all—the American approach to dating has always been a subject of confusion for me. When I asked, she said in a way that was no help, "I'm meeting people. I'm having a good time. But I love being single right now. Not having to answer any phone call or text message I don't want to."

"You are speaking about the opposite of my life," I said.

"I thought Jules is back in Paris right now."

"He is," I said. "That makes things even worse for our texting." I scrolled through my messages with Jules. She was amazed at the quantity.

"It's like you guys would die without texting every few minutes."

"Yes." I nodded sadly. "That's exactly what it's like."

The conversation, inevitably, returned to Rachel. Maybe it was the wine, maybe it was being at home, but Allison was more forthcoming about what she knew about "the affair." She felt conflicted, having helped Eric, her boss, make and rearrange appointments to manage his time with Rachel, even though he'd never explicitly told her what was going on. She said he was really good to her and although she was angry, like everyone else, she felt bad that the situation he'd gotten himself into was eating away at the company. Rachel, however, she had less sympathy for.

"She has that mortician's smile."

"The what?" I asked, and Allison pulled her cheeks into a frozen grimace with her fingers, her eyes flat and emotionless. I laughed until I lost my breath.

My flight back to Paris was the Friday evening before Christmas Eve. Since Rachel had allowed me only two days off, my return flight was less than a week later, on the 27th. The champagne business is dependent on the holidays, and Rachel said she wanted me to set up tables at the best Manhattan stores we'd sold to, leading up to New Year's, to help push stock before the big night. Even the morning of my flight, my schedule was full up until three or four in the afternoon—four stores and two restaurant visits— after which I was going to have to hurry to the airport. But Rachel called me just before lunch and asked me to come to the office between appointments.

I texted Rose and told her that I had a feeling something was wrong.

*You are overreacting*, she wrote back. *They are probably finally assigning you Marianne's work.*

It was the most likely explanation, so I tried to push the fears out of my head as I walked up to the building. Rachel was waiting for me in her office. Only once I sat down did I notice the CEO, Eric, standing by the far wall. Rachel wasted no time.

"Laure, your performance has been a disappointment. We're letting you go."

I looked into her eyes for a good ten seconds before I could speak. She didn't lower her gaze once.

"This . . . this is a total shock," I said.

"I don't see how that can be. We've been unhappy with you for some time."

"You never said a word to me," I said. "You never asked me to do anything different. I always did everything you asked. I completed every marketing plan. I've been meeting nonstop with clients. I've built relationships. I work well with Paris." (Only later would I suspect that some of those accomplishments were the very reasons she wanted me gone.)

"I didn't like that email you wrote to Maynesfeld House in September, as I told you on the record."

"*September,*" I couldn't stop myself from repeating incredulously. "When did you know you wanted to fire me?"

I looked over at Eric, who was standing with his arms crossed, sporting his usual, flattering three-day beard and a grave, inscrutable expression. Unlike Rachel, he could hold my eyes for only a second before glancing away.

A few strands of blond hair had fallen in front of Rachel's face and she swiped them away with an efficient flick of her hand.

"This isn't a negotiation," she said calmly. "Today is your last day. Please gather your things. Don't make this a scene."

"But you turned down my request to take Christmas Eve off so I could take an earlier flight to be with my family. Why would you do that if you were going to fire me?" I asked just to say it out loud, though there was only one possible answer. She'd done it out of spite.

I've often thought about this moment, because it was the same chance not to go quietly that I envisioned for Marianne. In my mind, instead of walking out in stunned silence, I stand and tell Rachel that I know she is firing me not because I am bad at my job but because I am *good* at it. Sometimes I bring up the affair that she may think she's doing such a good job hiding but which everyone on the floor snickers and groans about every single day. And I bring it up with Eric standing right behind her.

But I did neither of these things. In fact, I understood exactly what Marianne had felt in that moment. It was over, and Rachel—all of this—wasn't worth the calories it would have required to throw a fit. With every second that passed, Pringent and everything about it was shrinking in my mind, shrinking and shrinking until it was worth no more anguish than a pebble in my shoe. I had little to say to most of my colleagues, but from the disbelieving looks they gave me, I could see that whatever Rachel had hoped to gain by getting rid of me was unlikely to work. When I passed Allison's desk, she looked stricken. I mouthed, "I'll call you."

The one and only thing to Rachel's credit is that she didn't have Ben the doorman escort me out.

My short and inglorious career at Pringent USA had lasted nearly six months, or about the same amount of time I'd spent touring the U.S. on behalf of my uncle. I spent much of the flight back to Paris thinking as little as possible, alternating between sleeping and watching movies. I knew that given the time pressure of my visa expiration I should have started planning what my next step would be, but I was too spent. At the airport, my mother seemed happier than usual to see me, putting her hands on my shoulders and smiling while looking me over as if to verify there was no appendage missing. "There's my girl," she said, hugging and kissing me. We barely made it to the car before I started to cry and told her what had happened. Immediately, her goodwill disappeared. Instead of sympathizing, she began to berate me with peak exasperation.

"This is because you are too difficult!" she said. "You are too spirited, too loud, you never listen to what anyone says. You always think you know better than anyone else. I'm not at all surprised you were fired!"

Naturally, I cried even harder. When we reached the house, she apologized, but still made it clear that she thought I had somehow brought it on myself.

When I saw my father, he told me that while he was certain I hadn't done anything out of line, he wouldn't have been surprised if I had somehow made the situation worse. (My parents are either very insightful, very patronizing, or both.)

"She fired the other French girl, too, you know," I protested. "She was out to get the both of us. I felt it from the start; I just didn't listen to it."

"Why did she hire you then?"

"She thought I was stupider than I turned out to be. I don't know."

"I don't know either. I do know this. You were not happy. You did not respect your boss. In those situations, it's only a matter of time, one way or another."

After lunch, Jules came to pick me up. After months of listening to the roar of Benji's Ducati, seeing the chugging little Moby-lette made me laugh. I'd missed it. He gave me a long kiss and held my head in his hands, and said, "I'm so sorry, *mon coeur*, but everything will be all right." There we were again, puttering along the streets of Paris as we did when we were both still in school. I thought if I wrapped my arms around his waist hard enough we might be transported back to that time. But instead of two Parisian students, we were now two New York residents just back for the holidays. We went to his favorite bar, but he seemed a little restless. When I asked him what was wrong, I almost expected him to suggest that he drop his job and for us to move back. I waited for it so intently that when he actually did speak I was so unprepared for what he actually said that it cheered me up for the rest of the day.

"The only thing this place is missing is a good hamburger."

Thirty people came to my father's house for Christmas dinner: his two sisters and Uncle Alain and all their children. I was nervous about seeing my uncle—I didn't know what he'd say about my having been fired from the job I took after his. Would he think I'd impugned his good name? Question my general competency? But he was as accepting and encouraging as always, and I should have never doubted him.

We had a wondrous, enormous meal. The French are famous for moderation, it's true, but even moderation needs moderating— you can't do it every time. Every member of my family is a big eater and, even more, a big drinker. Leave it to the Americans to cherish a nearly fatless bird on a national holiday; to the French, the real king of fowl is the duck, rich and fatty. The wine had been hand-delivered from Champagne and Châteauneuf-du-Pape, and my father donated the spirits. It was about as good a menu as you can have.

After dinner, Uncle Alain finally pulled me aside, and changed my life for the second time.

"This just came to me, Laure. Do you remember the man we had dinner with in February, Mark Brodeur? He's an importer. He does everything himself and might need help. But he runs his business out of Westchester, so it would be far for you."

I did remember him, a tall, white-haired man who seemed to have a hundred stories and a hundred laughs at the ready. I remembered his cigars. I remembered the dinner probably the best of all. At the end of the night Mark had given me his card but I'd never used it.

My uncle had his number, and I called the next afternoon. I didn't expect Mark to pick up the day after Christmas, but he did.

"I remember you," he said. I thought I detected a small note of amusement in his voice.

There was, of course, no way not to tell him that I was out of work, so I got right to the point, saying only that I hadn't been happy where I was and had recently parted ways with Pringent. I bit my thumb nearly to the bone as I waited for a response. After a beat, he said, "I see. Well, I'm in Montreal until the new year. Would you like to come up on the third and talk? I'm always looking for help—but the *right* kind." I could tell he had a strong idea of exactly what the right kind of help was.

"Yes, of course, I can do that," I said.

Jules and I met Rose a couple of days later at the Ménilmontant bar, which was thankfully open. There was something strange but poignant about the three of us meeting in a Paris bar, when we would all see one another again in a week in our shared New York apartment. But there we were, sipping tea and coffee and eating *éclairs au café* beside frosted glass as though we had never set foot in the New World. We were all aware of this oddness, which felt even more like a time warp than my first Christmas home, because both cities, Paris and New York, were equally corporeal to me now, with New York the more immediate and Paris the more natural. It felt a little like being in two places at once.

"I don't know what to do," Rose said, echoing my own dilemmas from another time. "I want to live in New York, but Nico won't come back with me. He says it's too hard to find a job and he has so many more good opportunities here that he'll start to sabotage his career if he holds off any longer."

"It is hard, Rose."

She sniffed. "I don't know if he is trying to call my bluff about my wanting to stay in New York. He says he is trying to come, he's still sending out many feelers, but that there is no demand. He says the economy is no good. I suppose I believe him, but I'm so angry anyway. Maybe I am trying to call my own bluff."

Jules and I held hands under the table and murmured encouraging things. The most we could do was offer support for whatever decision she made, as much as we wanted her and Nico to make it work together.

The rest of the week went by quickly. I was at ease, at my mother's apartment, sleeping in my old bed, while knowing that a good opportunity awaited me in New York. But I was also supremely nervous just below my relaxed exterior, *because* I knew that a good opportunity, maybe the best I'd ever get, awaited me in New York.

Jules and I spent a subdued New Year's at a friend's house party. In our last minutes together in Paris the next morning, standing on my mother's stoop, Jules kissed me sweetly. I was definitely not going to let him come to the airport. He would be back in New York with his brand-new visa in just a few days, while now I was the one under threat of losing my ability to stay in the States. We'd switched places. We couldn't catch a break! But then again, we'd caught so many to get to this point. I needed just one more.

Jules was right, of course, though he couldn't have been as sure as he sounded. I got the job. But not before some trepidation and soul-searching. I'd thought hard about the hypothetical situation Jules had never actually raised—should we just call America quits and come back? It seemed more appealing once I looked up the commute I was going to have to put up with each day. But in the end the decision wasn't really that hard. I wasn't ready to leave New York.

I landed in the morning and only had time to stop by the apartment to change and shower before heading to Grand Central to catch the train to Westchester for lunch with Mark Brodeur. But just before I purchased tickets I received a text message: *My flight delayed. Let's do tomorrow if you are able.*

I was able, although it just meant another twenty-four hours of nerves eating a hole in my stomach. Instead of returning home straightaway I bought a sandwich and stood in the station's great hall, watching the business travelers back from the holiday criss-cross in front of me. I'd only been there once or twice, and nearly as impressive as the hall itself was the number of people who were no longer impressed by it. I made a vow to always be impressed.

I went back to my empty apartment, fell asleep on the couch, and woke six hours later not remembering where I was. I put on my coat and went outside to get something to eat. The ground was slick from light rain. It was the first Thursday of the new year, but the streets were oddly quiet. I couldn't remember ever feeling so alone in New York, not since my first few days in the city. Back then the solitude I'd felt was that of an alien. This was different. It felt like a city on hold—almost as if I'd paused it while sorting out my life. What I wanted more than anything was the power to press PLAY again, or, if it was about to start up again, to follow along and not get left behind. What I had been doing was, I felt, essentially American—rushing toward new experiences and chal-lenges, as if life were a great experiment. I'd been following its loose, improvisational script.

As I turned the corner onto Fourteenth Street, backtracking the route I'd once pushed my giant suitcases down from one hos-tel to another, I started to cry. Not out of sadness, but from an intense feeling of belonging.

I will tell you one last story about Pringent, with some ambivalence, because if I truly harbored no bad feelings and even felt some gratitude toward the company for forcing me to move on, then this story shouldn't make me happier to know it. But it does.

In late January, after I'd been working with Mark for a few weeks, my uncle called. I thought he just wanted to chat, but he was very excited. I started listening with polite curiosity, but it quickly turned into rapt attention.

"Laure! Listen," he said, sounding breathless. "I just spoke to a friend who knows many people at Pringent. Your old boss Rachel and the CEO, Eric, they separated from their spouses and took a long vacation together to Thailand. But hold on, that is not the story. It just so happened that at this time Jean Pringent was in New York and stopped by the office. He was there less than an hour before everyone started telling him how unhappy they were, how the business was going down, and of course how the two *rongeurs* had let their *feu* consume them and fired two good workers because of pettiness and jealousy. And Pringent believed them! But the affair was not his real concern. He called in an auditor and sat with them day and night as they went over the records, the ledgers, until they had proof that it was not only the culture of the office that had been poisoned, but the business itself. Satisfied, he found the resort in Ko Samui where Rachel and Eric were staying—with the help of the CEO's assistant, which should tell you how bad things had gotten—and instructed them to fly directly to Paris. He dismissed both of them within five minutes of their arrival at headquarters. They were told they would have no further access to the New York office. That was two days ago, and I have no idea where they are now. Perhaps they saw this as a sign and now live together in Paris, yes?"

It was a surprisingly romantic note for my uncle to finish on, but he can be forgiven. Our family tends toward optimism.

## Thinking About Wine

As a celebration of family—real or constructed—Thanksgiving is a wonderful holiday. But I still don't understand why Americans insist, with 100 percent seriousness, on cooking the most boring bird on the planet.

I'll at least repeat my small plea to kick up the occasion by avoiding the usual still wines we invariably serve at dinner, and try what the four of us did on the first Thanksgiving I ever celebrated: champagne and rosé, or just champagne, or just rosé. You can't go wrong.

Champagne hardly needs further introduction or praise. Rosé, however, is perhaps the most misunderstood of the French wines, and for that reason alone deserves special attention. I've had people ask me if rosé is made by mixing white and red wines. It's not (except for some rosé champagnes). Rosé is made from red wine grapes, but some producers add white grapes for a floral touch, as my cousin Guillaume does with the clairette grape. An extra step draws out the juice while limiting how long the juice stays in contact with the skins, depending on the producer's preference and the kind of wine desired. The two methods are *rosé de presse* (pressing the grapes to produce their tinted juice) and *rosé de saignée* (bleeding off the juice after macerating the grapes with the skins). The balancing act is in achieving the right color and flavor without letting the tannins overtake the wine's delicacy and elegance. Given how specialized this process is, you shouldn't think of rosé as something "between" red and white. It is its own affair altogether.

Rosé also has a reputation as a sweet, girly summertime wine, which leads people to clearer, lighter varieties. Provence produces the prototypical rosés—lightly colored, fruity, and dry. And indeed in Paris when the weather turns warm, the cafés all set up their outdoor tables and chairs and everyone sits in the sun and orders rosé from Provence. It's a beautifully tinted three-month movie, and then it is over. Look: if you just want a refreshing drink, stick with lemonade. Rosé isn't just there to cool you down. While it can't be aged long-term, it is more than capable of subtlety and flavor—and rosés can be, and frequently are, quite dry, not sweet. It allows you to taste the best parts of red wine grapes without the tannins. It is friendly and pleasant and more flexible than it is given credit for.

And this brings us back to Thanksgiving. As far as poultry goes, people often have strong opinions on whether you should drink it with red or white. *Pinot noir! Sauvignon blanc!* But I recommend a third way: try a darker rosé like the Tavel I ended up choosing. Tavel is an appellation in the southern Rhône Valley, and some of its rosés might surprise you—rather than the light pink wine of Provence, Tavel makes a deep red one, fruity and spicy with peach flavors. Though most rosé is best enjoyed within a year of harvest, Tavel rosés, along with some from Bordeaux, are an exception, and actually evolve well with another two or three years of aging. Rosé in fall and winter? Believe it. And try for yourself.

PART III

Harvest / Récolte

## 10.

...................................................................................

# The Older the Vines, the More Complexity

*Se bonifier avec le temps*

When you meet a bottle of wine, everything that has made it what it is has already happened. The aging, the fermenting, the harvest, the growth, the soaking up of the land through its roots—by the time it is opened by you, the wine's entire life cycle, leading up to tonight, is complete. It's the same when you meet a person—the lines on their face say something about who they are, but not how they got there. That story takes much more time to tell.

My mother always told me that something marvelous happens to a person when they reach a certain age: they're more resilient, more *themselves*. The same can be said for grapevines. A root system that has developed over decades is hardier and less susceptible to swings in the weather, able to handle too much rain or too little. Older vines may produce less, having lost the boundless energy and freshness of youth. But the wine they are capable of producing is less reliant on sheer fruit, and can be more balanced, more layered, more complex.

When does a vine qualify as an old vine? Nobody knows for sure. Or rather, there are plenty of opinions without consensus. Some say fifteen years and some say fifty. Even when you see *vieilles vignes*, "old vines," on a label, it doesn't tell you much. The grenache vines my uncle uses for his Cuvée des Cadettes are more than a hundred years old, and I can tell you that the product is quite good, but it's impossible to know how much is due to the age of the vines, or to cultivation techniques, or to terroir. When it comes to the art of viticulture—and life—the value of age is real, but difficult to quantify.

Time itself is no guarantee of quality. You can't simply tuck some vines away on deprived land, not prune them for half a century, and come back to make great wine, just as you can't drink wine your whole life without paying attention and expect to have magically gained wisdom. Though I'd grown up with wine, I'd only been paying attention for a year. Now it was the first week of 2008, and I was twenty-four. Who is wise at twenty-four? I knew what I *wanted* to know, but it was like something on a shelf just out of reach. No matter how I stretched and grazed it with my fingertips, I could not will myself to be taller, just as I could not will myself to reap another year's experience in a day.

I worried I would need it, though. Mark Brodeur had been importing French wines for longer than I'd been alive. At our dinner with my uncle, he'd been in a chatty, boisterous mood, but I'd also detected an intensity that my uncle didn't quite match, and I didn't know what to make of it. I didn't know what he would make of me.

My knees were weak as I got off Metro North in the small town an hour out of the city that was home to Mark Brodeur Imports. I'm not generally nervous in interviews, but things are always different when transatlantic stakes are involved. The fact that he was stubborn enough to run his business here, instead of in Manhattan, seemed an important clue to his character. My uncle told me Mark had long resisted expanding his business, but that he was one of the most passionate wine people he knew. I wondered if those two facts were related.

The village was so small that I'd barely stepped off the train when I found myself on the one-street downtown, a short strip of charming one- and two-story redbrick buildings trimmed in white. American flags were pinned to the telephone poles, and the shops had Christmas lights strung on their roofs. The only traffic signal I could see was a stop sign at the far end of the street where a few cars were making turns toward what I imagined were large beautiful houses with expansive lawns for their children to run around on.

Brodeur Imports was on the first floor of a small gabled building. It had been nearly a year since I had met Mark, and all I could remember was that he was tall and white-haired, with a voice that carried, and that I hadn't been able to keep up with the conversation at the time, the names of wines and wine producers that floated in and out like old mutual friends.

The door, stenciled with his name, was as elegant and old-fashioned as you'd imagine: a wide wood frame with a single large glass panel in the middle, horizontal shades askew behind the glass, and a round brass doorknob. It was a door I would later go in and out of hundreds of times and, aside from my desk, the thing about the office I remember best. Now I opened it for the first time, and there was Mark, standing from his desk to take my hand.

He was just as I remembered—the white hair and glasses, the slight downturn of his eyes matched by a slight upturn to his mouth that gave him a look of permanent bemusement. But everything that came out of his mouth in Québécois French was immediately serious and to the point.

"When we met you were helping Alain. You were traveling the country," he began, as if to remind himself.

"Yes, I was touring Moët's distributors."

"Moët, ah right. Tell me about what it was like and everything you learned."

I stammered a bit as I tried to describe the importance of making a personal connection with the sellers and restaurateurs. I said that I'd learned that every wine has a story, and that telling the story is invaluable to understanding the wine. I also said that the areas of the U.S. I'd seen were quite different from one another, but to my surprise nearly everyone I'd met was very enthusiastic and passionate about wine.

"Nearly everyone?" he interrupted.

I thought about the bad encounter I'd had in Nashville, but said only, "It's a business. I understand it's possible to be in wine just as a business, for the money, but I also think you won't be able to run the best business that way."

He nodded thoughtfully. "And Pringent. Tell me about Pringent."

I laughed nervously. "At Pringent I learned the details. I learned the difference between a medium-sized business and a giant business like Moët. It was not the best place for me, but it did help me realize I like smaller businesses, where you aren't just doing the same task over and over. You have wider responsibilities. And I learned what I want to do and what I want to be. It's not enough for me to be in the industry. I want to work with wine every single day."

He leaned forward, and his brow furrowed. "So you weren't happy with Pringent."

I shook my head. "No, I wasn't very happy. My boss was young and glamorous"—as I said it I realized that what I'd originally admired about Rachel was now what I counted against her—"but she was more interested in how things looked than how they worked."

He grunted. "You won't have to worry about youth and glamour with me," he said, and I laughed. He smiled in return, the corners of his eyes and his mouth nearly meeting.

Mark told me about his business. He *was* his business. He traveled to France to tour the producers. He made the deals to import the wine. He built relationships with the wholesalers and the restaurants. When they called, he was the one to pick up the phone. When there was a problem, he was the one to solve it. He wrote the checks, cashed the checks, balanced the ledger.

"I do everything," he concluded. "And I could use help," he said, opening up his palms. "But I want the person I hire to be able to do everything, too. I don't want someone just to do the books, or just to do the calls, or just marketing, or just dealing with clients. I want someone who can also talk to winemakers, go to tastings, pour the wine—and also clean the desk."

He gestured toward his expansive desk, which had neat stacks of paper and folders lined up next to his computer screen. "I clean mine every night. You would also be expected to clean yours every night," he said, pointing across the room at an unoccupied, smaller desk. He leaned back in his chair, interlaced his fingers across his stomach and paused, as if to let it all sink in.

"Most important"—he raised a finger—"I don't want some-body who is just here for a job. I am not just here for a job. I want somebody who loves wine as much as I do, if not more."

If this was a negotiation, he'd certainly laid out demanding and detailed terms. My knees were still quaking slightly, but no longer from fear. I couldn't remember the last time I'd been so excited.

❦

Four hours after I'd arrived, I returned to the station and boarded a train heading home. I couldn't believe how long the interview had gone. I'd done my best to assure him that the person he was describing was me—that I wanted to do it all, and out of love. My biggest concern was that I was too inexperienced for what he was looking for.

My head buzzed as the train slipped by the beautiful-sounding Westchester towns, crossed over the bridge into Manhattan, and went underground. If I'd convinced him, this would be my commute—three hours a day in total—but worrying about it now would have been like complaining about a gift I had yet to receive.

I was still alone in the apartment, days I spent in nervous an-ticipation. I bought some colored lights half off at a hardware store and strung them around the living room for a touch of fes-tivity. On Monday, Mark called to offer me the job. I was practi-cally shaking with glee—until he mentioned the salary, which was a little more than half of what I'd made at Pringent. He seemed to hear the surprise in my silence and added, with the firmness of a true dealmaker, "It's all I can do." He didn't condescend to say he was doing me a favor, but he also knew that without the job, I would be on a plane back to Paris within weeks, this time for good.

"What about the train?" I drew up the courage to ask. "Could the company pay for my train tickets?"

"I'm sorry, no," he said. "But the company will pay for lunch. I take lunch very seriously. That should be familiar to you, as a Parisian, no?"

I accepted.

Min and Derek invited me that night to a party at the Tribeca loft of someone they knew. I happily tagged along. At some point during the night, Min and Derek became uncharacteristically ardent, kissing each other as if I wasn't standing right there, so I walked alone around the duplex, dodging strangers who wanted to talk, looking at the giant canvases of abstract art, and then made my way back to the drinks table, where I found an uncommon Côtes du Vivarais red from the Rhône Valley—more rustic in its hints of blackberry and spice than typical Châteauneuf wines.

Min found me and asked how I was doing. "Aren't you happy?" she said. "I'm happy you're still here. I'm happy you don't have to go back to that nasty place."

"I am," I assured her, though I was close to tears. Complicated tears, of relief, frustration, anxiousness, joy. I've always thought that Min was a mind reader and a fortune-teller, so I listened closely as she squeezed my arm and leaned in to say something. "This is just the beginning," she said.

The first month with Mark was an adjustment, to say the least. On sunny mornings, I'd biked or even walked to Pringent. Now I woke up before sunrise, in full dread of the January air, and trudged through the slushy streets to Grand Central, where I rushed to buy a pain au chocolat and, if I didn't have a cheap French novel with me, the *New York Times*, and fight against the wave of commuters heading into the city. I felt like I was swimming upstream.

My first day, I got up early enough to shower, dry my hair, and apply a full face of makeup. After a couple of weeks, I started to put on my makeup on the train, and then I simply began wearing less and less. I wish I could say I gave it up out of feminist ideals, but the truth is I was just exhausted. Eventually I was regularly walking through the jingling front door of Mark's office with no makeup on at all. If he noticed, he never said anything. (My mother would have been horrified. She never goes outside without lipstick and since my teens has been pressuring me to at least put a little on to "emphasize the right things.")

The return commute was even worse, especially those first days when it was new to me. I left the office between seven and eight and still had an hour and a half of travel ahead. By the time I stepped into the apartment I was too tired to eat, and skipped dinner or ate cereal or toast and fell asleep in my clothes. When Rose came back in the middle of January her desire to go out was undiminished, but she was disappointed to have lost her dance partner. The nights she decided to stay in, she sat on the couch with me and read until I fell asleep with my head on her shoulder.

It was grueling. But I never questioned it.

Jules, also back, was now a working New Yorker, a fact that made me smile the dozen times I thought of it each day. The only problem was that his schedule had shifted nearly as much as mine, but in the opposite direction. I woke up while it was still dark, whereas his days started at ten in the morning and often went to eleven or twelve at night—the hours of a young start-up design firm scrambling to establish a client base. He was determined to prove himself, but was also working hard out of loyalty— something we both felt toward our employers. As he saw it, the design firm had taken a double chance on him, a French national with whom they'd had no previous connection. He wanted them to know they'd made the right decision. So I left while he was still deep asleep. He woke up at nine and walked to Fifth Avenue. I returned late at night, barely able to keep my eyes open, and would frequently be asleep by the time he got home. Some days we didn't see each other awake at all.

It was almost as if we were long distance! I whispered my goodbyes in the morning to his unconscious face, not wanting to risk waking him with a kiss. And he came home wired, wrists sore from a long day of drawing, with a hamburger in a bag, awake for another two or three hours watching basketball highlights on his computer. Long gone were our leisurely people-watching Whole Foods lunches and walks around the city. In a matter of months our lives had shifted into a more serious, more demanding gear.

Also, poor Jules had never experienced the punishing winters of the American Northeast, and it made him return to his old favorite game: things about America to complain about. "You didn't tell me it was colder here than Paris," he groaned. "My coat is no good now," he said, referring to his prized all-weather leather jacket, which was warm enough in France even when it snowed. Even after we bought him a new coat he'd loved in the store, he still grumbled. "There is something different about the air in New York," he said, sounding extremely certain for someone without any science to back him up. "I can tell, it goes right through the cloth much easier than Parisian wind."

But secretly I was glad to hear his complaints about winter. It meant he was no longer complaining about the noise, or the food, or the people who made up the living, breathing city. He had started, against every fiber of his being, to get used to it.

The commute and loss of time with Jules was worthwhile for one reason: Mark Brodeur. I've never quite understood the phrase "larger than life"—it seemed to be enough that he was more alive than almost anyone I've met. He had a deep-rooted awareness of life's gifts and grievances, and drew everyone's attention to them constantly. "Isn't life grand?" he liked to say. Or, in moments of frustration, "I'm not going to waste my life doing this." He was in love with it; he flattered and scolded it. Aside from his Québécois accent, he could have been French, with the sort of attitude I was accustomed to from my friends and family back home: stubborn, opinionated, always relishing the moment.

He also would have preferred that the earth split in two beneath his feet rather than miss lunch. Each day at one o'clock, no matter what we were doing, he heaved a sigh, pressed his hands against his desk, and said with the utmost gravity, "Time for lunch." My first day, I didn't know what to expect—he'd mentioned lunch when he offered me the job, but I figured it would be delivery or a sandwich.

He stood and gestured for me to come with him, and we walked out into the Westchester winter, the well-heeled local residents blowing puffs into the air and dodging the light tufts of snow that had gathered by the curb. At the end of the next block was one of the few buildings in town with a dark wood frame. The name above the door read LA MAISON DU ROI. It was French owned and operated, Mark told me proudly. Inside, we stamped the dusting of snow from our shoes, and suddenly there were hearty greetings being thrown our way.

"*Monsieur Brodeur! Bienvenue. Pour deux?*"

As we sat down, Mark introduced me, and everyone from the owner to the servers welcomed me with enormous, knowing smiles—it was clear he'd already clued them in to my arrival. As he unfolded his napkin he let out another, far more pleased sigh, and without cracking his menu ordered a French onion soup and a duck confit. He leaned forward to explain why he had ordered such a hearty meal, even though I hadn't asked.

"I go home now, there's no dinner. There's screaming, but no dinner. So this is all I have," he said, and spread his hands out over the place setting in front of him. He then told me that he had become a father for the first time in his fifties with his second wife, an American woman, and now had two small children. In fact, that's why he needed help. His wife had managed the office for years, but she had decided to stay home when the first child was born—five years ago. It had taken him this long to admit that he would eventually have to trust someone else around the office.

The French onion soup, which he insisted I also order, was too cheesy and oily and salty to be authentic. But Mark dug in with relish. As someone who went to France twice a year on business, he must have known what good onion soup tasted like—and yet here he was, smacking his lips over every spoonful. It had to be partially a form of pragmatism—it wasn't as if there were a dozen bistros to choose from—but his excitement was infectious, and so the soup wasn't so bad, really, I thought, as I took another sip.

"This life is what I want my daughters to have," he went on. "The good food, the French way of thinking. I want them to go to Paris and learn French—we don't speak Québécois at home. They should study abroad when they're in college. I lived there for a few years in my twenties, you know. I loved it. I worry about the American schools—the children are too prized, they are like little kings." *Petits rois*, he repeated in French, like an insult.

Though I'd been working for Mark for less than a day, he had no trouble unloading long tirades of personal details and opinions. I'm straightforward, but I'm not a big sharer, so I mostly nodded and clucked sympathetically. I was also biting my tongue to avoid arguing with him so soon in our working relationship. He had something of the old-fashioned belief in the supremacy of the Old World and the shallowness of the New, and I wanted to tell him that as someone who'd been born in France, it wasn't so simple. Everything that was great about France, I would have explained, was a double-edged sword. Our pride, for example, makes us susceptible to becoming defensive and small-minded, whereas the American way is to welcome everything, devour everything. It could be confusing, at least to an expatriate like me, but also exciting.

At the same time, not a day went by that I didn't wish New York could be just a little bit more like Paris—that it was easier to find a good croissant, that more things were built to be pleasing and to aid pleasure. The old ways, built on centuries of experience and experiment, *are* often more rewarding. In short, my feelings were complicated, which I was only starting to be able to articulate, as I began my second year in America. But I wasn't going to say all this to Mark on my first day of work.

Later, perhaps.

The next day at one o'clock on the dot, Mark sighed that same sigh and again we dropped what we were doing, retrieved our coats, and stepped out onto the chilly sidewalk. Only this time instead of La Maison du Roi, he took me to a nearby Japanese restaurant. Here, too, he was greeted by name, settled into a favorite table, and ordered a selection of sushi from memory. This time he talked less about himself and more about the business. He had a curious way of talking about the business—not with numbers, but stories. He told me about a winemaking family he had great relations with in Saint-Émilion, one of the more famous regions of Bordeaux—a father and three daughters, one of whom, he said, looked a little like me: tall, brunette, freckled, and spirited. For as long as he'd been in business he had imported their wine: two wonderful Bordeaux supérieur, Château de Macard and Château de Ribebon. The father, he told me—dropping his chopsticks to demonstrate—had very big hands, weathered from working so hard on the vines. He smiled and picked up his chopsticks again, while I silently interpreted the lesson he was trying to get across. I'd been so used to having to read the subtext at work, but ultimately, I decided that Mark was just telling me this man and his family existed, made good wine, and were an important part of his long professional life.

On Friday, we returned to the French restaurant, and as we hurried down the main street, jackets pulled tight against the cold, I realized that aside from a pizza parlor, these were the only two restaurants downtown.

As for actual work, the first thing Mark asked me to do was to update the fact sheets for all sixty producers in his portfolio.

"Where are your previous ones, so I can see how they were done?" I asked.

He hesitated, the first time I'd seen even a flicker of doubt on his face.

"Well, you see," he said, shuffling around a filing cabinet. "My wife did them before she stopped working."

"Five years?" I asked incredulously. "You've been going without fact sheets for five years? There's no way they're still good."

"No need to get excited," he said. "Some of the information I carry in my head, and I tell the sales reps everything I can. But you know how it is." He shrugged. I did know. Many sales reps had to be familiar with three to four hundred wines. If you didn't make things easier for them, your wines didn't sell.

Making the updates was not quite as straightforward as I hoped. The producers I needed to reach out to for information were in France, and busy. The winter is an important season— the vines are dormant and need pruning, a skill that takes a great deal of experience to master. You have to trim aggressively to stimulate the coming summer's growth. So the winemakers were often in the fields, or it was dinnertime and they didn't want to be disturbed. Many weren't diligent about using computers and printers and email, if they even had them in 2008. (Whenever the subject came up, they'd ask me, in typical fashion, how could computers possibly help them make better wine?) I sometimes faxed them, if they had a fax. And I needed to make sure they sent me everything, from a basic description of the vineyards to the proportion of the current vintage's blend—say, for example, a 2005 Bordeaux was 10 percent cabernet franc, 60 percent merlot, and 30 percent cabernet sauvignon. That gave a customer a clue about the balance of the wine. The more cabernet sauvignon, the richer, more robust and serious, and less exuberant the wine will be. When it is young, cabernet sauvignon can be severe, which is why it is often blended with merlot to make it fruitier and more drinkable.

We also included anything about the story of the vineyard to make it stand out. Family-run producers are often very good at making wine but don't always prioritize marketing. Their attitude is, "I make the best wine there is; why would you need help to sell it? It should sell itself!" They were proud of the histories of their châteaux, but didn't see what that had to do with sales.

They also hated sponsoring promotions and deals. At Château la Nerthe, I'd seen how effective incentives could be for our reps. Tell one that selling fifty cases will get them a free trip to the estate in France, and I guarantee you those fifty cases will get sold. But the wineries were reluctant to pay for the prizes.

By the end of January, I finally had the updates to show Mark, who nodded his approval and said to print them up.

"But this is just the information, it doesn't even look good," I said. I'd just typed up the facts in a long bulleted list. "We need a photo of each winery. We need them to be designed."

"I don't see why," he said. "The details are the details."

"No, no, no," I argued, used to explaining the ways of the contemporary marketplace to crotchety producers. "If something looks good, it gets more attention. That is always the way it is."

"You can do what you like," he said, raising his voice a little and waving at the paper. "I'm not paying for a graphic designer."

I retreated to my desk, surprised at how little he cared about the ugly fact sheets. He was exacting about most things but strangely indifferent about others, and this was clearly a case of the latter. But I was determined to get it right. And I had a designer in mind.

"How much will you pay me?" Jules said.

"I will pay you in smiles."

He considered. "I can't feed myself with your smiles."

"You're going to have to learn how."

He was already coming home at eleven. For the next few weeks I stayed up waiting up for him to help me design the new sheets, at a pace of two or three a night. It was child's play from a design point of view; he could do one in twenty minutes. But the cumulative effect was not only mind-numbing for him, it took away from his sleep and basketball-watching hours, no matter how much I tried to make it seem like a fun way for us to spend some time together.

"I should break up with you over this," he said drily. It was true. He was doing more than a thousand dollars' worth of work, gratis, just so I could prove a point.

"That's fine," I said, putting my arms around his neck as he clicked away. "But please wait until you finish the last ones."

Eventually I turned them in by dropping the stack triumphantly on Mark's desk and announcing that they hadn't cost him a dime. He flipped through them with his lips pursed, and my confidence began to droop. Finally he said, "You were right. Very pretty. I think it will make a difference. I don't know if it was worth your time and thus my time, but it's very nice. We'll have them printed for the wholesalers."

I told him my boyfriend had been helping me late at night, so I hadn't wasted any of his time at work.

He raised his eyebrows. "Sounds like a nice man," he said. "You also seem to be someone who it's hard to say no to."

Mark was careful with his money, to say the least, and his most common complaint was that everything was too expensive (everything except his wine, of course). I never went to his house but assumed it was large, and I knew both of his daughters were in private school and daycare. But he watched every penny, debating with me down to the thickness of the paper we used.

He was the opposite, however, when it came to knowledge, which he could never give away fast enough. Every day he was in the office, we went to lunch, where he would tell me about his wines and his trips to France and his crazier stories about disreputable wholesalers who liked to bounce checks. It was as though he was impatient because I did not know everything he did. Sometimes he'd say something like, "Remember when it appeared we lost that whole shipment?" referring to a time before I'd started. But when it came to the sixty producers he currently worked with, he never repeated himself. "You need to know my wines in order to do your job," he reminded me sternly. But what began as instructional lectures would always end up as discursions on the beauty of a vineyard, of a certain vintage, of a part of France, which occasionally turned into gentle ribbing.

"You are the niece of a respected southern Rhône winemaker and you haven't seen the Dentelles de Montmirail?" I shook my head apologetically, just the excuse he needed to keep talking. "Limestone ridges, not so tall, but quite striking. And all around the base, the vineyards of the Gigondas. So beautiful. You know the Gigondas."

I nodded, my other standard response when he was in the middle of a lecture. It was a Friday afternoon, and we had gotten back from lunch a few minutes before.

"Mmm," he said, a small smile on his face. As if the idea had just come to him, he reached into the cooler where he kept samples and retrieved a bottle, he told me, from a winemaker he had known for thirty years. He stared at it as if he could see the man's face in the glass.

"I don't want to tell you what to expect," he said. "Let's just taste." I'd passed the test of my diligence with the fact sheets, but this was a test I was not only unprepared for, but certain I'd fail. It was like the nightmares students have about quizzes they haven't studied for, where the questions are written in a completely alien language.

He took out a butler's wine opener, the kind that is not a screwpull but has two prongs of unequal length to both grip the cork and let a little air into the bottle so it can be removed. I've never been able to use one well, but they are effective for old corks that can fall apart easily. In just a few seconds, he had the bottle open and was pouring the wine into two glasses.

"Tell me what you detect," he said, and waited.

My throat was closed up. Among my friends I had no problem explaining every note; they didn't know any better than me. But now I was with an experienced professional, my boss, who had just presented me with a wine I had never tasted before and, it was clear, was not about to give me any hints. I worried that if I floundered, he would send me packing.

I forced myself to lift the glass to my nose and sniff, registering a vaguely familiar profile; it was like meeting a cousin of my uncle's wine. It was elegant and supple, the fruit and the alcohol wafting gently into my nostrils. I swirled and smelled again, the red berries becoming more apparent. Then I took a sip and let the wine run all over my tongue, let it interact with the air in my mouth before swallowing.

I nearly coughed out of nervousness and looked over at Mark, uncertain if he'd expected me to drink or spit. But he was happily drinking, too.

"Well?" he asked.

"Cherry," I said tentatively, the one thing I knew for sure—it's among the easiest and most common notes to detect. "Plus darker fruits. Mineral. A little toast or smoke in the finish?"

My hand was shaking. I put my glass down on a table.

"Mm," he muttered, the worst, most ambiguous thing he could have said. Then he nodded. "There's more—a little white pepper, a little leather and gravel. But I'll tell you what I really taste," and he took another sip and smiled. "I taste the south of France. I taste the feeling of sitting outside in the dry weather, on a rock at the chalky feet of the Dentelles de Montmiral." He sipped again. "Oomph," he said looking at the label. "It needed more aging. Another two years at least. *C'est la vie.*"

Still staring down at the label, he grinned and told me about the first time he'd met this winemaker, back when nobody would give Gigondas the credit it has today. It was the eighties. The family had been selling its grapes to other producers, until the son— a serious fellow, Mark explained—decided they should try once more to make wine themselves. Their Grande Réserve, Mark said, comes from grenache vines that go back to 1930, all together on a small plot—just a few acres!—in soil marked with white limestone and clay. The mountains had crumbled over millions of years to make this terroir. Millions of years, and the vines had been in the ground just a tiny fraction of that time, though long enough to extend over several generations.

"We humans are nothing, eh?" Mark said, laughing a little.

It had started to snow outside, dark flakes against a blue sky that was about to turn black. We both took another sip and looked out the window.

"That was a good beginning," he said, clearing his throat. "But you have to learn more." He wiggled the cork partway back into the mouth of the bottle. "This one I'll take home."

I consider this the first real tasting of my life, because of the care I'd put into it and because of the company, and because of what it awoke within me. Mark later explained that he wanted me to taste all his wines, a prospect that excited me more than I could describe. How often do you get to try dozens of excellent wines in the company of the person who has hand-selected each one? I could sometimes recall our fact-sheet description of a wine as we opened it, but the percentages and *Wine Spectator* ratings fell away as soon as the aroma hit my nose, and it would just be me, and the wine, and Mark intoning another one of his stories, in that little office in Westchester.

Mark was a firm teacher. Once I said I tasted oak, and he wasted no time telling me the wine was not barrel-aged at all. My face turned its usual Beaujolais red. To some extent a wine's notes can be subjective, but its prominent flavors are more objective (whether you like them is another matter). It's a matter of chemistry—a wine that tastes of cherry actually has compounds like those found in cherries. When I say nobody can tell you what you taste, that is true; but it doesn't mean you can taste just anything in a glass of wine.

Good wine will develop for a day or two after being opened, so sometimes we opened a bottle on a Thursday so we could try it again on Friday. I lived for those days. Every single one of my Mondays was oriented toward the end of the week when we would taste wine together. On Friday evenings I walked back to the train station drunk, not on the alcohol but on the wine itself, on the world of flavors and stories it contained, as if everything you could find on this earth could be captured in a bottle.

If I were putting together a satellite to send into space for the aliens to know who we are, I wouldn't send music and math and pictures. I would send wine. Those afternoons were more important to me than anything else I learned—anything. I have often wanted to tell Mark this. Now I have.

## Thinking About Wine

What makes a wine complex? It's not just the number of flavors it contains, but how they are expressed. In the nose, or on the tongue? At the start, or at the finish? What kinds of fruit do you recognize? What other earthy or mineral aromas and flavors? It's like tasting food at a restaurant and trying to figure out everything that went into the recipe.

To develop a language for talking about wine, you must first build up your knowledge of scents. The more familiar you are with the ways wine can smell, the easier it will be for you to know what you detect. And for that, there's just one thing to do:

*Smell everything.*

Out of all our senses, smell is the most underappreciated. I've read that most people say they would give it up before any of the other senses, and that is truly a shame. Smells are instinctive, primitive, they surprise you—and we aren't fully aware of their power. Most of the time we think of smelling as a passive act, that odors just come to us. But without *actively* smelling, you are cutting off at the start your ability to appreciate wine. It is the first important way you greet a wine and is inextricably linked to how it tastes. Cultivating your sense of smell, training it to be more active and precise than before, is the first step toward a greater acquaintance with wine.

So smell everything, and start to remember what you smell. Cut an orange in half and sniff it—this is easy. Do it with cherries. Blackberries. Try to tell them apart by the smell alone. Sit in your car and breathe it in—what do you smell? Leather, plastic, stale French fries? Every street you're on, every room you enter, take a big whiff. Go for a walk in the woods, or on the beach, and register every new odor. This practice has become second nature to me: when I'm doing laundry, I scoop up an armful of clean clothes and press it to my face. Every time I pick up my little dog to give her a kiss, I smell her at the same time.

Your relationship to wine will change completely. I cannot overstate this. Think about how limited your appreciation for colors would be if you didn't know what to call them. That is why developing a vocabulary—even a simple one—is important. No one can taste exactly what you taste, but learning the language of wine allows you to share the experience as closely as possible. When someone else tells you what they detect in the *nose*, you'll know they're talking about the aroma of the wine in the glass. When they go on to describe the *mouth*, you'll know they are referring to the taste and effect of sipping the wine. The initial sensation on your tongue is called the *attack*—but it doesn't end there. The flavors continue to evolve *mid-palate* as you hold the wine in your mouth. And even after you swallow, the taste and vapors will linger and develop for a few seconds, or even a minute—this is called the *finish*, and a long finish is for many people a sign of great quality and craft. Throughout all these stages the flavors, and the structure, develop and change.

First we'll go over the flavors, which I've divided into twelve basic groups, starting with the most important:

1. Fruit:
    a. Red: cherry, strawberry, raspberry, cranberry
    b. Black: black currant, black cherry, plum, blackberry, blueberry
    c. Citrus: lemon, lime, orange, grapefruit
    d. Tropical: pineapple, banana, lychee, mango
    e. White: melon, pear, apple

f. Yellow (or stone): apricot, nectarine, peach

g. Nuts and dried fruits: almond, hazelnut, fig, prune, raisin

h. Candied: compote, jam, cooked fruits

A full-bodied red will tend toward black fruit flavors, while a lighter red will tend toward red fruit. White wine is most commonly characterized by citrus, white, or stone fruit, whereas nutty and candied flavors can be found in both red and white. And here are the rest of the flavor groups:

2. Floral: orange blossom, iris, jasmine, rose, violet

3. Fermented: butter, cream, cheese

4. Wood: cedar, oak, pine, resin

5. Green: lemongrass, fennel, hay, fern, herbs, lavender, mint, tobacco, tea

6. Spice: anise, cinnamon, paprika, clove, coriander, ginger, nutmeg, white pepper, black pepper, licorice, rosemary, thyme, vanilla

7. Toast: coffee, toffee, chocolate, smoke, mocha

8. Candy: marshmallow, bubble gum

9. Animal: beeswax, leather, game, musk

10. Mineral: clay, graphite, chalk, gravel, flint

11. Earth: mushroom, dead leaves, truffle

12. Faults: cardboard, cork, mold, onion, rotten apple, wet mop, sweat, vinegar (may you encounter these the least!)

Once you've identified the flavors, you can seek to describe the structural identity of the wine: is it sweet or dry, fruity or earthy, light-bodied or full, crisp or creamy, expressive or closed? These impressions come from the tannins, the acid, and the alcohol, components the winemaker tries to keep in harmony, so that none overpowers the others. It's a delicate balancing act.

Tannins come from the skin and stalks of the grape, and you taste them as a dry, astringent sensation on your gums—try chewing on grape seeds for the same feel. They give a wine body and structure (and aging potential, since they mellow over time), but too much can be harsh and obscure the wine's flavors.

Acidity is expressed as the tartness on the sides of your tongue, and provides freshness to a wine, making the flavors bright and present. Acidity also allows a wine to age, preventing it from growing dull too quickly as it softens. Too little, and a wine will taste flat and "flabby," the flavors muddled and out of focus. But too much, and a wine will taste sharp or even sour.

Alcohol gives off heat on your tongue (think of how warm whiskey or other strong spirits taste). It helps give a wine body and weight—a southern Rhône with 15 percent alcohol sits in your mouth very differently than a 12.5 percent Burgundy. But again, too much or too little in relation to the other components can make a wine either oppressive or thin.

When all three elements are in balance, however, a wine is at its most pleasurable. Balanced wines can be velvety and supple, or rich and lush in fruit, or intense and opulent. The softer tannins and diminished acidity found in mature wines make them taste *round*. These are well-produced wines that have reached the right stage—a wine doesn't need to be aged a long time to taste round, remember. Wines that lack roundness can taste sharp or hard, on the other hand, and you'll find these described as angular, or even austere.

But remember, as with all language, the best any of these words can do is approximate what you taste in a wine, not capture it exactly. You'll never stop discovering odd and obscure flavors found in small and remote terroirs for which you may not have the right words. But even a basic vocabulary, and even the *attempt* to articulate the elusive pleasures of wine, will empower you to appreciate – and share—your experience, however imperfect the translation.

# 11.

## Wine Is Community

### La convivialité du vin

There are few objects that blend form and function as perfectly as the wine bottle. And when I say wine bottle I think first, as you likely do, of the standard "Bordeaux" bottle: a smidge under twelve inches high, two and three-quarters inches wide; straight sides with high rounded shoulders; tall enough to be elegant but not so tall that pouring is awkward; narrow enough to be easily gripped but wide enough to feel substantial; its neck a practical length without calling attention to itself. No one knows exactly how the shape was arrived at, but it can hardly be improved upon.

It's also a shape that invites sharing. On the table it cuts a dignified, unshowy profile—within reach when you need it, but never in the way of a sight line or conversation. Beer bottles are portioned for an individual, and it's uncouth to have an entire bottle of spirits on the table. Only the wine bottle is welcoming and communal, its colors attractive and soothing. I would never say you can't enjoy a glass of wine alone (I've certainly been known to do so), but it tastes better in company. Beyond the science of the chemistry in flavor compounds, a chemical reaction occurs in you, too, when you drink. If you love a certain wine because the first time you drank it you were with a close friend in Provence, then don't let anyone take that away from you, even if *Wine Spectator* pooh-poohs it. You can't remove memory from taste and sensation, and that sort of objectivity should never be your goal.

Wine is messy and imperfect and organic. Not organic as in the classification—organic as in *alive*. Of the earth. There is no lab for making wine, and there's no lab for drinking it. That's one reason I've never paid much attention to "taste tests" (except in good fun, with friends). Wine differs from person to person, from bottle to bottle, from day to day. When we use the more technical language of wine to try to capture it, it's only so we can share the sensation of drinking it. The greater experience, however, involves the language of emotion, and of memory.

After I first moved to the U.S., I started to make an effort to remember the wines I tasted. I wrote them down when I could, when a glass was notable, in a wine diary that did double duty as a journal of my life in New York. We drank that Marcel Lapierre Morgon, slightly chilled, when we first discovered the rooftop. I remembered the cool raspberry palate under the lights, with the city all around us, and Peter touchingly moved by it all. Or the minerality of the white Auvigue Mâcon-Villages I'd brought to face off with Alex's California wines, a flavor profile I remembered because I was worried whether everyone would appreciate it. In my store, I carry wines made by the Auvigue brothers, and whenever I drink one, I think back to Maya's kitchen, Alex taping over the labels, my mistaking Min and Peter for a couple. All of them stars—the people and the wines—in the constellation of my mind.

The last snow had just melted when Rose and Nicolas broke up. The distance was too much. Nico had been looking for work for more than half a year, and he finally took a job in Paris because he needed the money and a jump start to his career. She couldn't forgive him. He'd tried; she knew he'd tried. But to her heart it felt like a betrayal. They had been together for ten years.

The final decision came on a Saturday morning. There wasn't any shouting, but we heard Rose crying quietly. Jules and I stayed in bed. We had been nervously anticipating this for weeks, and he had a better idea of the other side of things than I did, having become friends with Nico when they'd overlapped in Paris. Rose eventually wandered in without knocking, looking as if she'd seen a ghost, and Jules made a hasty retreat. She climbed into bed with me and began to sob.

"Did I ever tell you?" she said as I tried to reach the tissues without leaving the bed, because she had a firm hold of my leg. "Nico and I made a pact when we were fifteen years old. We said we were going to move to New York together one day."

"You guys made it," I said, stroking her back. "You made it happen."

"Yes but"—she honked into a tissue—"we were supposed to stay."

I hadn't known until then that petite, inscrutable Rose was the most stubborn of all of us. But now that I saw it, it was obvious. Like so many other kids around the world, she'd had a dream of New York—its excitement and glamour, its energy and drama—and stuck to it, and nothing was going to pull her away, not even love. She hadn't just gotten off a bus from Indiana—she'd left her country and flown across an ocean to make a new life. It was the first time I truly perceived this difference between us. I'd come to New York for an opportunity, not a dream—and even though I loved the city, there was a limit to how much I would have been willing to sacrifice for it. As good friends as we were, she'd always been a bit closed off to me. Until now. I finally felt like I understood.

What's more, she'd left her job with the fashion photographer back in January and had been without full-time work for two months.

"I can't have a boss," she had explained. "Neither can you, you know."

I'd suspected she was right but I didn't want her to be—I loved working with Mark. "What are you going to do?" I asked. "How are you going to stay in the U.S.?"

She shrugged. "I'll figure it out."

*I'll figure it out.* It was this kind of tenacity that had taken me so long to fully recognize. Now it was two months later, and she was still here. I certainly wouldn't have pulled it off the previous summer if Pringent hadn't come through at the last minute. And I wouldn't have pulled it off this January if Mark hadn't taken me on. What did it say about how badly I really wanted to be in New York? I'd once believed I wanted nothing more, but if push had come to shove I wouldn't have given Jules up for it.

For Rose, there really was nothing she wanted more. Just when it seemed that she was going to have to move back to France, a move that would have reunited her with Nico, she wrote a short essay about her life in America for a magazine editor friend in Paris and then demanded, begged, and bribed her for help getting a journalist visa. Rose promised to handle the paperwork and the expense; she just needed the magazine to sign off on her as a correspondent.

"You wrote one article!" I said to her.

"So? It counts. Maybe I will write more."

After a relentless campaign, the friend came through, and Rose was safely a New Yorker for at least a little longer. She couldn't understand why I was so amazed. Her credo was that if you truly want something, you can always find a way to get it. She had succeeded; Nico had failed. Getting that journalist visa was probably the nail in the coffin for their relationship. It was all the proof she needed that he hadn't wanted it enough—hadn't wanted her enough. And it broke her heart.

Eventually Rose fell asleep. I was immensely sad for her, and also a little guilty, as if my sympathy for Nico—the realization that personality-wise I was more like him than like her—was a form of betrayal.

I quietly left her in my bed and went to the living room, where Jules was also asleep, his legs dangling over the arm of the couch. I got dressed and started my usual Saturday routine of walking to the Greenmarket in Union Square. Many mornings went this way, with the two of them unconscious, and me alone on the street, although normally I was rushing to the train station for work. Saturday mornings were among the most leisurely hours I had in the city, and the most anonymous, walking among the farm stands without having to say a word.

I always felt the most connected to strangers when I was alone on the streets of New York. When you are new to any city, your anxiety and uncertainty can be as distracting as another person. *Which way is the traffic going? Why are some streets numbered and some not? Why is everyone walking so fast?* When these questions quiet down, months or years later, you know you've become a part of the city.

It was early, but the usual mix of shoppers, people-watchers, students, and skateboarders were assembled on the southern steps of the square. I crossed over to the market. Though the air still had the snap of winter, hundreds of people were out among the booths and tables set up against the open backs of vans and trucks. The sun was out, and a big blue sky sat over the square. This, I think, is a big reason New Yorkers gravitate to public squares—it's not just the ground that opens up, but the air above, too, un-crowded by the tall buildings that make you feel like you're in a canyon.

These days, I only had time to cook on the weekends. Week-nights were a free-for-all. If Jules didn't pick up a burger, he would just cook a fried egg on white rice, the two mild but distinctive smells usually wafting through the apartment around midnight. At the Greenmarket I went from stall to stall picking up an item from each: a small head of cabbage, a bunch of carrots, shell peas, parsnips, potatoes.

I was relieved about Rose and Nico, because they hadn't been happy, but I was also scared. They were the first people I had met in New York, and the couple I'd hoped Jules and I could be. Their relationship was central to our circle of friends. It was Nico who'd introduced us to Peter and Min and Derek, whom he'd originally met on the soccer field of their corporate complex. I wouldn't have been surprised if they were still closer to him than to Rose. They may have been more sympathetic to him even, though they'd never tell her that. I didn't know what the breakup would mean, and it was strange to realize I'd now spent more time in the U.S. without Nico than with him.

As I circled back through the market one last time, I decided to invite everyone over for dinner that night to cheer Rose up, as if to declare that whatever happened, we would all still be friends. You may not be surprised to hear that I have a tendency to over-compensate. I walked to the wine store, deep in the kind of hyper-preparation I sometimes find myself in, and though it was still early, Jacob was in, reassuringly unshaven and in another heavy metal T-shirt.

"Where have I not tried yet, Jacob?" I said, pronouncing his name the French way, which always made him blush.

I asked *where* instead of *what* because I was more focused on the regions than on any particular producer. He scratched his chin, then pointed me to some Sud-Ouest wines. "These you don't see too often in the U.S.," he said. They were from Bergerac, in the Dordogne region—like Jules's family. Jules had taken me there several times as students to see the medieval castles over-looking the Dordogne River, and the famous Lascaux cave with its treasure of prehistoric human art. His grandfather still lived in the region, and Jules loved it. The Dutch tourists drove him crazy, but I didn't mind—everything was so beautiful. It was also the home of Monbazillac, the sweet wine we'd shared (accidentally) at our first dinner out together. Jacob told me the wines were a good value, given the region's low profile. I bought one white and two reds.

At home, Jules had his headphones on, watching clips from the basketball playoff games he'd missed that week. I tapped him on the shoulder to show him the wine. He looked at me, confused why I'd returned with so many bags. "From your ancestral home, remember?" I said, placing the bottles on the counter. "Jacob says this one is dry, with soft acidity," I said, pointing to the white. "This red is medium-bodied, supple, half cabernet sauvignon, half merlot. And this one is fuller, richer, more earthy. We shall see."

"You're thinking of wine, now?"

"Wine with my friends," I corrected him. "I don't see why not. Rose needs support. We should all be together."

Rose was in her room, lying on her bed, but her eyes were open. I asked if she'd eaten breakfast and she said no. I told her I was asking the others to come over for dinner, that I would cook, and it would be fun. She nodded mutely.

Rose was still in her room when Min and Derek arrived that night, Derek with a kind of frozen grimace on his face, and Min's expression a little crumpled, as if she'd been crying on Rose and Nico's behalf. I went to Rose's door and knocked lightly. No answer. Min shook her head at me. "It's okay," she whispered. Peter was late—he was always either ten minutes early or an hour late, nothing between—and seemed surprised to find us sitting quietly in the living room, which smelled of roasted chicken, not eating.

I handed him a glass of the white and told him Rose was probably not coming out. He lowered his voice and asked, "Have you talked to Nico?"

I shook my head, wondering if that was the wrong answer. "No, have you?"

He nodded, and I felt immediately embarrassed. It meant Min and Derek had talked to Nico, too. Maybe even Jules had. While I'd spent the day worrying too much about what was going to change, and trying to pretend it wouldn't, the others had done the appropriate thing and talked to their friend. Now, sitting quietly together around the coffee table, the evening felt like a wake.

Over the next couple of months, things did change. We didn't get together very often, all of us, to my regret. I didn't know if it was because of the shift in the group dynamic, or if it was because we were all working more than ever. Mark steadily began to give me larger slices of the business. While he was reluctant to let me speak to the producers when deals were in mid-negotiation (if I picked up the phone first and one was on the line, he would make a rapid *"fe-fe-fe-fe-fe"* noise from across the room while flapping his hand to signal that I should hand it over), he told a couple of wholesalers that I would be their main contact from then on.

"Gregory, I've hired a new associate. She'll be working with you. She's brilliant, and it'll be better for our relationship because I'm getting old and absentminded. You too? How would you know? Ah, ha, ha, ha." I would shuffle papers at my desk, pretending not to hang on to every word, trying not to blush with pride and nervousness. His *brilliant associate*. Mark had already begun taking me on sales calls, to dinners with wholesaler reps and restaurateurs. Following his lead, I didn't say too much. "Listen first," he said, and then proceeded to work the table with good humor and deep knowledge, until by the time the coffees came there was no doubt in the room that the best wines—at the best values—could only be found through Brodeur Imports. It was as though a spell had been cast, at least long enough to net Mark some deals and, even better, relationships.

Twice a month I went with him to the regional sales meetings, as I had with Moët. He spoke to the reps with no notes or preparation, conversationally rattling off the important facts as if they'd just occurred to him. Again, I stayed quiet, presenting the bottles to the audience, pouring tastes as I walked among the seats. I felt a distant kinship with the women on game shows who present the prizes, smiling not speaking. But I was watching everything he did, absorbing every word and gesture like a sponge. What I felt must be a common mix of emotions for an apprentice: envy, admiration, resentment, ambition. Looking back at my tour with Moët, I realized I must have come off to my audiences like a French wine robot, hardly comprehensible, repeating my presentation in an artificial singsong voice. Mark, however, spoke to a room as though he was having a conversation with each individual rep.

I asked him one day how he did it. He said, "No secret. Just remember it is always, always easier to do what you believe in. It takes energy to lie or to fake something. A tremendous amount of energy. Everything I say and do is true. I love everyone who loves wine. I love everyone who helps me get my wine out to as many people as possible. This is my joy. You understand."

I said I thought I did.

"No," he said. "That wasn't a question. I mean I know you already understand. This is why I hired you."

After the sales meetings, we would drive back to the sleepy little village in Westchester, and the modest storefront of his office, and continue working until seven or so, when he would rise from his chair, hitch up his belt, and say it was time for dinner— time, that is, for him to go home to his wife and daughters. He had a ten-minute drive. I had an hour-and-a-half commute. Although I could have tried to leave earlier, I didn't. I didn't want to miss anything. Sometimes he would open a bottle so that we could taste it that evening, and again the next day to see how it had changed. Wine doesn't have to be full-bodied to tolerate the exposure. It just has to be of high quality. Many perfectly enjoyable wines are meant to be consumed quickly, but to watch a good wine evolve over hours, over a day, is a marvelous thing. And so I stayed to the end every day of the week, on the chance it would turn into the master class I was always waiting for.

If it was early in the week there would likely be no tasting, and as we closed up I'd sigh to myself and board the train in the darkness and read my cheap French novel, or mentally go over everything that had happened that day. I never slept—my mind was too active. But by the time I reached home the exhaustion would hit. I'd never concentrated so hard, so unceasingly, on anything.

Most nights I was ready for a glass of wine, a small meal, and bed. Because of Mark's portfolio, I had been making my way through a swath of more affordable Bordeaux wines. Bordeaux is a huge, complicated region, with dozens of subregions and appellations. I'd tried several from the left bank of the Gironde River, in Margaux, which has bolder cabernet-based reds, and some from the right bank in Saint-Émilion and its neighbors, which use fruitier merlot.

But that spring I would frequently return not to a bath and bed, but a roommate standing in front of the mirror, wearing a sparkly top, slim pants that tapered to her ankles, and eyeliner that gave her face a sallow, sharpened look. Since the breakup, Rose had decided she no longer wanted to do, well, most things. She was not interested in going out to eat or sitting at home with ice cream and Netflix. She still wanted to dance, though, four or five times a week. She hadn't been single since she was fifteen, and without a boyfriend, without a job, she had an abundance of energy. She danced as though she had poison to shake out of her system.

"Come, Laure, let's go," she pleaded with a manic intensity, the opposite of her usual *froideur*. "Will you come with me tonight?" More often than not I wanted to say no. I was tired; I *had* a boyfriend who would soon come home. But I'd sit on the bed and think about how the night would be easier for Rose if I went, and begin to gauge just how little I would have to do to my appearance to avoid total embarrassment.

Most of the time, I didn't have to stay out too long. If the night was slow, we danced for an hour or two and came home, laughing, expended. But the chances were decent that she would catch a boy's eye, and, after several minutes of careful vetting on my part, I would leave on my own. Sometimes she slipped back into the apartment a couple of hours later; sometimes not at all.

"Hey, I'm a free girl," she said, a point of pride and lamentation. She missed Nico; she was also determined to live her life in New York, which she'd sacrificed so much for. "I can do what I like." She was right, of course.

It was, on the whole, a tumultuous spring. I don't just mean Rose's love life and its fallout. I was taking on more at work—which I loved—without yet feeling real empowerment. Jules and I were on our misaligned schedules, sleeping together every night but awake and in the same room a vanishingly small amount of time. And it had been more than a month since our friends had all gotten together in the same room.

One morning, in my usual rush to work, I ran into Peter in Grand Central. I was surprised to see him and wanted to talk to him enough that I missed my usual train. He told me he'd quit his job. "Couldn't be a cog anymore," he told me. He'd joined a much smaller company, which he said was just a stepping-stone on his way to doing his own thing.

He'd also recently gone through a string of bad luck, he told me—flights missed because of freak accidents, a mysterious stomach bug that felled him intermittently for several weeks, and an uncharacteristic dating dry spell. His long run of demi-girlfriends, as Rose and I had liked to call them—women he was with long enough for us to learn their names and meet a few times before they disappeared—had ended in March, and he hadn't seen anyone since then.

I realized that quitting meant he no longer worked with Min and Derek. I asked if he still got to see them.

"Not a lot lately. We've all been busy! But it's not like quitting means we're not friends anymore. That's why I don't need a girlfriend," he added, just before we separated to get to our respective trains. "I'm never lonely. I have you guys."

My only real window into mainstream American dating was through Allison, my old friend from Pringent. After I was fired, I didn't see her again until several months into the new year, when she called to say she'd gotten a new job, too, at New York University. When we finally met up at a West Village tapas restaurant, she launched immediately into everything I'd missed. It turned

out my uncle had heard a mostly accurate version: Jean Pringent
arrived on a surprise visit to discover a leaderless office. As people
started telling him what was going on, his narrow mustache, Allison said, quivered in rage. In his dignified and calm way, he set
up in the CEO's office and asked people to come and see him one
by one. Each reemerged with a tentative smile; Pringent hadn't
said what he planned to do, but he was clearly distressed. After he
brought in the auditors, he sat Allison down and said he understood the difficult position she was in but had heard that Rachel
and Eric the CEO were on a beach in Thailand. Which beach? he
wanted to know. She had the resort written down on her calendar
but felt conflicted. The best she'd been able to do, she told me,
was open the calendar to the right page and leave it on her desk
when she went to the bathroom.

She didn't know what had become of Rachel and Eric, just that
they were gone.

"And what about you?" I said.

"What about me?" she said, feigning ignorance. "Am I sleeping with a married CEO?"

"*Are* you?"

"If I was, the difference is that nobody would know." This she
said in a hush, and then broke into wild laughter. Though she had
no problems expressing herself, she was, I realized, a very private
person. But she told me she was seeing two men she'd met online
and had just had drinks with a third but couldn't tell if it was really
a date or not. Now she was at a decision point. She was trying to
break down where she was with each of them based on a complicated set of codes and cues, like who asked whom more questions.
But she hadn't slept with any of them yet—she had a five-date
rule—and that made it harder to pick.

"Rule? Why a rule?" I asked. I was mesmerized. Maybe this

reveals my age—I'm sure all the young Parisians are online-dating these days—but my experience has been that there are no "rules" for dating in France. There isn't even a French word for "dating." It doesn't mean you can't have a good time, the way Rose was as a single woman. But if you like someone, often someone you were introduced to through a mutual friend (like how Jules and I met through my friend Vera), you can take the time to explore those feelings without having to worry about the signals you are giving off, or whether the other person is seeing multiple people. Nobody *dates around*. You hang out, you hang out again, and if at some point you kiss, you are in a relationship. And if you don't, you decide to keep going, or to end it. That's it. The method has its downfalls, but I said a silent blessing for its simplicity.

Allison buried her face in her hands. "I need more time, but I'm running out. You get a certain number of punches in your card before it starts to become awkward, you know?"

"Awkward how? Why do you need more time?" I was getting more and more confused.

"I'm also Catholic!"

"So am I!"

"You're no help!"

"I still don't understand what you mean about the punch card," I said.

She tried to explain it to me, but it came out a jumble of statements about shame, expectations, religiosity, and confidence. She may have believed them all at once.

"Allison, I love you, but that is the stupidest thing I have ever heard."

"You're right, but I can't help thinking that way." She asked me to come with her to a wine store before she headed back to Hoboken. It had recently rained, and we linked arms for stability.

"What are you drinking these days?" she said. She knew I'd been making my way through the regions, but it had been months since I'd given her an update.

"Bordeaux," I said.

"Fancy!"

"Not always," I said. "Doesn't have to be. But it is probably the most famous, yes. My boss carries a lot of Bordeaux."

"Do you ever have a hard time deciding what bottle to get?"

"If you're going to make a joke comparing my taste in wine to your taste in men, I'll save you the trouble," I said, and her laughter echoed off the buildings.

We walked slowly around the store waiting for her glasses to defog. It was an elegant shop, sparely stocked, with shelves that highlighted the bottles nicely. Each had a careful description attached, with far more detail than the usual recommendations. I was impressed by the amount of information, and how unguarded the shopkeepers were with it. You would not have found a store like this in Paris that I knew of; in my mind they were still dense warrens, with dim lighting and bottles everywhere. Because she'd perked up when I mentioned Bordeaux, I helped Allison choose a rich, merlot-based wine from the less well-known appellation Côtes de Castillon to take back with her to Hoboken. I'd never tasted it myself but had tried similar ones that were drinkable young, soft and round, even chocolatey.

She kissed my cheeks—more firmly than a normal *faire la bise*. "Laure," she called after she'd walked down the street a few paces. "Now that we don't work together, who is going to pick my wine for me?"

"You're going to have to figure it out yourself!" I shouted back.

The first week in April the temperature topped seventy for a couple of days in a row and we knew it was time to open up the rooftop again. If I was a little trepidatious about everyone coming over, I shouldn't have been. We picked up where we'd left off, and no one seemed to blame Rose as I'd been afraid they would—just as I'd be afraid of pointed fingers if anything happened to me and Jules. Most of us were still holding out hope that Nico would surprise us by landing at JFK with a freshly stamped visa in hand, and everything would go back to the way it had been those first six months when we were just beginning to rely on one another.

After the long winter cooped up inside, I felt giddy to be again on the rooftop, looking around at these people who had become dear to me in the last year. We were all foreigners except for Peter and Derek—Peter was the son of Korean immigrants, and Derek was a gangly nerd who you could tell had lived through a prolonged awkward phase, which gave him a special outsider pass.

Benji's motorcycle may have disqualified him for outsider status, but he still pined in silence for Rose, especially now that she was single. He called almost every night to invite Rose to something or other—an art show, the opera. It sometimes sounded like he was just crossing items off a long list of every possible thing you could invite a woman to. Anything she needed, he was there for, quietly and patiently. One day when I was at work she texted saying the kitchen sink was broken. I called the super, but he was nowhere to be found. When I returned home, Benji's legs were sticking out of the cabinet, a toolbox open beside him.

Rose just shrugged, smiling, as if to say, *Hey, he wanted to!*

I woke up late that night and could hear Benji and Jules on the couch having a long, intense conversation I caught only snatches of—female pronouns, long pauses from Benji, hushed but animated exposition from Jules. In the morning I asked Jules what they'd talked about.

"Oh, guy things," he said, just to annoy me.

Those days, I was always trying to read Jules. With the arrival of the warm weather, he was complaining less than usual. I knew it didn't mean he was finally in love with New York, but he finally seemed satisfied, with friends he trusted, a job he was good at, and me. We had always talked about our lives as if they were inextricably connected, and made plans that way, but like Allison I was looking for signs and signals that we were on the right path. It was the planner in me. I've always felt that if I could guarantee my future, I'd be able to enjoy it more. Jules knew this about me, and liked to use it for his own amusement.

"Laure."

This was his favorite practical joke, which he played on me as often as once a week, and I fell for it every time. "Laure," he said from behind me, while I was standing in the kitchen, or just out of the shower in a towel. "Laure, I have something to ask you," he said in a serious voice that triggered in me a sudden desire to sit down. Every time, I thought he was going to ask me to marry him. And every time, his eyes watery and wide, his knee flexed as if he were about to lower himself onto it, he would pause for a heavy moment, and then ask something like, "Do you know where the mustard is?" And he'd laugh and laugh, uncontrollably, while I would pick up a pot holder, or anything, and hit him with it, chase him around the apartment, shouting, until we were on the bed and he had no choice but to wrestle the weapon away from me.

## Thinking About Wine

Bordeaux is the most famous wine region in France, and has one of the longest, richest histories of wine production, distinctive because of its busy port and huge international appeal. It is simply massive, with sixty appellations and a complex classification system I won't try to detail here, under which more than seven thousand wineries, or châteaux, operate. That scope is why I've saved it until now.

But you shouldn't be intimidated. Yes, Bordeaux can be among the most expensive wine in the world (although you will find the rarest in Burgundy). Because Bordeaux is so old and so established, a lot of its pricing is based not on the wine itself, but on reputation. This is to be expected. The market is heavily influenced by the standing of both the château and the vintage. In Bordeaux, more than with most regions, millésime can have a big effect on price. With Mark I was selling 2005—one of the best in recent history. Today, purchasing 2005 Bordeaux will cost you a pretty penny, far more than 2007 Bordeaux, for example, because of the former's reputation. But the benefit of having so many producers to choose from is that there are fabulous, small vineyards with affordably priced, good wine in any year.

Here are a few other things to know about Bordeaux. It has a "left bank" (southern) and a "right bank" (northern) in relation to the Gironde River. The left bank uses more cabernet sauvignon in its trademark Bordeaux red wine blend—as much as three-fourths—while the right bank uses more merlot. This has to do with the nature of the terroir. Never doubt how different the land can be on either side of a river. (The third grape, always in the minority, is cabernet franc.) The left bank wines are drier, fuller-bodied, and dark, with black currant (at its most intense, a cassis flavor), pepper, and woodsy notes. Barrel-aged reds taste of vanilla and licorice. The older wines will have hints of tobacco, game, truffle, even pencil lead. Yes, you read that right—this particular flavor compound is reminiscent of graphite. The right bank wines are fruitier: you'll taste prune, blackberry, and black cherry, as well as mint and violet flowers. In general—though not as a hard rule—these can be drunk younger.

The best châteaux of the left bank fall under a classification system that was organized in 1855 at the request of Napoleon III and is revered to this day. It's remarkable how long and how consistently the categories have lasted. And it's not just a rubber stamp—the wines made by these houses have been tremendous, the few times I've had a chance to try them. You may have come across these names before.

### PREMIER GRANDS CRUS CLASSÉS FROM MÉDOC, ON THE LEFT BANK

- Château Latour
- Château Lafite-Rothschild
- Château Mouton Rothschild
- Château Haut Brion
- Château Margaux

Five châteaux! That's it. They have formally been recognized as the best.

The right bank's classification is more recent, from 1955, with a more modern intention of updating it regularly.

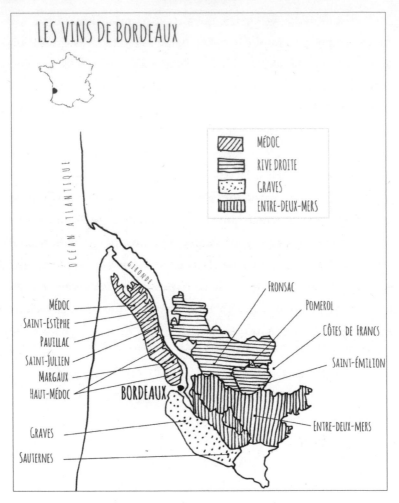

## PREMIER GRANDS CRUS CLASSÉS FROM SAINT-ÉMILION, ON THE RIGHT BANK

- Château Ausone
- Château Cheval Blanc
- Château Angélus
- Château Pavie

If Cheval Blanc sounds familiar, it was one of the wines I had the fortune of drinking the night I was in Nashville. We'd finished that same meal with a sweet Château d'Yquem, which is classified as the *only* premier grand cru supérieur in Sauternes. As I said, it's complicated!

But now that you have committed that to memory, forget it all. If you choose to spend your days chasing premier grands crus, you are welcome to. But I have also found something alluring about simply stumbling on them from time to time in particularly lucky moments.

Look: if you really want the best deal, don't buy Bordeaux. But it's still possible to build a rewarding relationship with Bordeaux without breaking the bank. Don't feel pressured to spend money on the prestigious names. Seek out something from Lussac-Saint-Émilion rather than Saint-Émilion proper. Look for one of the "lesser" vintage years, such as 2007 or 2008, which still produced good wine you can drink relatively young. Most of us don't store wine for a decade or more anyway.

If you want to be adventurous (and impress those people always searching for developing regions), look to the Sud-Ouest, the southwest, a huge area that stretches from Bordeaux to the Pays Basque. This is where you'll find Bergerac—the terroir is less highly heralded than Bordeaux's, but the same grapes thrive there: cabernet sauvignon and merlot. As you go deeper inland, such as Cahors, you find wines made 100 percent from malbec, a strong red grape that requires a lot of sun and yields robust wines. In Fronton, the grape is the négrette, which has a similar personality.

The Sud-Ouest is more a collection of small regions than a strictly unified one, but the wines have a richness and a rawness in common. Because the terroir varies so much from one appellation to the next, it's impossible to take it all in at once. But don't be daunted. As always, be patient and open—these wines are ready to make your acquaintance, new friendships that will only grow with time.

# 12.

........................................................................

## Wine Is Travel

### Le vin est un voyage

Can people change? I'm not sure, but I do know that as a general rule your natural characteristics round out and soften with age, even as they increase in complexity. And you can learn to see things a new way.

Each time I went back to France, my old friends would say the same thing: "Laure, you haven't changed a bit!" They meant it, I think, as a compliment—that I still had my youthful looks and Parisian sophistication, that I hadn't yet turned into one of *them*. (It would have taken a long time to explain that *they* weren't all that bad.) But I didn't want to be the same, and I felt my cheeks grow hot whenever anyone said it. What I really wanted was to be someone who had gained another sense, or power. I was definitely still French, but I was something else, too. I'd had an American infusion of the spirit and it had given me a newfound tolerance for risk, for uncertainty, for contrasting views. I'd left one job (if you count my brief tenure at L'Éléphant), had another expire, and been fired from the third. My closest friends were an assortment of people I would never have predicted. And I was the better for all of it.

This is the gift of travel. New places change your idea of what life can be. Our personalities have inertia—they prefer to stay still and sideways, like a bottle of wine. But unlike wine we benefit from being shaken up once in a while. Travel makes you see things differently from the moment you step out of the car or off the plane. You take in new words, new manners, and reconcile them with what you thought you knew.

If you're lucky and the place you're going is wine country— and more of the world than ever before counts as wine country— then you'll always remember a special connection between the wine and the land. That rosé you drank on vacation in Provence, for example; that wine will forever remind you of the place it's from, like a souvenir.

But the true power of wine is that it lets you travel without leaving home. I would never say you can only appreciate a wine by visiting its land—not everyone has that opportunity. A well-made wine brings its terroir to you if you pay attention to where it's from, what geographical features set it apart, who makes it, and what grapes are used in order to get the most out of the land. And through its flavor, too: by having a mineral taste because the vineyard is beside the famous limestone ridge of Burgundy, or by tasting ripe because the grapes were under the burning sun of the south. Together, these factors give you a sense of place, and a rich and rewarding way to experience the land.

Mark, with all his stories about the winemakers he'd "known forever," taught me the importance of intimacy. There's no other way to put it. The entire work of getting to know wine is removing the anonymity from it. You can easily drink a different bottle each night and forget the name of the producer by morning. But the rewards that come from closer consideration grow over time; drinking wine becomes more and more enjoyable. As long as you buy from small vineyards, you can rest assured that there is a person on the other side of the bottle, a family, a history tied to this wine.

Discovery takes work. And the more you do it, the more it teaches you about yourself.

The rest of 2008 went quickly—a sign my life in New York had shifted into a steady gear. We went strawberry picking in the early summer and apple picking in the fall. On the Fourth of July we sailed around Long Island Sound with friends of Peter's. When my two-year anniversary with America arrived in November, I kept it to myself, thinking it was a silly thing to be proud of, but when I got home from work that day, Jules had left me a cupcake featuring an enormous candle shaped like the Empire State Building. The next week Min and Derek held an election-night viewing party, and after the results were in and the country had a new president we all ran outside to join the rest of the city in celebration.

Winter was slow to come and mild when it arrived. Wanting to make the most of our weekends, Jules and I visited the overcrowded museums we hadn't been to before: the Frick, the Whitney, MoMA. Somehow, I'd gone two years without visiting the

Met, and we spent an entire day there. I would make the rounds of an entire exhibition and return to find Jules standing in front of the same painting where I'd left him. It was as though he was a planet and I was the moon trying to circle him, or I was an indifferent comet and he was a star. It's not that we were un-happy. We were both stable, in our jobs and our rhythms, but there was something missing—time, for one, since we didn't get much of it with each other during the week. Even though we fi-nally shared a bed, it was still a little like being long distance. I always felt this the most strongly on Sundays, after we'd crammed the weekend full, and I'd start to miss him before it was even Monday. But then the week would start and we'd be back in our busy routines.

Whatever I was feeling was subtle—too subtle for me to put my finger on precisely—but compared to everyone else, Jules and I were suddenly the most boring members of our friend group. A new pairing was taking up everyone's attention: at some point in the fall, Rose told me she and Benji had kissed, although she wouldn't say exactly when. (She didn't want to give me too much of a reason to say "I told you so.") She had cooled it off right away because she didn't feel ready, after a decade with Nico and a spring of brief encounters. That lasted maybe a week or two before they kissed again, giving her yet another reason to back off.

"What do I do?" she asked me.

"I wouldn't think about it," I said, because it was the advice I had been giving myself.

Even though it was too late to see any leaves, Rose and Benji took a weekend motorcycle trip to Vermont—"Just as friends," she told me—and they came back a couple. I didn't talk to Nico directly, but the others had, and reported back that he was dis-traught and relieved, at the same time, and wished the best for her. It took me some getting used to, seeing them together, even though I'd been predicting it for a long time. They spent more time at his place than ours, but sometimes I'd come home to find them in the kitchen, saturated in that buzzy happy glow of a new couple, and feel a little jealous.

On New Year's Eve, Min was drunk, her face a bright strawberry pink, when she told me she was thinking about breaking up with Derek. I had just returned from Christmas with my family and asked if something had happened in the week I'd been gone.

"No, nothing happened," she said. "But that's kind of the point. Have you noticed Derek and I have never gone on vacation?" She continued before I could answer. "Six years together, and zero vacations. Visiting family and going to weddings doesn't count." I tried to think back over the past two years I'd known them.

"That can't be true," I said.

"When then?"

"There was the time . . ." I started and then drifted off.

"I don't know what his priority is," she said. "But it's not me."

"He loves you," I reassured her.

"Love's not enough sometimes. I feel like we are in a rut I don't know how to get out of."

It was an unexpected announcement coming from Min, who was always the most positive among us. But she was also a ruthlessly practical and efficient person. Once, we all showed up at a restaurant for Rose's birthday and realized we'd made a mistake with the reservation—there was no table for us. While the rest of us agonized and passed the blame around, Min quietly disappeared and reappeared saying she'd talked us into a walk-in at Nobu, even though we were a party of seven on a Friday night.

If Min had known that I would immediately begin a personal crusade to force Derek into a vacation, roping everyone else into the effort, she probably wouldn't have told me anything. But as it was, the campaign worked. We nagged and shamed him until they made plans to travel in March. And where else? To France!

They told us over dinner one night, and I could see how excited they both were, how something quiet but charged had come back into their relationship. Derek was asking questions like, "Is it mer-CI or MER-ci?" Then I started to say that it was still cool weather in Provence in March and maybe they should consider June instead, until Min shot me a look that shut me up immediately. She was not about to risk losing this opportunity by messing around with the dates. They had to go on vacation, and go as soon as possible.

They were gone for two weeks, and we heard nothing the whole time—radio silence. We knew they were spending a few days in Paris, going to see Maya and Alex in Aix, and then staying on the outskirts of a smaller Provençal village. We waited. Even on the day they flew back—no news. I waited a few days and then invited them over.

The people who came over looked a lot like Min and Derek but didn't sound exactly like them. Min was more or less herself, but at a slightly slower, less demonstrative pace. Derek, however, was more clearly different. He had never been abroad before, let alone on an extended vacation. He'd had a glimpse not only of a different life, but a version of himself who was happy and relaxed, who had the time to put his relationship first. It changed everything.

"Oh, man," he said three or four times in a row before responding to a question as simple as what they ate. "Oh, man," and he ran his hands through his hair as if communing directly with his memories. He was still Derek, with the sardonic delivery and the low rolling laugh. But he looked about thirty pounds lighter— and most of that was from stress. His eyes, usually pulled tightly inward beneath a furrowed brow, were wide open beneath a smooth, broad forehead.

"No phone, no email," he said in disbelief.

"I didn't think he could do it," Min said, smiling. But he had.

The first two days in Provence, she said, he was still himself. "Where are we going now? What are we doing next?" he kept saying. She refused to answer him, until he finally stopped asking. They did no sightseeing. They stayed in the village the whole time, walking to the center square for the farmer's market in the mornings, having a regular afternoon coffee, switching off between cooking and going out. One night, they ate only bread and cheese and drank wine—the local rosé.

"Good food, good wine," Derek said in reverie.

"Good company," Min added, squeezing his hand. She was glowing.

"The best company," he said, looking at her. Suddenly, the rest of us were no longer in the room.

They were engaged a week later.

In the end, I was the one who went to France that June when the weather was warmer. Everything leading up to it felt of a piece. Like a pianist who has been practicing for years, I had some sense of my skill now. I knew my regions, I knew the producers I liked from my own explorations, plus the sixty in Mark's portfolio that I now knew very well. When I visited Jacob's wine store these days, it was like entering a room with hundreds of people, some of whom I'd gotten to know fairly well, some whom I could recognize but not quite place, and some whose names and faces were new to me. Some names, the big companies, rang a bell even if some of the individual labels were less familiar: Jadot (Burgundy), Bouchard (also Burgundy), Chapoutier (Rhône), Jaboulet (also Rhône).

I'd grown in confidence. My tasting sessions with Mark were no longer tentative. I wasn't afraid of being combative, worrying that he'd think me amateurish and young. I was comfortable saying that a certain wine just needed to open; he would say nonsense, it needed more aging. I would say there was a touch of roasted coffee in the finish; he would pause, then shake his head and say it was cocoa.

Our working relationship changed in other ways, too. I was spending more time out of the office—either conducting Friday sales presentations by myself or going on wholesale tours at stores and restaurants in Westchester, western Connecticut, New Jersey, New York City, and Long Island. I had, in many ways, come full circle. But instead of making sales calls on behalf of one producer—my uncle, or Pringent—I was now representing several dozen, of which I only had time to talk up a few to each customer. They all bounced around my mind like the names of friends, with qualities and personalities and stories I knew by heart because they'd been told to me so often. I'd tasted nearly all of them by now. Passing them on was like recommending someone I knew. It was not just a job; I was proselytizing.

How far I'd come! Just two years earlier I'd been a bumbling brand ambassador with a few dozen English words and memorized talking points, relying on charm and a French accent to make my way. I was no longer pretending. I knew and meant every word I was saying. For one, now that I was in my second year with Mark, I could easily and directly compare the previous year's wines to this one—and what a difference it was. The year before I'd been tasting and selling 2005 and 2006, both fantastic years in Bordeaux. Now we were working with 2007, too—not a bad vintage, but not as good as 2006 and especially not 2005. Those two kept flying off the shelves by the power of their reputation (and largely living up to it). I tried to avoid making direct comparisons, but there's only so much you can do: the wine magazines and the ratings websites do it for you, and the customers pay attention. Once a year like 2005 is anointed as special, the price goes up and the wines sell fast, especially when it comes to Bordeaux. (The irony was that even for a year as special as 2005, the wines would not reach their full potential for a long time, whereas a vintage yielding more straightforward wines, like 2007, can mature sooner. Depending on the wine, it might have made sense to drink a 2007 *before* a 2005.)

After sales calls, I would return to the office exhausted, and Mark would remove his glasses to look at me and say, "How did it go?" I briefed him the way you respond to your father when he asks you about your day at school—this many cases, that interesting new store, this enthusiastic rep, that unimpressed restaurant, all relayed as impartially as possible.

"Very good," he said, replacing his glasses. "Write up a report for me by the end of tomorrow."

I have many good qualities, I'd like to think, but completing tasks I don't see the point of has never been one of them. "But I just told you what I did," I said.

"Yes, thank you," he said, his tone shifting from paternal to professorial. "But I need the paper for my records. I can't remember everything you say."

"Pah." I slouched down in my chair. He went back to what he was working on, and it might have ended there, if it wasn't for my mouth: "I don't know why it's so important."

He let out an impatient grunt.

"You don't have to know exactly why it's important. I do—and it is my company, I hope you remember." He said that whenever we disagreed, and I hated it. "And," he added, "I don't know why you are wearing jeans here now. Don't you have nice slacks? You didn't used to always wear jeans to the office and I don't like it. We try to be proper here."

Clearly, cracks were starting to show in our working relationship. Part of it was that I was overly sensitive to any perceived slights or lack of trust. And Mark, as I've said, was a frank and emotive man who loved to talk and argue. It seemed like a recipe for disaster, leading to a Marianne-level blow-up that could easily have cost me my job. I didn't know why it had been so easy for me to talk back to Mark, when I'd been so acquiescent to Rachel— possibly because I felt more comfortable around him (in no small part because of our shared language), even as I resisted his authority. But whenever it seemed like we were on the verge of a bigger argument, he would immediately clam up, study me intently with those brown, slightly downturned eyes, shrug, and turn his attention elsewhere. Only now do I see that this was an act of generosity, saving us from a bigger fight. By any measure, I was getting a little ahead of myself. A year of intense apprenticeship did not equal three decades in the business, no matter how much he wanted me to know what he knew.

When we visited distributors, Mark often let me present to

sales teams on my own, but on the days he did it himself, it was clear I was to play the assistant, pouring the wine, smiling at the reps, and saying nothing. It was frustrating to switch back and forth. Once, after a presentation in New Jersey in which I'd hardly said a word, I talked too much on the car ride back. It was uncharacteristic bluster about how much I'd learned, how good I was at making deals and communicating the wines' stories, how I always got great responses from customers but he didn't see it because it was only when he wasn't around. Then for some reason I started to talk about how much I missed my family. I told him about my older brother and his children, who lived in Luxembourg and with whom I Skyped whenever I could. I described my parents' supportiveness—I knew they'd be happy no matter what I did but I thought they were secretly pleased I'd ended up in the family business.

It had never been like this, with me talking and Mark listening. And when I noticed how long the car had been filled with my voice, I went quiet. Mark said nothing for a minute and I watched the trees pass outside the passenger window, wondering if I'd said too much. Then he said, "My next trip to France is at the start of June. Why don't you come with me? The company will pay. It will be good for you, and you can see your family as well."

It was the last thing I expected him to say. The last two times he'd gone to France I'd stayed behind, managing the office. I wasn't sure what had changed, but considering the added cost, the fact no one would be there to answer phones, it had to be a vote of confidence of some kind. As it always seems to, it took me only a millisecond to say yes.

I flew to Paris a weekend early. It was like a warm bath of good feelings. Even though my mother was annoyed at me for waking up late the two days I was with her, I couldn't help but smile at her and tell her how happy I was to see her. (It only made her suspicious of me.) My cousin—one of the daughters of my mother's clan—came over for lunch, and filled us in on the latest news out of Champagne: Uncle Charles had all but completely handed the reins over to my cousin Charles-Henri.

"Well, it's your turn now," my mother said to me, and to my cousin, and from the tone in her voice I could tell she meant more than just the business.

Mark arrived on Monday. I picked him up at the airport in a rental car and we drove southeast, toward Aube, Champagne. Aube is on the southern end of the province, known for its Côte des Bar region—too far from Montagne de Reims for me to see my ever-crankier uncles. I was nervous enough about traveling with my boss. We'd spent plenty of time together in the car around the tri-state area, but this was another level. It's hard enough to be with someone you're close to and trust when all your awkward and embarrassing habits and tendencies are inevitably exposed while on the road.

Brodeur Imports did not have a big roster of sparkling wines, but you always want a few; otherwise you're practically begging clients to work with other importers. Our first visit was with a winemaker, Françoise, who had taken over the vineyards when her husband died, renamed the label after herself, and now ran the business with her children. Her signature blend was three-quarters pinot noir and one-quarter chardonnay—the pinot gave it a nice structure, and it tasted of dried fruit, toast, and hazelnut, with a lovely yellow color. When we pulled up to the *maison*, a modest

stone building at the base of the hill, Mark and Françoise embraced like old friends. I was surprised. She was middle-aged, gray
hair hanging in wiry trails down both sides of her face. Her hands
were rough to the touch. I tried to remember if she had been one
of the easier or harder people to work with on the fact sheets.

"My assistant," Mark said, proudly, I thought, and Françoise
turned her appreciative eyes on me.

"Shall we walk out to the vineyard?" she suggested. We climbed
a gentle slope into the bright green rows. There is something
beautiful about the neatly ordered vines on rolling land—man's
(or in this case, woman's) influence in an open, natural setting. It
was remarkably cold for June, even by Champagne's standards. I
hugged my cardigan closer to myself and had a hard time keeping
up on the uneven dirt path. I stumbled and nearly dropped to a
knee, gasping. Mark turned around in concern, took one look at
my feet, and roared with laughter.

"You're definitely a beginner!" he said. My face grew red—like
a fool I'd worn open-toed shoes, while Mark and our host were
both in sturdy boots. They stopped to closely examine a chardonnay vine; satisfied, Mark stood up, murmuring something I
couldn't hear. A small breeze caught his attention and he lifted his
eyes over the vines and inhaled deeply, and smiled to himself. He
was thoroughly in his element.

Mark always told me he had no dreams of making wine—if
wine was his religion, he was more of a missionary than a monk—
but visiting the producers he represented was as important a part
of the process as drinking the wine itself. We were similar in that
way—my childhood visits to see my family in Ambonnay were all
the evidence I needed that I was not made to be a winemaker—
but I was more drawn to city life than he was. For Mark, West-

chester was close enough to Manhattan for him to conduct business without having to live there. And though he was a great salesman, a part of him liked the steadier, more routine pace of his life as it was, suburban, under his own control. It was in Aube that I realized I couldn't do exactly what he did. I didn't quite want to be the middleman, connecting winemakers and wholesalers, even as I found the most pleasure in discovering and maintaining relationships based around wine. I couldn't put it into words, but I knew I wanted to work directly with the average wine drinker.

We were many miles from my family's land, and the hills here were gentler than the Montagne de Reims but it felt familiar anyway to be among the vines. We spent another full day in Aube, during which we had lengthy meals with Françoise—going over the business a bit, but mostly talking about the wine, how the winter had been and how the spring and summer were shaping up. We walked into the vineyard again, and this time I borrowed a pair of boots. Mark wanted to show me the differences, aside from color, between the smaller, compactly bunched pinot noir and pinot meunier grapes, and the larger chardonnay grapes, something I'd never paid much attention to even on my family's land.

Then we drove on, further south into Burgundy to see a husband and wife team in the Nuits-Saint-Georges appellation. I'd never before stepped foot among Burgundy vines—perhaps the best example of the heights a partnership between man and the land can reach. Nuits-Saint-Georges does not have any grand cru vineyards—we'd passed the best of those just to the north, in the Côte de Nuits—but the wine is still highly respected, and good bottles can be had at a value, at least in terms of Burgundy. We were far from Champagne now: the sky a deeper blue, the building roofs a glazed red.

The only night we spent in anything resembling a town was in

Beaune, the wine capital of Burgundy. We rested for a bit and then met for dinner at the hotel restaurant, where Mark told me he dined every time he passed through. It was our first meal alone in France. We could have been back at Maison du Roi, by the office, except for the sheer quantity (and quality) of local delicacies piled on the table: snails with butter sauce, unpasteurized cheese you can't get in the States, a light and delicate mille-feuille (Napoleon) for dessert. It was the kind of meal you can't even find in Paris. Everything we consumed was sourced within miles of where we were sitting. Everything—food, drink, environment—was in perfect harmony. We ate four courses each and went through two bottles of local Côte de Beaune wine: a Pernand-Vergelesses white, lively and elegant with honey notes, from Domaine Vincent Rapet, and a Pommard red from Domaine Chantal Lescure that was deep, earthy, elegant, with a long finish.

We were, by the end, with no business to attend to in the morning, quite drunk.

"I come here every year, but always alone," he said, eyes moist with happiness. "Even when my wife was helping with the company, she wouldn't come on these trips. This is my first time eating here with company. I'm glad to have it," he said, and touched his glass with mine.

"I've been worth every precious penny, no?" I said to needle him.

"Every penny," he conceded.

We had never drunk this much together—not simply tasting, but going through entire bottles. It had all the unexpected and liberating silliness, mixed with a slight fear of doing something wrong, of the first time I'd gotten inebriated in front of my parents.

"And you, Laure? Working with me has been worth your precious time?"

"Every minute," I said right away. He raised his eyebrows as if he'd been expecting a sarcastic response and was surprised to receive an earnest one. I knew that I'd started to become impatient, had lost perspective on how much further I had to go, and how lucky I was to have a boss and mentor who wanted to see me get there. Just being in France with Mark had reminded me of this fact, and had revived more than a little gratitude in me. There was no real doubt in my mind that the job had been one of the greatest experiences of my life.

We had long finished everything on the table, but we lingered. There was something Mark wanted to say, I could tell, that he'd been working his way up to.

He cleared his throat. "I've never liked having assistants," he said. "I only have one when I desperately need it. I don't have a big business, but it's big enough for me. I like to work alone. And I may not be the easiest person to work for. I liked working with my wife—I can trust her. It's hard to find someone you can trust. This, in the end, is why I don't hire many assistants. I'm too trusting. My company is like one of my children, and my assistant is like one of my children, too. Maybe a niece," he corrected himself. "So that's why I don't always hire for the position. It's a big deal to add someone to your family and you can't do it lightly," he said with an air of finality. I had to blink to hold back the emotion that threatened to burst, especially after all the wine. I probably would have failed, if he did not then let out an immense belch, and sit back in his chair, looking as satisfied as I'd ever seen him.

The next day, after we recovered, we continued south along what the French call the Road of Great Wines, the Routes des Grands Crus, leaving behind the limestone ridge that is the backbone of Burgundy and the reason for its great terroir. We drove on through Beaujolais, past the steep slopes of the northern Rhône. We didn't have time to stop, but Mark took a route that added nearly an hour to our drive so that we passed more vineyards. We drove straight through the heart of the Côtes du Rhône Villages, along barely paved roads. The land was flatter here, and as far as I could see were rows of syrah vines. Vines upon vines.

We arrived, finally, at the feet of the Dentelles de Montmirail—the Lace of the Mountains: lace because of the white limestone, the jagged, exposed range that catches the sun like a row of stone candles. It was the place Mark had described to me on our first lunch together, a year and a half before. Its Gigondas appellation is the chalkier, more rustic cousin of Châteauneuf-du-Pape, and the grenache, syrah, and mourvèdre vineyards were cut into the mountainside on small plots. The road narrowed into a groove in the rock. We bumped along in silence—Mark's least natural state of being. Either he was still impressed by the sight he had seen many times, or was letting me take in the view unalloyed.

I wondered if I would have had the same emotional reaction if I had never moved away from Paris and one day found myself here, perhaps having taken a drive with my uncle. I didn't think so. We would have traveled in a straight shot from north to south, and everything in between would have meant little to me, even as a child of wine country. I would have dozed off, daydreaming about whatever my job was—writing briefs for a nonprofit, crunching numbers for a think tank. The vines, a constant fixture of my childhood, would have been nothing more than a fuzzy backdrop, like a pattern on wallpaper. "Look, look," my uncle would have said, and I would have opened my eyes, maybe let out an appreciative murmur, and gone back to sleep.

But now the entire map of France had been remade in my

mind; every square foot had taken on new meaning. We drank Gigondas and walked in the glimmering reflected light of the mountains. At this higher elevation, it was even cooler than Burgundy. The wine was plummy, earthy, spicy, powerful—invigorating, like the land.

After two days, we drove back to Paris, and after another weekend with my parents, I returned to New York—not a changed woman, per se, but a humbled one. Even before we landed I knew where I would have to go next, that summer, even if I didn't know yet exactly why.

## Thinking About Wine

The next time you visit a winery, don't just drink the wine. Walk around the vineyard, if you can. (Wear closed-toe shoes!) The appearance of the vines can tell you a lot. If they are pristine, with shiny leaves and clear earth around their base, that is a sign the winery is availing itself of modern fertilizer and pesticides to help maintain a consistent crop that can be harvested en masse. I've seen wineries like this in France, and these are likely the vineyards you imagine or have seen in pictures. They look sterile. They are the result of mankind imposing technology on the land, which has been the standard way of making wine for a very long time.

But I've also seen winemakers who let wild vegetation grow between the vines, who don't use synthetic sprays to eliminate insects, weeds, or microbes. The vines (and whatever other plants want to tag along) are fed with compost instead of industrial fertilizer. Compared with standard vineyards, these vineyards are unkempt, even *dirty*. But dirty in the best way, as this is a sign of organic grape cultivation. Yes! Everything else these days can be organic: why not wine? Organic wine is a complicated concept. As with all "organic" labels, qualifying for it requires following a set of protocols that differ from country to country. In fact, a lot of winemakers may use organic methods to grow their grapes without bothering to get the label. This is yet another reason to learn something about the producer—the label can't tell you everything.

There are good reasons organic wines haven't yet taken the world by storm. It's difficult and expensive to care for vines without the help of synthetic fertilizer and pesticides. You have to watch them carefully, day and night, for signs of any of the big three diseases (downy mildew, Oidium, and Botrytis) instead of assuming the chemicals will take care of everything. In short: it's a pain. Is it worth it? It depends—if you believe it's better for wine to speak to the character of the land, and that a land's character is more naturally expressed without presticides, then yes. In fact, 85 percent of the wine I carry in my store is organic.

Cultivation, though, is only part of what makes a wine. There's the actual production—sorting the grapes, crushing them, fermenting the juice, adding sulfites to preserve and prevent microbial growth. Yes, sulfites; you might not have realized that almost every bottle of wine you drink has a tiny bit of sulfur in it. Even if no sulfites are added, a small amount will still occur naturally.

That leads us to another category: natural wine. You may have noticed this label showing up more frequently on wine bottles. If organic wine covers cultivation, natural wine includes the actual production, too. It means the grape juice ferments under its own natural yeast, with nothing added, and the wine is stored without added sulfites. Without added sulfites, wine is more fragile, vulnerable to spoilage and oxidation. Red wines can get away with it a little more because the tannins in grape skins are natural antioxidants. Some winemakers who avoid sulfites will add an inert gas like nitrogen or carbon dioxide to keep the wine away from oxygen; if you buy a bottle with added gas, it may appear to fizz for a few minutes. Don't worry! You can decant it if you wish— once oxygen is introduced, it will calm down. Because you have to be so careful with natural wines, I currently only carry ten, out of three hundred total.

Natural wine doesn't necessarily taste better, I should say. Some people choose to buy organic and natural wines because of health concerns; they think the sulfites are dangerous—although in low amounts they're not—or prefer to avoid herbicides and pesticides. I'll leave it to science and history to decide whether there really is anything to be worried about on these fronts. But I don't think it's a fad, either. It's part of a long-term trend, and a mark of progress. Organic and natural wine production is kinder to the land. Why not take care of the land that takes care of you? That more and more winemakers (and winesellers—like me) are approaching their business this way is part of a smarter, more conscientious relationship with the earth. It allows the wine to be as direct and respectful an expression of the terroir as possible.

# 13.

## It Always Comes Back to Terroir

### On revient toujours au terroir

Everything comes from the land and is of the land, whether it is a grape or you or me. Just as your environment and culture have helped make you who you are, so terroir does for wine. It can be easy to forget this in the U.S., where so many cultures and regions coexist within a hard-to-define sense of what America *is*. The wonderful way it is always changing, always shifting—the very thing that drew me to it—can also be frustrating, whereas a single strong tradition, like we have in France, provides guidance but also breeds conformity.

So what do I believe now, with the benefit of hindsight? Is one way better? The truth is, they're not as different as they seemed to me when I first arrived in New York. I could name a few stubborn and small-minded corners of America, and am often inspired by the innovations of French culture. At best, you can learn from both. And no matter where you are, you need a supportive community to flourish, and good wine is no different: it needs fair weather, a well-timed harvest, a careful attendant. There will be things you can control, like your methods, and things you can't, like the sun and the rain. The best winemaker in the world cannot make great wine from bad land, though a bad winemaker can squander even the most fertile soil. And the best wine is wine that has a sense of place. You can take the trimmings from the oldest, most heralded rootstock and transplant it to another country, and the wine won't taste the same—it may be better, it may be worse, but it will most certainly be different.

Just recently, I was working with the winemaker Sylvain Pataille, from Marsannay in Burgundy. He has two cuvées whose plots are right next to each other: Clos du Roy and Longeroies. One is fresh, smooth, easy to drink, and the latter is deeper, full-bodied, stronger. I asked him what the difference was in his production techniques, to make such different wine.

"Just a road," he said.

"What do you mean?" I asked, confused.

What he meant was that his methodology for both cuvées was exactly the same. All that separated the two plots of land was a narrow path. Same technique, different wines. That is the power of terroir.

Like it or not, we are irrevocably a product of our time and place. True satisfaction comes from embracing it. It took me almost three years to learn this. I'm still learning it.

Mark Brodeur loved to work, and wanted the same from me. He'd made it clear from the start how he saw me as an extension of him. In the twenty months we had worked together, he'd allowed me one week off for Christmas and a few days here and there. I had no benefits (although he was reluctantly paying half my health insurance) and there was no official vacation or sick day policy. If I came in to work sick I could tell he was proud of me for doing it. So I wasn't sure what he'd say when I asked for a week and a half in August to tour California with Jules.

"What will you do?" he asked, his eyes nearly closed in deliberation.

I smiled. He was too easy to tease. "I don't know. Just Disneyland."

"Humph," he said, shaking his head. "If you are not going to drink the wine, then I don't know why you are going, and I can't let you go. I'm disappointed in you, Laure." He really did look like I had let him down, until I admitted to the prank and he gave me the time off.

I hadn't flown within the U.S. since touring on behalf of Château la Nerthe, and I hadn't been to California since that first February, two and a half years before. I was thrilled about the prospect of visiting it again, after I had seen and learned so much. There was a natural symmetry to it.

Lately I'd been spending two or three days a week away from the office. I would go up to Westchester on Monday to collect several bottles, which I'd bring back on the train like a bag of rocks over my shoulder. At home, Rose or Jules would meet me on the landing, take hold of a strap, and help carry the bag up five floors to our apartment, where I'd carefully place the bottles below the air conditioner in the bedroom (I couldn't afford a wine cooler). On the days no one was at home, I had to lug the bag up the stairs myself.

I went on sales calls, taking a few bottles with me—in the summer no one wants full-bodied reds, so I carried plenty of white and rosé. To Queens, or Port Washington, or the Upper East Side, or the Hamptons, on a morning train. Once I went all the way to Montauk at the very tip of Long Island. I dressed in white linen. A sales rep picked me up at the station and we went around to the stores and restaurants. These were beach towns, with elegant main streets where the wealthy strolled, restaurants spilling over onto the sidewalk, and the smell of the sea. I thought back to when I'd first started these kinds of sales calls as a young woman who could barely put five English words together, with a raw palate and some memorized lines. Now I was confident, knowledgeable, opinionated, and able to make small talk—even make others laugh (the test of true fluency I had set as a goalpost).

Sometimes, I just picked a sales destination myself and went on my own. The routine was, by now, second nature. Drop me off in front of any store with a bottle in my hand, and I'll walk in and sell a case. It's easier to pitch something when the product is good quality, and Mark's wines were. I never had to lie—a luxury in any business—and I never stopped being grateful to work for someone who cared more about spreading the gospel of great wine than making an easy buck.

Wherever I went, on Fridays I returned to Westchester, and Mark and I would put our feet up on our desks and I'd tell him about the week while he clasped his hands behind his head and nodded, his lips pursed: such and such cases of $x$. Such and such cases of $y$. Sold under this rep's name. Or with that rep at my side—Who? You know, the guy who . . . Oh yes, he's good. Then, debrief complete, Mark would open a bottle for us to taste.

When we tasted, there was nothing else in our minds but the wine at hand, and for a few moments it felt like we were in France again. Mark's face would change, soften, and the memories would flow about the winemaker and her family, about the first time he drank this wine, the weather that day, the shoes he was wearing, the look on his wife's face. Although I didn't quite have the memories he did—and definitely not as far back in time—I knew even then that these Friday afternoons would later be some of my best.

At the beginning of August, Jules and I left for San Francisco. Peter, who'd grown up in the Bay Area, was there for a long visit divided between work and family. He picked us up at the airport.

"Did you guys just come from the beach?" he asked us, eyes wide.

"No," we said, smiling, arms around each other's waists. We thought it was just Peter being Peter. "Why would you say that?"

"You look like you're already on vacation!"

"We are!"

"No, I mean you *look* like you're already on vacation." He meant we were relaxed; we had sunglasses on; our shirts were haphazardly buttoned; we were in sandals; we were smiling enormous smiles. Apparently it takes most New Yorkers—and perhaps most overworked Americans—a full day after landing anywhere to get into "vacation mode." We had made the transformation before the plane had even backed away from the gate.

Peter drove us to the South Bay. Jules and I both sat in the back, as a joke, but also to be close to each other. The last few months had been rough on us. We had been arguing, not unlike our first couple of months in New York, but for different reasons. In the early days of our life together in the city he'd been unmoored, anxious, resistant. A lot of tension came from his disdain toward the whole experience, how much he hated everything I loved—the people, the bustle, the unpredictability. But as he approached his two-year anniversary as a New York resident, the things that had bothered him most he had grown, if not affectionate toward, at least accustomed to. He still disliked the noise of bars but no longer complained as much about it and could even tolerate it long enough to meet friends for a good portion of the night. He didn't whine about the cuisine, and his work schedule had eased enough that he was no longer subsisting on egg-on-rice. He frequently got home at a normal time, and because I was spending most of my days in or around the city, I, too, returned to the apartment in the early evening.

But our renewed closeness raised its own set of issues. Previously, the only quality time we spent together during the week was while we were asleep. It's very easy to be kind to each other in your sleep. Now, expectations were raised. We were suddenly an active couple again, and our preferences and rhythms often didn't line up. I had energy in the evenings. I wanted to try all the new restaurants popping up on our stretch of Eleventh Street, go to every rooftop bar, spend every night for a week in Williamsburg to see what the fuss was about, meet every friend of every friend. Jules wanted to watch basketball, develop a taste for Scotch with Peter, and go to the Bronx Zoo and the Coney Island Aquarium (he enjoyed animals so much I often thought he preferred their company). I didn't understand it, but we tried to compromise—and I did truly love seeing his face light up at the sight of elephants. But more than once he didn't show up for dinner, and I

texted, called, and finally apologized to our friends and, frantic with irrational fear, ran home to see if he was all right. He was invariably asleep, oblivious to all alarms and ring tones, and I shouted and shouted until he rolled off the bed onto the floor.

I wasn't proud of us at this time. It seemed every few months there'd been a new twist, another challenge. *Would it ever be simple and easy?* But our story was the story of every long relationship, I told myself, and we were still tender, and reassuring, and devoted. I was still his *coeur* and he was still my *loup*. The same traits in him that drove me crazy—stubbornness, a deep idiosyncrasy, single-minded pursuit of his passions—were the same ones that made me laugh, that charmed me, that led me to desire him like no one I'd ever known. He still tricked me with false proposals, and on Saturday mornings, before I went to the Union Square Greenmarket and he fell back asleep, we told each other half-remembered, half-imagined dreams of ourselves in five years: children, bicycles, picnics (although we never mentioned in what city).

I couldn't imagine a life without Jules.

❧

Unlike our friends back in Europe, we'd done little vacationing, having put everything into proving ourselves at work. This trip to California was important. I kept thinking about how well a vacation had worked for Min and Derek. So here we were, even *looking* like we were on vacation. In the backseat we smiled at each other, unable to see each other's eyes behind the dark sunglasses. Once again, the bright California sky didn't fail to amaze me. In the distance were pale yellow mountains.

Peter took us to his hometown. We ate at a sidewalk café and

marveled at our surroundings. It seemed idyllic—the pedestrians moving at a leisurely pace, everyone in shorts and sandals, with bright smiles, casually exuding money. For each person who passed, Jules and I played a game: did they work for Google or Facebook? Peter was intensely embarrassed by us. We spent the night at his parents' house. They were gentle people who treated Peter with great love but a little gingerly, as if they hadn't raised him themselves but had found him in the woods.

Then he drove us up to San Francisco, where we spent the night in an affordable bed and breakfast established in a traditional old Victorian house. It was adorable, and we slept well in a bright white double bed—the only downside was a shared bathroom. On the whole, Jules seemed to find the city puzzling. He hadn't expected the hills, or the beauty of the bay, or its compactness. It was cool and windy. Overconfident in my memory and navigational instincts, I got us lost on a walk I swore I had taken the one other time I'd been there and we ended up at Fisherman's Wharf. Our feet hurt, but as soon as Jules heard the sea lions he went running to see them.

The real excitement for me began the next day, when we picked up our rental car and drove over the Bay Bridge and north, into Napa Valley, into the heart and soul of the American wine industry. It got much hotter as soon as we left San Francisco. It was a hundred degrees. The hills, yellow with green patches, were still all around us in the distance, but in all the spaces between, for miles in every direction as far as the eye could see, emerged the vines, the crooked trunks, the canopies well-kempt and bright with leaves.

I was driving. Jules had never gotten a driver's license, even in France—yet another source of tension. I looked away from the

road in quick glances to see if I could spot the camouflaged grape bunches, the heavy green of the sparkling and white grapes that in this climate would be ready for harvest now, in early August. My heart drummed in tune with the thump of the tires on the road.

"The next winery, I'm pulling over," I said. I couldn't stand to be in the car any longer, with the grapevines—and their end product—so close. As soon as we stepped out of the car, the heat hit us. Even closing the car door nearly burned my hand. The tasting room was twenty feet away across the gravelly lot and it seemed like too far to cross under the desert sun.

"I can't drink wine in this weather, you are insane," Jules replied, but I wouldn't be dissuaded.

The tasting room wasn't like anything I had ever seen. In France, you often don't even find tasting rooms; at the older wineries in particular, you'll sometimes just get the winemaker in his or her office, paperwork everywhere and an antique computer in the corner, standing by a table that has been hastily cleared so a bottle can be retrieved and opened. This Napa room, however, was high-tech: enormous, with a large L-shaped marble-top bar and several employees behind it, all spread out, wearing matching shirts and smiles. And in the other corner a gift shop, where you could buy prepackaged cardboard boxes of wine, inscribed wine glasses and bottle openers, even shirts like the ones worn by the staff. I turned around slowly, openmouthed, taking it all in.

Then we navigated the tasting fees—tiered pricing for three, five, or seven wines. In France, no château would charge you to sample their wine (though this is starting to happen at a few famous estates); it's simply not the same touristic activity as it is in the States. Inside it was well air-conditioned and full of people—boisterous, even, like the first minutes of happy hour, but at eleven in the morning. One couple seemed to be paying careful attention to the contents of their glasses, but everyone else drank quickly, nodding to each other, progressing from whites to reds without pause. Would they remember what they tasted tomorrow, or a year from now? I couldn't say. Everyone, at least, was enjoying themselves.

But I also hope they were able to find a way to give the wine their full attention. In all your days, so few of them will be spent drinking wine at its source. Those days are special.

Jules still refused to taste the wine. Even though most of the wineries were a pleasant sixty-eight degrees inside, he stood just beyond the line of customers at the bar, fanning himself with our road map. I tried to convince him that spitting the wine out would keep him from overheating, but he complained that even the tannins on his tongue and gums made him hotter. So I tasted and spat, and described my impressions to him, and he listened with the attention and amusement of a child being read a story.

"This is good, minerally, very dry," I said about a sauvignon blanc, and he smiled at me. I was the only customer using the spittoon.

"This is bold, plummy, so much alcohol, I think a little bit of chocolate," I said of a cabernet sauvignon.

"A lot of personality!" I said of a Bordeaux-style blend. (And when the attendant turned away for a moment, I added in whispered French, "But too young. Definitely needs to age.")

The story I told was spinning out from my mind and senses with each new wine. We—I say *we* because it had started to feel like a joint endeavor, even though Jules wasn't putting anything in his mouth—finished with a classic California zinfandel, which once dominated the California wine landscape but has for a while been pushed out in favor of cabernet sauvignon. "Strong aroma," I said as I lifted the glass to my nose. "High alcohol content. This will be interesting." I sipped. "Dark berries, very peppery. So much berry. Jules, you must smell it." Like a mime, he sniffed and nodded.

We slept in a motel that night, the A/C window unit on high. In the middle of the night I felt restless and slipped outside without waking Jules—easy enough. It had cooled down after the sun set, and there was almost no moisture in the air. The sky was not totally black but a dark gray-blue. In the darkness I felt the presence of the vines and their precious cargo. I smelled the earth, the vegetation, carried lightly in the night breeze. And I felt a great richness in the land, but one that I didn't belong to. Does that make any sense? Even as I stood in the middle of it, admiring all of its grandeur and vitality, I was at a distance. It felt so big, all of it: California, the U.S., the land between here and the home I had made for myself. The cellars were big, the vats, the destemming machines I saw on a winery tour. Everything was new and clean, expansive and bold and young. There was so much happening, and so much being invented. I felt it deeply, but also knew that it was going to roll on with or without me.

It was only my first night in California wine country, but all the pieces were coming together—why I wanted to come, why it meant so much to me, and why it felt so symmetrical with my first trip so early in my American journey. It was like a bookend. I'd wanted to touch this side of the country one more time before scooping up everything the U.S. had given me, and taking it back to France.

I'd been considering it for months, I realized, but only half-consciously. The business trip with Mark had felt destined, put-

ting me in closer touch with my terroir. For nearly three years, I'd
been drinking French wine almost exclusively; I wanted to know
it above all others. It was the wine that was mine, that was me. I
hadn't anticipated this awareness dawning here, standing on a
concrete deck along a roadside motel between two towns, surrounded by fifty square miles of grapes. But there it was.

It was time to go home.

I didn't say any of this to Jules until our second night, which we
spent in Sonoma. It was just one valley over from Napa, but it was
a different world. The wineries were more relaxed, the environment more bucolic, slightly cooler. The zinfandel was still high in
alcohol, but softer, more velvety. The unoaked chardonnay was
crisp, with a greater portion of tree fruit like apple and pear. It's
easy for oak to overpower a chardonnay, especially if the barrel is
new, but I tried a couple that were beautifully balanced, buttery
and rich without losing their delicacy and freshness.

I'm sorry to say I didn't write any details down. I was enjoying
the wine, but my mind was elsewhere. We ate dinner at a casual
American bistro with garden seating—desert shrubs of a green-
gray color in pots between the tables, and lights strung overhead.
I cut into my squab, feeling truly like an explorer in a strange land,
while Jules poked at his seafood pasta and sipped his wine, which
only now in the cool evening was he willing to drink, and waited
for me to notice him smiling.

"What is it?" I said, somewhat disingenuously.

"You tell me!" he said.

There was no delaying any longer, though I knew it would
mean something different as soon as I said it out loud.

"I'm ready to go back to France."

"You don't want to grow old here? Raise little American children? We can move to California."

I looked around the garden, at the alien plants. "I miss my family. I miss France." I shrugged a fundamentally French shrug that I had mostly dropped in the last couple of years.

"What do you want to do?"

"I don't know. Something in wine, still."

"You came to America for wine," he said. He'd yet to say anything about his own feelings.

"Yes and no. I came for the experience and for the language. I stayed for the wine."

"And I came for you."

The way he put it in such stark terms broke my heart a little. It was true that between the two of us I had done more to shape our life together. If Pringent had never called me at that party in Paris, things might have turned out differently. Jules might have found a position he loved somewhere, and we could now be in England, as I'd originally planned, or even China. I might still have worked in wine, but for an old business, learning the old ways. Or I might have left the industry altogether.

We found another motel, and in bed before we fell sleep I asked him to assure me again that he was willing to leave New York, too, even though he'd spent two years assuring me that he was happy there.

"Yes," he said. "I may be used to it, but it's still not for me."

"You'll have to watch your NBA at odd hours."

"I know."

I was entirely wrapped up in his limbs, in the center of a sagging mattress. It was not a position I usually enjoyed for more than a few minutes, but tonight it felt like the most comfortable place in the world. I started to drift off, and Jules, his voice still clear and awake, said, "How long are you thinking? There are a couple of projects at work I'm attached to the next few months and I would feel guilty leaving them in a bad position."

"I understand," I mumbled, and then drifted off. Unlike the previous night, I slept soundly the whole way through.

❀

I woke up as refreshed as if I'd slept for three days. All of my muscles felt loose, as if I'd had an intense massage.

I wanted to spend one more day in Sonoma, which was bigger than I'd expected. We drove toward the coast where the cool-weather pinot noir was more likely to thrive. In the morning the remnants of fog retreated back over the hills separating us from the sea. The vineyards here were like patches of carpet on the steeper slopes. In France, California has a reputation (to its detriment) for brash reds, but these weren't it. The pinot noir was lush, dark, slightly vegetal.

The rest of the trip carried us along like a receding fog. We drove south not only because I thought Jules should see Los Angeles, but because I'd heard that some Central Coast wines were starting to make a name for themselves. On the famous Highway 1 somewhere between Monterey and Big Sur we pulled into a state preserve overlooking the ocean. It was dark, but the moon was bright.

"Do you want to sleep here?" I said. It would save money, but mostly it just felt exciting.

"Right here in the car?" Jules said. He shrugged in the glow of the dashboard. "Why not?"

We felt like children. A great weight had lifted, knowing now as we did that our time here was coming to a close, and we couldn't stop giggling, in relief and also a bit of hysteria. As strange as it had been to try to make a life in the U.S., it was also going to be strange to leave.

We tilted our seats all the way back and rolled toward each other so we could hold hands over the cup holders. Through the windows we'd left open a crack I could hear the ocean crashing against the cliffs. I'd just drifted off when I was woken by a bright light through my eyelids, and the tapping of metal on glass. A man in uniform was speaking to us. It took me a few seconds to reach full awareness, and I had to shake Jules violently until he woke up, too.

"You folks can't sleep here; are you crazy?"

"It's just so beautiful here, officer. We are tired, we thought we would just sleep for the night and continue driving in the morning."

"I'm a ranger, not a cop."

"Ah, pardon us," I said. "We were just so tired."

"Well, you can't sleep here. It's illegal," the ranger said, which was news to us. (We'd done it often in France and Spain.)

So we drove on in the dark, disappointed to be missing the view—it was too late to find a motel, and we couldn't justify spending money on the few hours of night remaining. We exited at a small town to the south, and we slept until dawn in a parking lot, squeezed between two cars to hide from view. (This would be the last time I spent the night in a car. To this day I have fond associations with American motels: their spare, basic arrangements, the fundamental need for a warm bed they fulfill, the freedom they afford travelers who don't wish to plot out every last hour of a trip.) We spent the next day stopping at as many wineries as we could, first making our way through a cooler hilly area and then continuing eastward where the land was broader, drier, hotter. We sampled the California staples, bold cabernet sauvignons and chardonnays that were a little subtler than the Napa varieties. I tried a couple of Rhône-style wines, too. I was impressed by a few that I tried, which managed to balance the usual dark fruit with softer tannins and the spice and leather notes I always enjoy.

In the late afternoon we had a picnic at one of the wineries, under a trellis with flowering vines providing shade, in view of the acres and acres of pre-harvest, heavy grapes. The atmosphere was relaxed and uncrowded. We sat on opposite benches and the California light was as special as the clichés indicate, and even more so here, softer, shining on every one of Jules's eyelashes.

"You really wouldn't want to raise kids here?" he teased again.

"Here, maybe," I said. We had a bottle of one of the Rhône-style wines we'd bought in the tasting room. The wine was a dark violet with a radiant center where the sun pierced it. We sat across from each other, ankles intertwined. It seemed like we had stepped outside of time, entered a place where we could talk about anything without consequence. None of it, even the decision to leave, would be real until we returned to New York.

We spent another night in the area, and then drove south and met up again with the coastline before Santa Barbara. I thought Jules might hate Los Angeles, but he ended up loving it, the way a child loves the circus: the spectacle, the impossible standards of beauty, the never-ending Sunset Boulevard, and the Santa Monica pier. We drove up into the hills to meet friends of Jules's co-worker, a man and two women. First all three kissed Jules on the cheek one by one, and then each turned to me and kissed me on the lips. I looked at Jules with wide eyes—*What California custom is this?* But he was too busy laughing to notice. They offered us pot, which we declined, and then invited us into their hot tub, where they kept suggesting we take off our suits and relax. Jules couldn't stop giggling and wouldn't listen to my increasingly alarmed suggestions that we head back. When we finally left, Jules wouldn't stop joking about it. "What's wrong?" he said. "Two women together is a beautiful thing. You don't think it's beautiful?"

We flew back to New York midweek. We landed in Newark and took the bus into Manhattan, running alongside the marshlands until the Empire State Building appeared in the distance. Jules had a catlike half smile on his face, as he slept in the seat beside me, and I wondered if he was dreaming about California— the Los Angeles hills, perhaps. I, however, was wide awake.

I didn't want to leave the U.S. right away. But I'm not a patient person, and once an idea gets into my head it invariably begins to grow in size like a snowball rolling down the mountain, triggering an avalanche of thoughts and actions. Back at work the next day, Mark greeted me in a restrained manner, as if he'd hardly noticed I'd been gone, but soon he was waving his arms, telling me that everything had fallen apart while I was gone, which I could see for myself: there were stacks of paper everywhere and two empty bottles on the floor by his desk.

"Give me a report," he said, with every ounce of seriousness, and put his hands behind his head and leaned back in the way he did when I told him about my sales calls. He wanted to hear about what I thought of California and its wines.

"If I'd known this was going to be for business research I would have made you pay for it," I said. He scoffed and smiled.

This is how fate works: chance conspires with opportunity. The next week I began a round of sales calls in Manhattan. I'd long planned to visit the stores near my apartment in the East Village, but had been saving it for after California. I avoided Jacob's, as I was too regular a customer to avoid a conflict of interest. But even so, canvassing my own neighborhood was both heartwarming and surreal. It had been a long time since I'd walked so many of these streets on a weekday morning. I ended up on Avenue C, just a couple of blocks from Rose and Nico's old apartment—the location of my first, lonely night in New York.

I knew nothing about the wine store I was standing in front of, which had opened after we'd moved to the new apartment, as I stepped inside with my heavy bag to a jingle of bells on the door. But it is a moment I will never forget. The space was tiny, just a few hundred square feet, but every inch was thoughtfully used. There were tall shelves against the walls and a row of shorter racks in the middle. I scanned the rows nearby and recognized only a couple of the labels; the owner was sourcing small producers. The signs for the regions were nicely designed, and every bottle had a handwritten tag around its neck. A solid wood table stood to one side for tastings. The owner stepped out from the office to greet me. I was surprised to see a young woman.

"Are you Laure?" she said.

She couldn't have been too much older than me, meaning she was the youngest store owner I'd met—and one of the few women. She was small, with red hair and large expressive eyes, and a big voice, a big laugh. She was pushy, I could tell, and frank. Just my kind of person. She bought three cases that day, one of rosé and two of a Crozes-Hermitage Rhône (a medium-bodied syrah of soft tannins but good spice, fitting for summer barbecues), and asked if I would come back Friday to conduct a tasting for her customers. I agreed and gave her my direct line, marked her in my book, and left, trembling.

I returned Friday evening, walking down the familiar streets with a small knot of anticipation in my stomach. Meeting the shopkeeper had excited me. She was my age, with a business she ran herself. It wasn't a possibility I'd ever seriously considered. It turned out she also owned a cheese store next door, and had brought over bread and cheese for the tasting. There was a small crowd, mostly younger, with one middle-aged couple. All the patrons seemed to live within a few blocks and know the owner. And everyone was excited, if tentative, smiling big smiles the way Americans do and nodding at one another. The owner seemed the happiest out of them all—genuinely pleased to see people in her store having a good time. After the tasting, I asked her how long she'd been in business.

"Little over a year," she said. "But I've aged ten."

I laughed then, though I filed that unintended advice away.

I couldn't sleep that night, or that weekend. Jules and I had planned to meet Min and Derek in Central Park, because he'd somehow gotten them to agree to go to the zoo with us, but I couldn't focus on what was happening around me. At home, Jules took one of my tasting bottles, a Bordeaux that would be too old to use as a sample by Monday, poured two glasses, sat me down, and said, "What is it?"

He'd reminded me at the start of the week that he had several months of projects lined up at work, and I'd reassured him that I understood. But I hadn't promised I'd stay in New York until he finished. And now I knew I couldn't.

"I am going to open a wine bar and store in Paris," I said.

"That's perfect!"

"I think I have to go first, to prepare."

"Soon?"

"Soon."

He sipped his wine, his lips moving as he let it swirl around in his mouth. "You know I can't go yet," he said.

I put my hands on his knees and kissed his cheek. "I will get everything ready for us."

"Why now? You can't open something that quickly. Do you even know where? What it will look like?"

I shook my head. "No," I said. "That's exactly why I have to go now. So I can research, so I can be prepared. I don't even know how French business works, really. I only know American business. It will take time."

He exhaled. "I need four, five months," he said. "At least."

"Do you have to stay?" Now it was my turn. "They can find someone else. Your colleagues can pick up your work."

He shook his head more vigorously than I had. "No, they took a chance on me two years ago. I can't leave them suddenly like this. I'll tell them my plans, but I have to help them finish. The work already has my personality in it."

We were quiet for a minute, then. Opposites attract because if one person happens to be headstrong and stubborn, the other often needs to be able to softly receive the blow, like a hammer hitting a pillow. When we first started dating, I'd thought it was obvious that I was the hammer and Jules the pillow, but at some point it had shifted, and for a while I thought it was the opposite. By now it was clear we were both hammers. That it had worked out this far was nothing short of a miracle.

And aren't miracles often the most likely explanation?

I told our friends on the roof one hot August night. I couldn't sit still, so this time I was the one pacing while Peter sat in my usual chair, selecting songs from his iPod. I kept waiting for the right moment, and the right moment kept passing. Just when there was a pause in the conversation, Derek stood up for a refill of wine, and the talk turned to weddings. I smiled and stayed silent, a boulder in my throat. Min and Derek began to make overlapping comments about their band versus DJ preferences. I'd told Rose the day before, and we cried and she admitted she wasn't surprised, that I was meant to go home and she was meant to stay, that was the difference between us.

Finally, I just blurted it out, in the middle of an entirely different conversation. There was quiet, and then a hundred questions at once: *Did something happen with the job? What was Jules doing? What was Rose doing? Why?* I answered as best as I could, even though I still didn't know many of the answers. I knew I wanted to leave in a month or less, sometime in September.

In the distance, just above the water towers, fireworks started going off, far enough that we couldn't hear them, small colorful starbursts on the horizon. They were clearly professional, though not as impressive as the ones on the Fourth of July. We lined up by the edge of the roof and watched without speaking until the last one faded from the sky. Even then, we lingered for a minute before going back to our seats and our wine. I felt embarrassed to have ruined the atmosphere. Everyone looked at me, and I felt tears gather in my eyes.

Peter started laughing first. Soon we all were. The silence had become unbearable.

But I still had one person to tell.

It's never easy to quit. For every person who gleefully shouts, "You can take this job and shove it!" there are a hundred more nervously biting their tongues, breaking out into a sweat at the idea of letting down the company, their colleagues. It speaks to our better natures, how hard it is to leave even a place we complain about constantly.

Days passed, and I didn't say anything to Mark. I was in the office three days in a row, which was unusual now, so that we could go over some business, and each day I would sit at my desk going over the words in my head while he hummed and flipped through papers across the office. "Ah, *déjeuner*," he said, like always, and we strolled together down the sleepy sidewalk to La Maison du Roi, for French onion soup for him and a salad niçoise for me.

Then it was Friday, and I knew it wouldn't be fair to let it go past the weekend. I was planning on leaving within a month, around the end of August, since nothing really happens in August, when the whole of France shuts down. The whole day I tried not to nibble my lower lip clean off. He went to fetch a bottle of wine, and before we even took the first sip, I told him quickly, like ripping off a bandage.

He put his glass down and let his head drop with a suddenness that made his glasses slide forward on his nose, and nearly fall off entirely. When he lifted his face again, it was red—with anger.

"This is not cool. This is not a cool decision. I taught you so many things. I taught you everything you know!" he said. "I spent a lot of money on you. Training you, feeding you. I trusted you. Now you're leaving me like this. It's going to be very hard on me, very difficult to be by myself again . . ." He drifted off. Now his glasses were in one hand while he massaged his brow with the other.

I picked up my bag and left. I managed to hold back my tears until the train began to move out of the station and back toward New York.

On Monday I went to my appointments in Brooklyn as planned, over the bridge Jules and I had once taken to see drummers in Prospect Park. I didn't call to check in with Westchester. I imagined Mark would need another day to recover, but around lunchtime my cell phone rang.

"I'm sorry for my anger," he said. "I did not think about why you wanted to leave. I was thinking about myself. Now I understand. I support you. Go, go be with your family. Go start your business. You learned everything so fast, it helps to be a natural. I knew in my heart I couldn't keep you. I will be there for anything you need."

It was better than I could have hoped for. I wasn't prepared for how touched I felt. I canceled my appointments for the following day and went up to Westchester instead. When I entered the office Mark lifted his head a little to acknowledge my presence, grunted, and turned back to his reading. I sat at my desk and conducted business as usual. I made a few calls to a wholesaler, tallying up the sales I'd made on their behalf (a mutually beneficial arrangement if there ever was one). As soon as I hung up, he turned to me. "Let's eat early today," he said. "I feel like sushi." We stood and met by the door, but before opening it, and without thinking, I gave him a hug. He patted my back paternally and said, "Yes, yes. Yes, yes."

Three weeks later, I was on a plane back to France.

Drinking wine is a string of moments. Each sip is discrete—you lift the glass, allow the wine to infiltrate your nose and run over your tongue, and put the glass down again—but most people will remember it as one continuous experience, unless they're really paying attention. If you don't notice each moment, they blur, rather than connect, and instead of a braid of pleasures and observations, you are left with only a fuzzy memory. You remember you did *something*—but not what it felt like to do it.

It's the same with life. The years go by like *that*. If you don't pay attention to everything you see and do, every nerve tingling, every firing synapse, then the experience cannot touch you. You are cutting off your memories before they even have a chance to form.

I wanted to fill my final month in New York. I spent many nights with my friends, laughing, dancing, and drinking wine. I didn't want a goodbye party. I told everyone just to remember the one I'd had before I got the Pringent job. And I bought champagne for them all, spending a whole paycheck on a different cuvée for everyone—I knew they would drink together and wanted them to be able to taste a few different ones: Drappier for Rose and Benji, Roederer for Min and Derek, Jacques Lassaigne for Peter, even a bottle for my old colleague Allison, who always complained that sparkling wine gave her a headache. I gave her a nice Larmandier-Bernier Cuvée Longitude, and later she told me she felt fine after drinking it—better than fine. There were thankfully few tears. I said I was coming back to visit soon, which was true. Jules would still be here, and Min and Derek's wedding was in the spring.

Rose moved in with Benji just days before I left, and maybe that was why there were more smiles than frowns this time. It felt as though I were giving her to him for safekeeping. I helped her carry some stuff to his apartment, which was tidy and spare, but not impersonal—his own photography was on the wall, enough to get a brief glimpse of what it was like to see through his eyes, an intense, slightly off-center gaze. We cried a little, but the sadness paled in comparison to the wonder we felt when we thought back over our friendship, how unlikely it had been, something both of us could not have predicted and now couldn't live without. We'd been born only miles from each other, and there was a chance we'd never live in the same country again—but we promised that would never get in the way.

Jules was moving into an affordable place on Fifth Street, rooming with a woman he'd found on Craigslist. We were giving up Eleventh Street completely, and the loss of the roof felt like an especially tough blow. For the first time, I let Jules come with me to the airport to help with my giant suitcases, help I hadn't had when I first arrived in New York.

"So?" he said.

"Isn't this funny?" I said. "We've switched places. I would have never thought this would happen."

"I'll be back in Paris soon."

"Take care of the city for me."

"It's going to have to take care of me."

We kissed very hard at first, but ended with a light peck—like a kiss good morning, the kiss you give when you know you're going to see that person soon. Then I was on the plane, holding my breath as it lifted off and up over the water. Only when we turned to point northeast and I could no longer see the skyline of Manhattan, did I really start to cry.

The journey is different for everyone. It had always felt as if I'd been going in one direction: up, up, and away. I'd gone to America and watched as France grew further and further behind, until suddenly it was right in front of me.

That's all I've really wanted to tell you. It's one story, looked at a dozen ways. I went across an ocean to find myself. Then I came home.

# Epilogue

## One More Thought About Wine

I cannot tell you in this little space everything that has happened since I returned to Paris. Maybe I will another time. I have my own store and wine bar in the 17th Arrondissement, carved out of a converted carpenter's studio. I named it L'Ébéniste du Vin— "the cabinetmaker of wine." Having grown up in the 12th Arrondissement, in Bercy, which was the center of Parisian wine trade for hundreds of years (and where, if you remember, my grandfather managed the wine trains coming in and going out of the city), I knew very little about the 17th and that side of Paris.

It was a few months after I returned to town. Maya was visiting from Aix and staying in the 17th with her cousin. "Come have lunch with me here, it's a cute area!" she said—and who can refuse

Maya? It was terrific to see her. She was as effervescent as always. We ate salad in a brasserie near the Batignolles market. Across the street, outside the window where I sat, I saw a FOR SALE sign on the industrial-looking façade across the street. For a moment I could have been in New York.

"I knew you'd come back, but I didn't know when," she said. "I thought it could have been another five years."

"How did you know I'd be back? We never really talked about it."

She looked at me as if I'd asked her how she'd added two and two. "I knew your heart was here."

After lunch we walked around arm in arm. We saw young professionals, families with strollers, a growing neighborhood. But there were still the signs, and sometimes the shops, of its past, too—woodworking, leather making, cobbling, haberdashery. It was changing fast. I hoped there would still be room for me when I was ready.

Months passed. It felt as if I was building a nest, piece of straw by piece of straw. I worked as a rep selling Brazilian liqueur, saving what money I could. I looked for an apartment for me and Jules. It would be our first home together, just ours. My mother helped, tsk-tsking at every place we looked at. I thought she just didn't want me to move out, until we saw one place together, in the fashionable Marais, that was beautiful. The building reminded me of the West Village, with its big striking blue door and wide wood stairs going up to the apartment from the courtyard. It had an "American kitchen," which in French means an open kitchen. It was January, and I felt the promise of the new year ahead of me.

I kept finding straw. I furnished the apartment as affordably as I could and had time to be exacting—Jules was taking longer than he thought and wouldn't be back until April. I sent him pictures.

We talked every day about the time we would be together. It was what we held on to. Long distance again, there was no fighting. We texted good morning and good night, as always, only now I was the one several hours ahead. Our home was all I thought about, and how he was going to come soon and make it complete.

When I went to pick him up at the airport, we held on to each other without letting go for twenty minutes. I took him back to the apartment he'd only seen in photos. We made love. Then, the sun bright through the window, we sat on the edge of the bed and, over the course of the afternoon and evening, until it was dark in the room and I had to stand up to turn on the light, we broke up.

At the same time that I'd been single-mindedly preparing for Jules's arrival, another feeling had been turning itself over deep in my breast, waiting to see how it might make itself heard: that we were not right for each other. I didn't know it, but a similar one had been speaking up in Jules's heart. And only when we saw each other again in the place where we were to truly start our lives together did those feelings recognize each other, and begin to talk, sadly but truthfully. That's the best explanation I can give. It will have to do.

There's no resealing a bottle of wine once it's been opened— the wine is already changed, and changing. You can plug it, keep it for another day or two, but you cannot make the bottle whole again, the way it was before being opened. And that's okay! Most of the time, if you are lucky, the wine was enjoyable. Sometimes it was spectacular. But when it's gone, it's gone, and all you can do is remember it.

I still see Jules once in a while around Paris, and we laugh about his eggs on rice, how stubborn he was, and how bossy I can be. The only one left in New York is Rose. We talk when we can. I picture her sometimes, chin up, walking briskly on our East Village streets, the way she did that November day we met. It makes me feel like a piece of me still has a claim on the city.

In April 2011, I walked into a real estate agency in the 17th Arrondissement, accompanied by my father, and asked them to show me some commercial spaces that afternoon. Nothing I saw felt quite right, and near the end of the day, the agent showed me yet one more old decrepit restaurant space. As I left, disappointed, I noticed an unusually wide storefront with tall windows across the street. It was a carpenter's studio. I made the real estate agent follow me inside. My father only smiled; he knew me. The space was beautiful, like a cave, the walls made of mortared stone. I knew instantly that it was my store.

"He's been here for thirty years," the agent said. "It's not for sale."

"Why don't we ask?" I said. The carpenter emerged from the rear, a tall, dignified looking man of about fifty, smelling of sawdust and sweat. He greeted us curiously; we didn't look like his normal customers. I asked him a little about his store and the neighborhood. He was friendly in his answers. Then I asked him point-blank if he was looking to sell his studio. His look of mild surprise deepened. "How could you have known?" he said. "I've just started looking for a bigger space closer to the center of the city."

He wanted time, and I had plenty of that. But I had to fight resistance from everyone I knew. *Are you sure you want to do this? It sounds very hard. You have to close late. Do you really want to work until 2 A.M. if one day you have a family?* Even some of my closest friends and family said to my face, "You can't open a bar—you're a woman."

We closed the sale on September 30, 2011. It was one of the best days of my life. I was determined to open before Christmas, which was going to require a lot of construction. Everything had to be perfect. I wanted to reuse all the old oak in the space, and pair it with clean steel. I wanted floor-to-ceiling shelves. I knew the types of tables and chairs that would be intimate and comfortable, solid feeling yet light, inviting people to linger. I wanted fresh flowers on the bar. I knew which wine glasses would be perfect—and I wanted more than just your standard white and red glass shapes, but several kinds to suit each inimitable wine.

Americans love a happy ending, and so do I, so I'll say that just about everything went as I'd hoped. I opened l'Ébéniste that December. The bar was all I thought about; the last thing I expected was any romance. But I met my husband, Max (this is another story), and in March 2013, we opened a seafood restaurant and oyster bar. The wine bar logo has my profile stamped on it; the restaurant, L'Écailler de l'Ébéniste (the oyster seller of the cabinetmaker), has his. By the time you read this, our next restaurant, focusing on grilled meat and traditional French meals like *coq au vin, blanquette de veau, pot au feu, and cassoulet*, will be open as well.

I want to help my countrymen and -women learn about the wine that comes from their land, to understand and embrace the many changes happening around us every day without fearing the death of tradition, to not be afraid or too proud to appreciate creativity and trying new things. Chic wine bars are a dime a dozen in New

York, but still a relatively new concept in Paris. And there are more places like mine now opening every day. I love it.

In French *tu* is a casual way to address someone you know, whereas *vous* is the more formal mode. At all of my establishments we use *tu* with our customers; mostly they are charmed by the gesture of warmth and intimacy. (Sometimes they are put off. Not infrequently, these are the same customers who demand to talk to my general manager, a man who works for me, and ask if I am his wife.)

Hardly a day goes by that I don't think about my time in New York. The old ways are beautiful, time-tested; they are what make France great. The new ways will make us even better. My mother was right: I am a champagne baby, and that means that wine is my heritage, my passion. But she didn't know that one day it would be my mission to make champagne babies of us all. Without forgetting our rich history, we should always approach wine as we should approach life: with an open, willing heart, our five senses, our thirsty minds, ready for anything.

## Acknowledgments

I've changed names and identifying details of many people and some places in this book. It is a memoir, after all, which means it's about me. I don't need to drag others into my story more than they already have been. But all those who helped make this book possible know who they are, and I cannot thank them enough for being in my life.

## About the Author

LAURE DUGAS was born in Paris to a family of winemakers and has worked for some of the biggest names in champagne. After three years in New York City, she moved back across the Atlantic to open a wine bar and store in the Batignolles neighborhood of Paris. L'Ébéniste du Vin was such a success that a year later Laure and her husband opened an oyster bar next door to it, then opened another restaurant in early 2016. Laure Dugas lives with her husband and daughter in Paris.

## About the Type

The text of this book was set in Janson, a typeface designed in about 1690 by Nicholas Kis (1650–1702), a Hungarian living in Amsterdam, and for many years mistakenly attributed to the Dutch printer Anton Janson. In 1919, the matrices became the property of the Stempel Foundry in Frankfurt. It is an old-style book face of excellent clarity and sharpness. Janson serifs are concave and splayed; the contrast between thick and thin strokes is marked.